Cinders

Cinders v Charming

⚖

A personal account of domestic violence and the family courts

Cristina Weds

New Clarion Press

First published 2010

New Clarion Press
5 Church Row, Gretton
Cheltenham GL54 5HG
England

A catalogue record for this book is available from the British Library.

Paperback	ISBN-10: 1873797532
	ISBN-13: 978-1873797532
Hardback	ISBN-10: 1873797540
	ISBN-13: 978-1873797549

Typeset in Garamond by Paul Leather, PLGraphics, Coventry
Printed in Great Britain by imprintdigital.net, Upton Pyne, Exeter

for Orla, Eva and Enya –
you know who you are

Contents

1

The fairy tale

It all started well some years ago with a white wedding. We should have lived happily ever after, just as they do in fairy tales.

But someone forgot to write the sequel for Cinderella. The story of Cinders and Charming is crying out for a sequel. Why don't they do the one about how Prince Charming turned into a domestic abuser and how Cinderella was expected to stay with him to keep up the fairy tale image? Or the one where the matrimonial palace is sold to fund the divorce settlement and they fight for custody of the kids in the family courts?

This is the story of what happened after the three-tiered wedding cake was cut, the confetti was thrown and the last guests left in the limousine. This is what happened after the words: 'They lived happily ever after. The end.'

*

It was difficult when people came to visit us. We had a fairy tale to keep up. Anyone who has visited television studios or movie sets will know what I mean. There are façades of buildings without proper interiors. The outsides look fantastic; they form the settings and backdrops for many a film and television programme. You'd never know that they weren't real; the exteriors of the buildings look so convincing. Unless you walked around them, looked behind the façade, you wouldn't be able to tell. An abusive marriage is like that. Often the façade is wonderfully convincing. It can look like a fairy tale. Behind the fabricated illusion of reality there is a different story.

There was a very different story behind our façade. Outwardly we were very respectable; highly educated and intelligent. Both of us had been to university. My husband was a teacher. I had done a variety of things. Before we married I was working for an MP at the House of Commons. We lived in a pleasant leafy area in London in a £400,000 house, surrounded by affluent neighbours, good schools and a prosperous environment.

It all started off well. While we were living together, before we got married, I travelled in to the House of Commons by train and Tube to work. It was just before Tony Blair and New Labour first came to power and there was an excited, anticipatory feeling in the air about the upcoming general election. After work I went home in the evenings to an old-fashioned man who never cooked and was unable to open a can of beans. When I first moved in, I went through the kitchen cupboards. There were out-of-date tins of food. Some of them had passed their use-by date ten years ago.

When you live with someone who never cooks and you are interested in healthy eating and a good diet, you naturally start cooking for yourself. And it would be rude to feed oneself and not offer anything to the other person in the household. That way you fall into cooking for him too. I didn't see a way around that. He wasn't going to cook. I had to if I was going to eat.

In the beginning I didn't have to cook every night because I met friends after work. I often ate out in the evenings. I walked straight up the road from the House of Commons towards Leicester Square. I met friends at Cranks, the vegetarian restaurant, several times a week; or we'd look out for venues which combined eating with music or poetry readings. I was earning plenty of money; I liked trying unusual places to eat.

Westminster Cathedral was just down the road. I went there for Mass during my lunch break from work. Often I skipped lunch to get to Mass. I was conscious of being hungry, but I was also conscious that there were plenty of hungry people around.

The tramps and homeless guys hanging around the cathedral often approached me for money. I didn't give money but I bought food for them. I got into this after buying pizza from a place near the station with a friend of mine who was a Franciscan friar. He stood out like a beacon with his long brown robe and bushy beard. He looked like the twelfth-century St Francis mysteriously transported into modern London with its bumper-to-bumper traffic, loud noise and neon signs. We bought a take-away pizza and he asked my permission to give it and the bottle of cola we were carrying to a tramp. The homeless guy was thrilled by the pizza. He walked away clutching the big white cardboard box, wolfing down the triangular slices, with the coke tucked under his arm.

My friar friend said he needed the loo and went in a nearby café. Meanwhile I offered to get another pizza so we wouldn't go hungry, and while he was gone I went back and bought a second delicious cheese-topped pizza. The tramp must have spread the word about free food, however. By the time the friar came back, I'd bought and given away another pizza and we still had nothing to eat.

Skipping lunch didn't bother me. Instead of the food I enjoyed the smell of incense in the Byzantine gloom of the cathedral interior, sitting under the glittering mosaics in the half-dark. I had a job to get there in my lunch break but I managed it. I'd narrowly get back on time. Sometimes I was held up on the Tube. One of my co-workers was late for work a number of times. 'You'll have to do something about the Tube system,' she said to our boss. 'It needs sorting out. You should bring it up in the House.'

Of course we all had our own ideas about what he should bring up in the House. Late and overcrowded trains were a favourite topic with the staff. I had to set out at some unearthly hour to get to work. I didn't do a scientific survey but it felt as though two out of three trains on the Thameslink service were either late or didn't turn up.

The colleague who shared my concerns about the trains was a pleasant but anxious character. She cautioned me against carrying full cups of coffee up to our office from the dining room below, saying that I was likely to trip and scald myself and I should never carry a cup up the stairs if it was more than half full. On learning that I was a northerner unused to London, she instructed me to be careful about being jostled off busy pavements into the path of traffic because 'plenty of people' had come to London and found their 'ankle sliced off' by a passing car. I looked around for these maimed foreigners when out shopping for clothes with her, but thankfully never encountered any.

When my anxious colleague went on holiday my boss called me into his office and said, 'While she's on holiday, do you think I could get a full cup of coffee?' I thought that was decent of him: he'd obviously noticed her anxious proclivities and hadn't forced her to face her worst nightmare by asking for a full cup until she was out of the way. For that week we went wild on full-to-the-brim drinks.

I was more myself at work, where I felt at home working for a fellow northerner, albeit one who was shortly to become a Lord. I wasn't entirely myself at home. I was often careful about what I said. It started in a small way; too small to register in my consciousness. I was beginning to tone myself down. It began subtly, however, and I did not notice the creeping restrictions because they came about through the levers of approval and disapproval.

I was spending too much time with other people, my then fiancé, Jack, thought. I had coffee or spent time with male friends whom I had known long before I met him. When you are first in love with someone, you interpret restrictiveness, control, in flattering ways. 'He cares excessively about me' is how you read it.

Gradually Jack began to whittle away at my friendships, making it clear that I shouldn't spend time alone with other males. I protested that I was trustworthy; these were old friendships, there was no harm in them. But he persisted in seeing them as rivals. With hindsight you can say it was one of the signs which should have warned me that something was wrong. Back then I had not experienced the abuse that would follow and I interpreted this control as a flattering jealousy that would die away in time as he saw that he had nothing to fear.

I went out less frequently. I watched television at home and read books. The controversial *Panorama* programme featuring Diana, Princess of Wales, was aired. In the programme she talked about her marriage and how there were three people in it. She also believed she had been spied upon by the security services.

Jack detested the Princess of Wales. He was convinced she was to blame for all her marital ills. She was manipulative and conniving, he argued. I felt differently; I liked and admired her. But I suppressed my opinions without noticing I was doing so. It was easier than arguing; although arguing was not the right word to describe what happened between us. If I held a different opinion from Jack, I was either ridiculed or humiliated for holding it. Educated, intelligent, middle-class people didn't hold certain opinions, according to Jack. I was made aware of my working-class roots as though they were something to be ashamed of.

Arguing took place next day in the office. My employer was pacing up and down, furious. He was going to write to the BBC and complain about the *Panorama* programme. *Panorama* was a serious programme for dealing with important issues. What had happened to the vital issues of national interest and importance?

He asked me what I thought. I disagreed with him and argued the point. I wasn't interested in the salacious details of an adulterous marriage but I was horrified at the idea of Diana's phone being tapped, of her being watched. What about freedom and personal privacy in our democracy? How could you justify listening into people's private conversations if they were not criminals or a terrorist threat?

The MP agreed that the security services were probably watching Diana. He wasn't interested in that. *Panorama*'s stooping from serious issues to interviewing the Princess did concern him. We were on different tracks, each concerned with different principles. I was interested in civil liberties and the steadily encroaching powers of the state; I thought that what organisations acting on behalf of the government did to individuals was of major importance. It may not have been the focus of the programme; most people were interested in the Diana/Camilla/Charles love triangle, but I felt an important point had been overlooked.

I was pleased not to be asked to write the letter of complaint about *Panorama* on his behalf. At that moment I was only interested in the implications of the security services apparently having no restrictions on what they could do to individuals. If you were a member of the royal family and couldn't protect your privacy, what hope did anyone else have?

I pressed the point. 'Get back to the machine,' I was told. He meant the computer.

I was taken aback. Get back to the machine – just like 'get back to the kitchen sink'! That was disempowering talk from a Member who was supposed to have the rights of women and gender equality close to his heart. I wanted to laugh, but I didn't dare. I tried to suppress my laughter while he was in the room. What a hoot! Here was a champion of equality of opportunity telling a woman to get back to the machine, to assume the inferior, menial role because he couldn't take her arguing with him and sticking to a point of principle. It was too good a joke to miss and I seized on it for a dinner party anecdote. It always got a laugh.

There was another irony in being sent back to the machine. He hated that 'machine'. He was scared of it; never touching it. He couldn't even turn it on. Once the computer crashed and the office ground to a halt while it was out of order. I tried to explain the problem to him. He gave me a computer repairer's phone number on a crumpled piece of paper and then scuttled into his office, slamming the door. He wouldn't come out again until the computer was up and running. I could feel technophobia seeping out from under the crack in the door.

Overall, though, he was a kind, generous employer, happy to give his staff responsibility and trust them to get on with the job without butting in or looking over their shoulders every minute. He was a real honest-to-goodness northerner, with a few idiosyncrasies, but fundamentally good-hearted. He was kind to everyone who worked for him. I was grateful for the kindness. At home I was beginning to walk on eggshells. I noticed that Jack was sensitive to quite small things. I couldn't predict what would trigger major irritation, but the moods seemed to increase on him as time passed.

I had a couple of friends over one weekend. Jack took an especial dislike to one of them: a confident, well-educated and articulate feminist. While we were in the middle of a discussion in the kitchen, he suddenly left the room, offering no excuse. I was perturbed. Something was wrong. It was obviously another of those incidents which had triggered a disturbance in him. When I could get free without being rude, I followed him out of the room.

I found him upstairs, pacing up and down, angry. My friend and I were 'silly giggling lesbians, disrespectful of men', he said. I was stunned at this head-on, unprovoked attack. His line of argument was that I'd been infected with specious feminist nonsense. He continued in the same tone. I began to feel guilty, to think back over the conversation.

It was difficult in the face of someone else's utter certainty that I was wrong to maintain my own position. It is hard when you are emotionally involved with someone. You lend weight to their criticism; try to see their point of view.

I was puzzled. I couldn't see what my offence was, but I had clearly made him angry. This was embarrassing. I didn't want our guests to feel uncomfortable. I tried to smooth things over, to apologise. We could sort things out later, but we shouldn't desert our guests. He wouldn't return to the room where the others were. He began to raise his voice. 'You can get out of the house. Leave now. Push off.' I didn't want my friends to hear. They would have been worried about me, no doubt have urged me to leave. I missed a warning sign there. Why wasn't I telling myself to get out?

I did take my friends to a nearby pub. They had a good time. I was on edge, worrying about my reception when I got home. What had caused such an outburst? What had I done? I was mystified. Wondering about it gave me a headache. I couldn't enjoy the afternoon.

Later in the day I went home alone. Nothing had changed. I was a reprehensible person with bad attitudes towards men, I was unfeminine and I had lesbian friends. A note of pleading crept into my tone; the pleading would increase later on in our relationship. It made no difference to his attitude, however.

I had two choices. I could stay frozen out and unable to unravel the mystery of what I had done. Or I could go somewhere else for the night. I rang up one of my friends who had been there in the afternoon and explained that I needed a bed for the night. I travelled across London by train, upset and worried. I'd slept in a sleeping bag on the floor of my friend's room many a time, but this was the first time it hadn't been a happy occasion. Jack hated my friend. That was bad news.

It was just the start of Jack hating my friends. Gradually, one by one, they were frozen out. He disapproved of them and they began to pick it up. They called less often and were constrained when they phoned. Often Jack would pick up the extension in the other room and join in the conversation. It was difficult to object to this. He would say that couples had no secrets from each other. If I had nothing to hide, why couldn't he join in?

I began with objections to this. I was used to seeing these friends on my own. I had known them for years. Because we were a couple, it didn't mean I had to give up friendships. Of course not, he countered, we would simply share our friends, see them together. That's what couples did.

Something seemed wrong about it, but it was hard to argue because it was always couched in terms of openness and sharing; he put it in a positive light and made me feel unreasonable if I disagreed. Why would I want to be secretive? Were the friendships disguises for something else? Perhaps I wasn't trustworthy after all?

I wasn't prepared for any of these arguments. It was like trying to stand upright on a rug which is being dragged across the floor at speed. I couldn't get a footing. The word 'control' didn't come to mind until much later on in our relationship.

At work, my boss offered to show me where I could get a good view of the Queen arriving for the Queen's speech, which was nearly upon us. I turned it down. 'No thank you. I'm a republican.' I had held republican views for practically as long as I'd been interested in politics, which was absurdly early, as far back as my primary school years. On this occasion it was he who was taken aback. 'I'm a republican too.'

We surprised each other. Why was he telling me what was self-evident? I assumed that anyone who had a real commitment to equality of opportunity should be a republican. You couldn't believe in equality of opportunity and in privilege gained by birth at the same time. And why was a republican watching the spectacle of the Queen trotting down the Mall in her carriage? If you were a republican, you didn't enjoy titles and baubles, pomp and circumstance and the elitist mumbo jumbo that went with it.

My boss didn't see the connection between disapproving of the monarchy and refusing to look out of the window to watch the royal carriage.

I didn't watch the procession to the House of Lords. But I did watch a video at home starring Tom Cruise. Jack interrupted me, tumbling into the room in a ferment. I stared at him, amazed.

'Why are you watching a video with Tom Cruise in it?'

'I like Tom Cruise.'

'Are you telling me you fancy Tom Cruise?'

'Loads of women fancy Tom Cruise and watch films because he's in them.' He was still the hero of *Top Gun* with his dark good looks and white teeth, before the media fell out of love with him over Scientology.

I wasn't picking up Jack's tone. To my amazement, having a crush on a film star was a sin – because, of all things, he knew someone who knew someone, who knew someone else, who knew Tom Cruise. And if I knew Tom Cruise personally, I would prefer him to Jack and that was disloyal and unfaithful. And it was only because Tom Cruise was a big movie star and unavailable that I couldn't meet him, but it was still the same as if I could meet him. I was being unfaithful by watching Tom Cruise on television.

I couldn't follow all this. It made my head reel. I was being unfaithful by watching Tom Cruise in a movie? It was surreal. I couldn't take him seriously; it was way out, cult stuff, yet he was deadly serious. I wanted to say, like John McEnroe, you cannot be serious! But it was serious. I wasn't allowed to watch Tom Cruise in future in case I had fantasies about running off with him, which could turn into possibilities if Tom Cruise weren't Tom Cruise.

I tried to argue the point. 'But Tom Cruise is Tom Cruise. I'll never meet him. Anyway, I can tell the difference between the movie character and the real person. It's just fantasy. I only like Tom Cruise in character in the film. I know that he isn't like the character in real life, any more than Richard Gere is an officer and a gentleman or

Christopher Reeve has super powers. It's just escapism.'

No argument I put forward was accepted. They were all shot down. I was reduced to compliance. This was not a sixth-form or university debating society. I could argue the hind leg off a donkey if my viewpoint was respected and listened to. I didn't care if others held a different viewpoint; I enjoyed the debate. But in the atmosphere of home I couldn't debate intellectual points of view, have a difference of opinion and enjoy the argument. I wasn't expected to argue. I was being difficult, nasty, manipulative and unfeminine if I argued. I should agree with Jack because he knew so much more than me; he was older and wiser.

The turn these discussions took was often personal and nasty. I was ridiculed and demeaned, told I was spiteful, deceitful. Nothing had prepared me for this behaviour. I had a strict rule of conscience; you didn't use personal attack on anyone who disagreed with you. You could attack arguments and principles but not people personally.

For Jack, personal attack was justified if you disagreed with him because anyone who disagreed with him must be morally bad, and their opinions didn't count. He didn't phrase it that way, but that's how it panned out. Time after time I would express an opinion, only to be traduced or humiliated for holding it.

One time I made a comment about the IRA. I said that I supported their republican aims and their desire for a united and independent Ireland; but that I didn't support violent methods under any circumstances. This opinion caused a massive upset. The second part of my assertion – that I didn't support terrorism or violence in any form – was overlooked. In his eyes I had expressed support for an organisation that murdered people.

He went on and on for weeks about it. He brought it up at every opportunity. He slipped in snide remarks about my support for terrorism and used it to impugn my integrity months later. I was an IRA supporter and my political views on all subjects were therefore morally dubious. I had no right to an opinion.

I tried to expand and discuss the issue philosophically, in a reasoned way. I'd done philosophy in my first year at university; reasoning was my first form of defence. But there were no defences against someone who was willing to use personal attack and insult to win the argument.

I lived in two separate worlds which didn't connect. At work I was passionate about what I did, about helping people. I got involved in people's problems and I worked hard to resolve them, whatever they were. Constituents came with a whole gamut of problems: housing, education, immigration, difficulty with intransigent organisations or local councils.

Some constituents assumed you were like Directory Enquiries or the *Yellow Pages*; a few would even ring the office if they couldn't find a parking space or their plumbing was leaking. I retained my patience and politeness with those who thought we were the emergency services and tried to make helpful suggestions, put them on the right track.

I put a lot of effort into facilitating meetings on behalf of haemophiliacs who had been infected with AIDS due to contaminated blood. Some of them were not likely to live long and the cogs and wheels of government turned slowly. I was desperately sorry for their plight, and touched at their gratitude for my help. It was humbling given what they were suffering.

A couple of reporters from a newspaper dropped in. They wanted a photograph of my boss. But not just any old photograph; it had to be staged. I watched bemused as they rearranged the office, bossing the staff about into this position or that position. Finally they decided they needed another MP in the picture. A pal of my employer worked just along the corridor. He was sent for. The two MPs were ordered into position. It looked as though they were having a boxing match; my boss was balling his fists. The idea, the reporter said, was to show the daily cut and thrust of politics.

I looked at my colleague across the room, who had been asked to rifle through a mound of papers for the camera. She looked at me and shrugged.

'You can sit in that chair and do your shorthand,' the reporter told me. I stared at him. 'I don't do shorthand. It's not my job.'

'Well, look as though you're doing it. Hold your pad and pen like this.'

I held my pad and pen. I felt very miserable. 'What's up?' asked the other MP kindly.

'I have to sit here and pretend to do shorthand which I can't do, and I feel very strange acting this way.'

'You'll have to get used to it if you're going to work here,' he said good humouredly. 'I'm afraid there's a lot of pretence.' He played his part well, sitting dutifully on the sofa, under the notice board which was cluttered with football rosettes, while my boss pretended to box the opinions out of him. I still have the original photograph on my shelf, which serves to remind me that things are not always as they appear to be.

It was interesting watching the new generation of Labour politicians; the ones who were to become familiar faces in government over the next decade. They weren't like any of the working-class socialists I remembered from childhood. I'd grown up in the 1970s on a council estate where a three-day working week, the ever present threat of redundancies, the struggle to make ends meet, strikes, trade unionism and employer/worker strife were stark realities. Posh socialists were a strange sight.

None of this was of interest at home. Home was another world, completely cut off. Jack worked from home, teaching pupils of all ages, coaching them to pass entrance exams for highly thought-of schools in London. He hadn't gone out of the home to work in years. My world of work was of no interest to him. He expected me to become completely absorbed in his world. I compartmentalised my two worlds while I was still working, the parts not linking.

There was a point at which I felt low enough to talk about things to someone outside. I wrote to a monk friend. Telling a monk was like going to the confessional, what I said would never go any further.

I was on my way out to the post box when I was stopped by Jack. 'Where are you going with that letter?'

I was carrying it openly. 'I'm going to the letter box.'

'Why didn't you show it to me first?'

I was nonplussed. Did people have to seek approval from their partners before sending a letter?

'Couples have no secrets between them,' I was reminded. Why did I have to sneak away and post a letter without him seeing it?

Every reason I put forward was countered and twisted to make me look bad. I was secretive and up to things. Why didn't I trust him enough to show my letters? What did I have to hide? The trouble was, I couldn't open the letter. It did have something about Jack in it that I knew he would be upset by. It contained worries about his controlling behaviour. I didn't call it control in my letter, but he would read it in a negative way. I was implying that our relationship wasn't perfect, that he wasn't perfect; I was letting the outside world into our relationship.

I said I wouldn't send the letter. I took it back upstairs. I had to rewrite it and delete any reference to Jack. I brought the letter downstairs again later in the day for him to approve. The letter contained a positive account of my life with Jack. It retained the façade. Our real relationship was hidden behind closed doors.

This supposedly was all for my own good. He wanted us to have the 'perfect' relationship and I should work on the flaws in my character. In the beginning I tried to say it was two-way: what about his faults? What was he going to do about those?

The conversation always got shifted on to other ground at that point. 'My faults are irrelevant here,' he insisted. 'This time we are talking about your character flaws. Why do you always change the subject when we are talking about you? Partners should point out each other's weaknesses and help each other to change.'

I was told, 'You are argumentative; it's just a way of evading taking responsibility for yourself. You're afraid to discuss your faults because you know I have a point and you don't want to face it. Honest people can face their faults and deal with them.'

Another occasion would be the appropriate time to talk about him, he said. Unfortunately that other occasion never came.

Jack had all kinds of reasons for being touchy that made me feel sorry for him. He seemed to have encountered an unnaturally high number of women in his life who had misunderstood or even exploited him. I felt sorry for him. When we argued, he reminded me of these women; how badly they had treated him; thinking about it made him unhappy. It limited what I could say. Inexorably my hands began to be tied and my tongue tied. I could not say anything without upsetting him, treading on sore spots, opening old wounds. I felt I had to protect him.

I had a private face and a public face. I began to look forward to the times when I was home on my own and Jack went out, when I could relax. I was held to account not only for every single utterance I ever made, but also for my facial expressions and even my thoughts. I could be asked suddenly, at any moment, what I was thinking. If I was slow to answer, which I often was, I was deemed to be prevaricating, thinking up a dishonest answer.

If my facial expression was not agreeable to Jack, he would cross-examine me on what it meant. 'What are you thinking?' This question came often and it was a dangerous one because my answers were mostly deemed unsatisfactory. The strain of trying to be perfect and to avoid criticism became enormous. I was continually nervous and jumpy. Sometimes I concocted defences ahead of time, anticipating criticisms that were likely to be made. Living became a see-saw of avoiding harsh criticism on one side and seeking approval on the other.

The option of getting out presents itself less and less. That prospect wears away as your self-esteem drops. You are becoming isolated. Your friends are falling away because they are no longer welcome at the house. They sense that Jack doesn't like them. It makes it hard for them to come. Even if they are prepared to put up with his coolness or downright rudeness, they inwardly sense things might not go well for you afterwards and they don't come out of consideration for you.

There is no one to challenge him on your behalf; no one to remind you that you are a good person, with opinions that are worth something.

I gave up work when I became pregnant and the outer world just dropped away. It was me and my husband within the four walls. Jack wanted a big family and me at home to look after the children. Going out to work was out of the question.

2

Behind the façade

⚖

It was after the birth of our first child that Jack first used physical violence. Until then I had been on the receiving end of verbal abuse and criticism, which had increased during my pregnancy, but it was the appearance of the children which seemed to unleash worse aggression.

One of the earliest incidents of violence in our marriage happened when our first child, Madeleine, was only a few days old. There was a disagreement over something trivial. I threw away our dog's cushion, which had burst in the washing machine. I had committed a major crime. I had thrown away something without Jack's permission. That was not allowed. I was not allowed to throw away so much as a duster without his say-so.

Jack's voice was increasing in decibels as he paced about the room, raging about the cushion. He always paced frantically when he was angry. 'You are a domineering, calculating, controlling person. You have no right to throw away my belongings. You never consult me. It is my house, who do you think you are?' He went on in the same vein for a whole day. It escalated. He couldn't let it go.

Next day, Jack was still ranting and raving. I was lying on the bed with our new-born baby. I had just finished breast feeding. Unexpectedly, Jack picked up a wooden chair which was by the door and paced back into the middle of the room with it. With calculated swipes he began systematically demolishing the glass light shade that was hanging over the double bed. In between each smash, as the glass tinkled and fell down on to the covers, he paused to watch my face. The fear and terror I felt must have been visible. I was stunned and shocked. He wanted to see the fear on my face; he was actually watching it. Instinctively, I covered my baby daughter by leaning over her and sheltering her face with my hand as the glass fell about us.

I felt unreal afterwards; too shocked to take it all in. Lying amongst the shards of glass, trying to pick them out of the bed covers, I kept going over the scene in my head, the glass falling down, his furious face, the unexpectedness of it. Did it really happen? Part of me wanted to deny it had happened. It was too horrible to believe.

Looking back, I think that shock removed me one step from the reality of what had happened because I did nothing about this incident; I told no one, I couldn't fully face the reality of it. It might have been something I'd seen on television; my mind seemed to slip sideways on the facts. I could visualise the images afterwards; they kept replaying in my head, but I had no coherent thoughts and no explanation for what had happened. I simply put the incident in a drawer in my mind and closed it up.

The next situation arose when I asked Jack if he would make me a cup of tea. It was the sole request for a drink I ever made in the whole duration of our marriage. Only once in seven years did I ask him to make me a cup of tea.

I had been breast feeding for a long period. Our first child seemed to need hours of breast feeding a day. It was draining. I often felt dehydrated. I was reluctant with my first baby to let her cry while I attended to other things. With subsequent babies I was more relaxed, but I found it hard to let Madeleine cry. After having been stuck in a chair, feeding an insatiably hungry baby for ages, I was desperate for a drink.

Jack was passing through on his way upstairs, so I asked him politely if he would make me a drink. His sudden outburst, a violent riposte, was startling. Nothing had provoked it. He told me, 'You are the most controlling person I have ever met. You don't even know how controlling you are; and so manipulative. You can get your own drink, you bitch.' He continued to make bitter comments about it for the next day or two, rubbing it in, assuring me that I was full of self-deceit and that my real motivation was control.

Scenes like this became regular; they left feelings behind which were painful and difficult to deal with. Shock was a common feeling: disbelief, emptiness, sick feelings in my stomach, helplessness, fear, anxiety, dread and confusion. Day after day I seemed to find myself alone upstairs, looking out of the window over the rooftops, crying, feeling bewildered, trapped, all normal life at an end.

Even in the midst of this devastation, though, appearances had to be maintained. Like a Stepford wife I dutifully opened the door smilingly to well-heeled parents and their offspring who came for lessons, or to the odd collection of stray aristocrats and celebrities from Kensington or Mayfair who dropped off their dogs for us to look after when they went on holiday. I pored over recipe books and hosted dinner parties for Jack's literary or thespian friends, none of whom knew the real story behind the carefully constructed façade.

I was an intelligent person. My instinctive response was to talk, to understand, to explain and to sort out. To my frustration, arguments were never resolved by means of reason, compromise and forgiveness. There was a bog standard approach to all our disagreements and it involved my backing down, admitting that I was completely in the wrong, and conforming exactly to his standards of behaviour. There was no variation on this theme. It was repetitive and relentless.

If I refused to toe the line or raised questions about his behaviour, it would raise the stakes to an unbearably high level. He could not tolerate any kind of questioning. The level of menace would always rise when I sought to assert myself as an independent human being with thoughts and feelings of my own.

A number of violent or distressing incidents involved our children. There is no lever so effective in getting a woman to toe the line than to use her children against her. He lost his temper one Christmas, just two months after Madeleine was born. We were staying with a relative. His temper got frayed again. I called him 'touchy'. It was a red rag to a bull.

Rather than shouting, yelling and pacing as he would have done at home, he went for a silent punishment. He pulled the bed covers off. It was mid-winter outside and snowing. I was left chill and shivering on one side of the bed, bereft of any means of covering up. I hugged the baby to me, trying to keep her warm. At two months old, she was far too small to stay warm effectively without any covering. I pleaded, begged, for a return of the covers but to no avail. Jack was seething. To make the point he kicked out at me and then turned his back on us, wrapping the cover around him so that he was wrapped warmly inside it like a sausage.

I carried the baby downstairs after half an hour or so of shivering. I could see that Jack's anger was going to be an all night affair, as it generally was if he lost his temper.

There were no covers downstairs. I found a woolly jumper on a chair which someone had left around, and wrapped Madeleine in it. Held close to my chest in a sweater, she managed to sleep, unaware of the bitter cold outside. By contrast, I was uncomfortable all night. It was as cold as Narnia. There was even an orange lamp-post outside, and a pretty white covering of snow on the ground. But there was also a feeling of dread in the pit of my stomach. It was justified. Jack's anger did not diminish in the night.

He got up in a black mood. When we were alone in the house, the shouting started. He was going to take Madeleine back to London without me, breast feeding or not. He grabbed her out of my arms and began walking up and down furiously. Madeleine started to scream. He wouldn't hand her over for feeding but continued to pace up and down with her gripped tightly under his arm like a rag doll. He opened the front door and headed off down the street towards the car with her. A neighbour, overhearing Jack's threats and my pleadings for him not to take Madeleine away, came running to help. Jack's anger and belligerence turned on the concerned neighbour for interfering. The neighbour called the police to stop him taking Madeleine.

I was scared by the time the police arrived. If I had made a complaint against Jack, I would have paid dearly for it, so I downplayed his behaviour, taking some of the blame, making it appear we had rowed loudly and alarmed the neighbours. The police went away after telling us both off and giving us a pep talk about disturbing the neighbourhood.

I was made to pay for this visit by the police. Any involvement by other people always led to my being punished either physically or emotionally. Jack could withdraw emotionally for weeks on end. His anger would not lessen with the passage of time.

It was difficult in many ways. I had given up working outside the home. The only thing which I was allowed to do was to take on the teaching of some of Jack's excess pupils because then I was under his control in the house. Teaching and reading books saved my sanity because at least I had an intellectual space to function in, even if it was completely private and inward.

The more interesting pupils to teach were the ones whose parents gave you a free hand and you could spend the time trying to inspire a passion and interest in ideas rather than simply cramming them with facts. Parents brought their children for tuition for a range of reasons; some were Chinese wanting to learn better English, others were having difficulties at school and needed help keeping up; a number of them came for exam coaching to get them into some of London's top schools. It was evident that some children were doing it under duress from their parents and you could tell that any interest in books or education was going to drop away the minute they were out from under their parents' authority.

I loved teaching, although some of the pushy middle-class parents were a shock initially. I'd grown up seeing people read books because they were interested in ideas, not because it gave you a competitive advantage. I enjoyed watching one kid who was completely turned off school light up when we abandoned a more traditional approach and spent the lessons just talking about the ideas in George Orwell's *Nineteen Eighty-Four*. My experience with this teenager made me swear to myself that I would never try to hot-house my own kids. I didn't agree with those parents who counted success as getting into particular schools and the children coming out with a string of A grades. To my mind, education was no use unless you gained a life-long pleasure from learning and a genuine passion for knowledge.

Despite the teaching, I had no money of my own. Jack was in complete control of the finances and it gave him the power in our relationship. When he was angry, it was excruciating having to ask him for money; it was a powerful weapon of control. Most often he would refuse to hand any over. Other times he would throw the money on the floor just to see me having to crouch down and grovel in order to pick it up.

The humiliation of having to pick up the money from the floor where it was scattered burned. After doing it a few times while he shouted insults, saying I was a gold digger, a dead loss, that I had married him for his money, I finally snapped and refused to pick up the notes from the kitchen tiles. I swore I would go hungry first. The fridge was empty but I was prepared to go without food for as long as it took. It took several days of hunger before he was prepared to hand over some money with anything like politeness.

I had to find ways of buying things that didn't involve asking Jack for money. Regularly I was reduced to taking back gifts I'd been given for birthdays or Christmas, and exchanging them for money. The parents of pupils who came to the house for tuition were particularly generous with gifts. Many of the presents had to be redeemed for cash to provide money for food or clothes.

Jack kept thousands of pounds hidden amongst his books.

Ironically, he had three thousand pounds, in the form of ten-pound notes, inside *Treasure Island*. I saw the money go into his books but I did not dare touch any of it. I dreaded even to ask for a pound because of the shouting and degradation that I would have to endure.

I found it demeaning to have to beg for necessities, even to have to ask for money for sanitary towels. I never dared ask for money for clothes. He never seemed to care about how few garments we had. I was embarrassed because other people noticed our general shabbiness. I had one pair of shoes, never more than one pair, and at one point they wore into holes. I wore them with holes for three months.

I was dependent on the clothes other people gave us. My parents gave clothes for presents, and friends gave me their hand-me-downs. There was endless stressful contriving just to be able to buy a child a pair of shoes. They never had proper new shoes. More often than not it was a pair of cheap pumps or trainers.

Jack controlled all the clothes the children wore. If someone bought an item of clothing as a present and he did not like it, I would not be allowed to dress the kids in it. He disapproved of bright colours, lace, frills, anything he considered to be fussy. Anything that little girls might like, he was sure to disapprove of. It was frustrating to be in possession of a perfectly good item of clothing and not be able to use it, especially given how few clothes we had. This control over our baby daughter's clothes very quickly started to expand into other debilitating forms of control.

3

The treatment of Madeleine

⚖

When our second child was born, the eldest – only 14 months old – was jealous. She had been the only child, now she had to compete for attention. Sometimes she took her feelings out on her baby brother, as jealous children naturally do. She scratched Ben's face from time to time or tried to climb on my knee while he was breast feeding.

Some of it was amusing, like the time she tried to put the baby in the bin, or the time she put a box on his head and said, 'You look better that way.' She just needed a good dose of attention and affection to reassure her that she wouldn't take second place now a new baby had come along. Instead, after she had tried to scratch her brother, Jack took her into a room and made her stay there for hours on end. I wasn't allowed to take food into her, merely water.

Jack expected her, at one and a half years of age, to offer an apology for scratching Ben. She was expected to show contrition for her actions or she could not be let out. The scene only ended late in the afternoon when Madeleine fell asleep and Jack decided to call it a day because he was tired of watching her and waiting for an apology, which of course wasn't forthcoming because she had no idea what was going on.

Like many children, Madeleine scribbled on the wallpaper and denied having done it. There can barely be a child alive who hasn't done a similar thing at some point. Even the great Isaac Newton used to scribble on the walls as a kid. His home in Leicestershire still bears the marks of his childhood graffiti on the walls.

One childhood friend of mine had proved such a destructive and compulsive scribbler in the house that her parents had been forced to give over one bedroom wall entirely for her to scribble on, so that she wouldn't deface the rest of the house. I had drawn on wallpaper myself as a child. I drew rings and circles around the patterns of the expensive suede wallpaper in my bedroom; and even picked away at the slightly sticking up edge of the wallpaper near the skirting board, with the help of a cousin, until we had worked our way halfway up the wall, systematically stripping it bare.

According to Jack, however, Madeleine's action in scribbling on the wallpaper at the top of the stairs was no less than 'disturbed'. Even worse, it was my fault. No doubt she was disturbed because I was disturbed. I had a flawed personality and I was passing it on to my daughter. She, poor little mite, was expected to show an adult kind of remorse and understanding for her actions.

I was in an impossible dilemma when my husband disciplined my eldest child. If I stuck up for her, I made things no better because my opinions carried no weight with him, and it might even make things worse because he always reacted aggressively and angrily to any challenge. I sometimes tried reasoning, pleading her cause, but mostly I had to shut up and try to soften things for her behind the scenes.

There's a scene from *David Copperfield* which sticks in my mind. After being beaten by his abusive stepfather, the evil Mr Murdstone, David is confined to his room. The kind servant, Peggotty, secretly brings him a sandwich to eat. I tried to make up for things in this way when Madeleine's father wasn't there because I couldn't help her overtly without making things worse.

My husband was a strict disciplinarian. The kids had to eat every scrap on their plates. They were not given normal plates of food, however. Only two or three mouthfuls of food would be placed on their plates, and if they cleared it, they got a little more. The reasoning behind this, Jack explained, was that if you gave them control of their food, they could use it as a lever against you. For someone who made a science out of control, he was paranoid about the possibility of anyone attempting to control him, or about anyone resisting his control.

If Madeleine didn't clear her plate, she was left sitting there for an hour or two. Jack would go off next door and do his own thing, leaving me to supervise her. It was agony. I was afraid to go against him in case she came in for the brunt of his anger. Sometimes I resorted to eating the food myself, pretending she'd eaten it. But I was scared. She was so little that I feared she might give me away by saying something.

Meals and food became tortuous affairs due to the endless irksome rules. Jack had a rule about eating cheese after every single meal, having read somewhere that it preserved your teeth better than brushing them. What the science was behind it I never found out, but it was extremely tiresome to remember. I couldn't afford to forget these numerous and complex rules, however, because I was nagged and bullied into submission.

There was a ban on sweet stuff. The children were not allowed anything sweet. If I ate chocolate or sweets, I had to dispose of the wrapping secretly. One means of doing this was to put the empty wrapper inside the card tube of a used loo roll, fold up the tube and dispose of it that way. I often consumed sweet foods in the toilet or bathroom so that I wouldn't be caught.

Madeleine found her own way around some of this control which we didn't find out about until much later. She responded by finding a cavity beneath the counter where she ate, and secretly depositing unwanted food in it. She was very clever at pushing it into the hole so that we did not notice. It only came to light much later on when the smell of rotting food prompted Jack to investigate the causes. When he took off the side panel of the counter, I had a recognition shock at this act of subterfuge. It was along the same lines as my hiding the sweetie wrappers.

Under Jack's control, the natural work of parenting lost its fun, joy and spontaneity. It was completely regimented, thought out like a military operation. It was parenting by ideology; we couldn't even learn from our mistakes because Jack didn't admit that he could make any mistakes.

4

Keeping the rules

Secretly disposing of sweetie wrappers became a metaphor for my life. One of the disturbing facets of abuse is that it forces you into dysfunctional behaviour. In order to save yourself from punishment you have to lie, to dissemble. An unnatural way of living becomes normal. I was always hiding something; afraid that I would be caught and punished.

One of the tiny details Jack insisted on in the house was the number of sheets of loo paper I was allowed to use when I went to the toilet. I was instructed to count out three sheets and no more. This was inflexible and rigidly enforced. I did not lower my dignity to ask whether I could use more when I was menstruating. I simply used more than the stipulated amount.

But disobeying rules carried risks. We had an old-fashioned 1930s style of loo. Sometimes it didn't flush effectively, leaving evidence of more than three sheets in the bowl. Woe betide me if this happened, as it did occasionally. The excuses I had to come up with, stuttered excuses about diarrhoea and extra-heavy periods, were puerile and embarrassing. Not only did the bellowing start all over again, but I was forced to listen to lectures about reducing household expenses.

My mother saw some of these things when she paid us visits. On one occasion I was looking forward to her arrival and planning to meet her at the station. Unfortunately, I succeeded in upsetting Jack again. I was prohibited from leaving the house and ordered upstairs. In order to ensure that I didn't try slipping out, Jack seated himself on the bottom stair in the hall. Short of jumping out of a window, there was no way to leave the house. Being confined to the upper storey was becoming a regular thing.

I felt sick, waiting for my mother to arrive, wondering what she would make of me being locked into the house. She was horrified when I tried to whisper to her what had happened, hoping Jack wouldn't hear. She tried to waken me up to the fact that I was demoralised and completely under his thumb. Incredibly, I was putting his abuse in soft focus and blaming myself at this time, so I couldn't grasp what she was saying. It merely increased my confusion. Part of me was still thinking I could fix things, if only I worked harder at it.

My mother threatened to report Jack to the social services for his treatment of Madeleine. I was horrified. Not only was I in denial about his behaviour, but I was terrified of the consequences. My husband worked with children. What if reporting him to social services wrecked his livelihood?

My mother was banished from the house for threatening to go to social services. I was forced to choose between my mother and my husband.

There was a worse incident when my third child, Jools, was a few months old. This time I had cleared out a medicine cabinet which could be reached by the children. The medicines I threw away were long out of date. Because I had not asked for permission, however, I was in the dog house. I wasn't even allowed to explain myself; I was just subjected to another explosion of fury. I had a flash of rebellion and decided that this time I was going to hold my own opinion and stick to it. It was extremely rare that I pushed my luck in this way. It was usually easier to knuckle under.

I was holding Jools in my arms in the hallway while I argued with Jack. Unable to stand me voicing my own opinion for once, he lashed out in a temper. Clenching his fist, Jack battered at my head in a fury until I went down, then he continued hitting me with his fist when I was on the floor.

I tried to protect Jools as I fell. I was terrified, in a ball on the floor. There was no escape. I began screaming when he started punching me. I desperately hoped that the neighbours or a passer-by in the street would hear my screams.

When he finally stopped hitting, I struggled to my feet with the baby. Jack opened the front door and shoved me out into the garden.

It was cold. I had no coat and shoes, and no outdoor clothes for the baby. I stood there in the garden, shaking and trembling. I couldn't think what to do for the best. It seemed ages that I waited, but it didn't look as though Jack was going to let me in again. I didn't dare go to an immediate neighbour for help because I was too terrified of what Jack would do to me. He would regard it as the utmost of betrayals. I thought I would end up paying for it for the rest of my life if I turned to anyone in our street.

The baby was cold and hungry. He started crying. I couldn't stay where I was. I ran past a friend's house, hoping I wouldn't be spotted from the windows. If I was seen, I knew the family would come out and there would be awkward questions. I was terrified of them finding out: I was still at the stage of not wanting anyone to blame my husband for his behaviour. I scuttled past their garden hedge and gate as quickly as I could. With no shoes on, I made no noise. Hurrying across the main road, I knocked at the door of Jack's friend.

I was tear-stained and shivering. The baby was snivelling. It was obvious without anything being said that something was wrong. I was in such a state that more than the beating-up emerged. Some of my pain, frustration and incomprehension at the state of my marriage came out. Don promised to speak to Jack for me. He said I could stay with him for a few days if I preferred.

I looked around Don's house. I felt despairing. It was the house of a long-term singleton, totally unsuitable for a mother and young baby, even if I hadn't had two other children who would be missing me. I was worried about them. They must have heard me screaming and being beaten. They had been next door in the kitchen while I was being attacked in the hallway. They must have heard everything. I thought of my four-year-old and three-year-old alone together, hearing that scene. I felt a horrible ache inside at the thought of it. I had to go back.

Don prepared the ground for me. He reassured me that everything would be okay. There would be no come-back. Jack was ready to make peace. I wasn't fooled by his reassurances. I knew exactly how it would be. My husband was going to be furious and punitive. I was going to pay each and every day for god knows how long for exposing his behaviour to another person.

I had my ears boxed, my head knocked on the corner of the banister, dinner thrown on my head while the children watched in silent, fearful astonishment. Shock and pain removed me from the immediacy of it, though. It was like watching some silly cartoon on a television screen, standing there with food on my head, a slice of bread sliding down my shoulder, while the children stared at me from the other side of the table, wondering what I had done to make

Daddy so cross. For he made sure that they knew I had done wrong and that I deserved punishing for it.

The thing that most gave me that feeling of dread in the pit of my stomach, however, was fear for the children. Anything could trigger a sudden eruption by their father: the most trivial of incidents, such as Ben playing with his sister Madeleine's hair clips. He was no more than a toddler when he put his sister's clips in his hair and pranced about in them. Jack burst into a violent rage, shouting that they were 'disgusting'.

My little boy patted his head admiringly. 'I like them.' I trembled for him. Surprisingly, he did not come in for the hiding I expected. That was reserved for me. Later I was stormed at: I was confusing my son about gender roles, emasculating him. It would be my fault if he turned out to be effeminate or gay.

I tried to calm Jack's rage. Dressing up in your sister's clothes was a natural childhood thing. That was how kids developed, they tried things out. And Ben had been funny, patting his head like that. But it wasn't funny to Jack; it was deadly serious. And, as usual, it was entirely my fault. I was teaching my son to be a sissy. Of all things which Jack dreaded, his son would probably turn out gay.

It was impossible to reason on the subject. I gave up. Inwardly, I was just thankful that my son hadn't been punished, that it was me bearing the brunt of his father's anger. If Madeleine transgressed in any way, she generally was punished, and harshly. Any challenge to his authority by a female sent Jack wild. He was different with the boys, going easier on them.

I was not allowed to cut my hair or Madeleine's hair because Jack believed that women should have long hair; it was unfeminine to wear it short. One day I trimmed Madeleine's fringe, which kept falling in her eyes and bothering her. He screamed because I had cut it too short. 'Don't ever cut her hair again without asking me for help and advice,' he bellowed. 'She's fucking ugly.' My precious little girl was standing in front of him as he shouted it.

I could not make any decisions on behalf of the children without Jack's permission. This could be embarrassing. Sometimes friends or neighbours would issue me with invitations or ask if my children could come round to play with their children. The one or two times I took it upon myself to agree, I was in hot water for ages over it. It was embarrassing having to prevaricate and make excuses when I was put on the spot by someone who expected me to give an answer. It became easier just to say no, or to cite prior appointments, rather than to confess that I couldn't lift so much as a finger without permission.

Jack generally disapproved of other families. He feared any influence on the children except his own. The children's lack of friends worried me. No one else was considered worthy of educating them or influencing them.

All the children's reading matter was checked and vetted by Jack. I came back one afternoon with a lovely storybook called *The Magic Paintbrush* from the charity shop in the high street. To my disbelief, it was confiscated because there was a nasty emperor in the story and Jack said that authority figures should not be shown in a bad light because it might corrupt the children.

Wicked stepmothers, witches or evil women were okay in stories, but not evil men. If a story showed a man in a bad light, he went to the lengths of rewording it, or giving a moral commentary on it so that the kids wouldn't be badly influenced. Even the version of *Hansel and Gretel* that we had on the bookshelves came in for rewording when he read them the story; Jack made sure that the way the children in the story were abandoned was all down to the wickedness of a woman. He changed the story so that the father came out of it well.

Along with book censorship there was the problem of sleep deprivation. Often Jack would sleep in another room for weeks on end and I would be left alone in our bedroom. I dreaded going to bed when he was angry because I would find him suddenly bursting in after I'd gone to sleep, turning on the light and shouting at me.

Jack would burst in at midnight, rant and rave, and pace the room while I was cowering in bed. I dreaded his nocturnal rants in the quiet of the night. I was sure the neighbours could hear through the walls. He would keep this up through the night, storming in at regular intervals. It was impossible to sleep in the hour between each outburst because I was sick and terrified, anticipating the next one.

Another favourite ploy was to bang his door furiously in the night or to put his music on loudly, so I could hear it through the wall and stood no chance of going to sleep. And I hated him waking the babies, who would cry. There was nothing like the screams of a baby who had been startled out of sleep to make my heart sink.

By four or five in the morning, when Jack finally decided to go to sleep, it was time for me to get up with the kids and start another day of looking after them. Sometimes I was so exhausted that I could have fallen asleep on my feet.

Begging and pleading had no effect on him though. It was difficult to unlearn this. I instinctively pleaded when I was at his mercy. If anything, it made him worse; it fed his behaviour rather than reduced it.

5

The wake-up call

There was a wake-up call while I was pregnant with my fourth child, Mia. I had begun to get very worn down. I had been told too many times that I could get out of the house if I didn't go along with things. This time I was going to have my say. I went into a room which Jack considered one of his own private rooms. There were two rooms in the house which were out of bounds to the children and to me. One was his study, the largest room in the house, from which he worked. Originally it had been the sitting room. The other private room was upstairs.

His upstairs room was closed off. A child gate had been put across the entrance, ensuring the children could not get in. I climbed over the gate with difficulty. 'I want to sort things out,' I said. 'We have to talk about what is going on.' He reacted with fury, telling me, 'Get out of the room and get out of my house.' On this occasion I wasn't taking it. 'It's my home too and I'm not going until I've had my say this time.'

He began hitting me around the head. Instinctively, I dropped to the floor, trying to protect myself. What followed was a kick in the back. Then he walked over me, left the room, and went about the business of the day.

I lay there on the bedroom floor, numb with shock. I was only a short period away from giving birth. For me the kick symbolised something. It said everything about our relationship. Vulnerability would always be despised, taken advantage of. I had to face the fact that my husband had a real streak of cruelty in him. He appeared conscienceless. Nothing moved him. Not even the well-being of our unborn child.

I went into labour with my fourth baby. I called on a neighbour called Eva to help. Her family was friends with Jack. Eva was highly intelligent and Jack had taught several of her siblings at school. He'd thought well enough of her to invite her to teach with us, since we had more pupils than we could manage. She had told me to call her when the contractions started. She was shopping in central London when I telephoned and she hared back through the traffic. I was cooking for Madeleine, Ben and Jools when she arrived. 'For God's sake,' she instructed, 'sit down and take a rest. I'll cook.'

Jack stuck his head in at the kitchen door. 'I'm tired. I'm going upstairs to have a sleep.' He came back down again several hours later, after his rest. He was carrying a book.

I was in serious pain by this time. Jack opened his book and began reading out loud. He started to laugh at what he was reading. It appeared to be a medieval tract about the evils of women. Eva told him to stop. It wasn't funny.

'It doesn't seem to be amusing you,' he said, and continued reading aloud. Eva looked at me. 'You've got to tell him you don't want him at the hospital,' she told me. 'I'll come with you instead.' I could hardly think for the pain. But I knew I'd never dare ask for a friend rather than my husband to come with me, even if I had to put up with hearing how evil women were on the way to the hospital.

Jack had been talking about selling our house and moving. He wanted to move to France. He felt we were tired and overworked in London; that it had become a stressful city to live in. He wanted to move to the countryside. I agreed to it at first. Then I began to get cold feet. If things were bad in London, how would they be if we went abroad, away from any sources of support and away from anyone who spoke our language?

I imagined myself stranded, penniless, friendless, on the receiving end of his temper in some remote rural location where nobody could hear if I screamed for help. In the end I dug my heels in. I wasn't going to move. He announced that he was going to sell the house over my head anyway. He called the estate agents round. The house was going to be put on the market whether I liked it or not.

I was being forced into making a choice to stay or to leave. The ground was being prepared whether I willed it or not. Mentally I had to face facts about my relationship that before I had evaded. I was suddenly faced with the stark realities of my marriage. Until this point I had always put the abuse in soft focus, explained it away and excused it.

Now, faced with the real possibility that I'd have to depend totally on my husband, alone in a foreign country with him, things began to seem much more serious. Eva admitted that she was having bad dreams about the whole scenario. In the last few weeks of my marriage she came right out with it. 'You can't possibly go. It will be a disaster.' It was unnecessary. I had finally worked it for myself.

Eva's family invited us for Easter breakfast that year. In Eva's Catholic family, Easter Sunday was very important. They traditionally had a special family breakfast on that day. Jack didn't want to go. Originally, Eva and her family had been Jack's friends – it's how they slipped in under the radar when all my other friends were gone – but they had become supportive towards me as they saw my predicament at home. Whether I liked it or not, they had been witnesses to some of his abuse and they didn't like what they saw. Even though they didn't challenge him overtly for my sake, because they didn't want me to reap the consequences if they remonstrated with him, it had become apparent to him that they weren't on side the way they had been.

I'd begun to open up to Eva a little about what was going on at home. I was utterly jolted by the kick in the back when I was pregnant and I told her about that; also about how surreal it had felt to have him walk over me and continue with the business of the day as if nothing had happened. Eva tried to help me to understand some of the behaviour that was going on; but we were equally flummoxed for a name or label to describe it. It wasn't simply about poor impulse control, losing his temper and then making up. It was impossibly rigid behaviour that wasn't open to challenge at all.

Eva suggested trying different strategies to deal with Jack. Over the space of a year, I tried altering my behaviour in a number of ways. I tried emotionally withdrawing from Jack and trying to keep as much distance between us as possible. I tried the opposite approach: deliberately shouting back at him one time in response to being bellowed at. I wasn't angry; it was calculated to see if it had any effect. In response, I had my nose pulled long and hard until my eyes watered. The withdrawal strategy hadn't worked either. He simply wouldn't let me withdraw. He would act provocatively, deliberately entering my personal space, keeping me awake at night to prevent me from putting that distance between us.

Neither Eva nor I could come up with any strategy that worked. It was hopeless of remedy, and if I ever went round the corner to Eva's house these days, I would find Jack ringing up and ordering me to come back. He made it practically impossible for me to go out. He even retained the key to the petrol cap of the car to prevent me from going very far. If I went any distance, I'd run out of petrol. Shopping was very stressful because I constantly feared I wouldn't have enough petrol for the journey. If I tried popping out round the corner after the children were asleep in bed, he argued that it was not convenient; he needed a meal cooking, or he wanted to go out himself, or he needed to walk the dog.

I was frightened to go home after I had spent time with my friends because I was grilled about our conversations and no answers I gave were accepted. I was lying. I was hiding things. I preferred my friends to him. I was disloyal. He would kick me in bed when I came home, turn over so hard in the night that he hurt my limbs or banged my head.

The kids were enthusiastic to have Easter breakfast with our friends. Eva had two children of her own who had become friends with my children. But Jack prohibited our going. We were all very disappointed.

That month in 2002 I suddenly snapped. I had been worn down over the years, bit by bit. Just before Easter I was locked out of the house by Jack and left to wander the streets for hours on end with all four children. Eva, in her home round the corner, spotted me from her bedroom window, wandering the neighbourhood. She came down and offered to accompany me home. She was due to teach a pupil in my home anyway, so it wouldn't look odd for her to come with me to the door. I was scared to go home, even with her.

'He'll have to let you in if I'm with you,' she insisted. That wasn't the point. Yes, he would let me in if there was anyone there to observe him; but I felt sick through and through at the scene that would come later on that night when no one was there to see it: another night of screaming; another night of sleeplessness. It was the last straw that broke the camel's back.

I didn't know when I got up that Friday morning how close I was to breaking. It was Good Friday. As soon as I got up, the war of attrition resumed. Jack began by yelling at me about moving house. We were going to move whether I objected or not. He was putting the house up for sale in the next few days. I looked him full in the face, perhaps for the first time seeing him as he really was. He was impervious to me, not guessing what was going through my mind. He paced up and down. I was paying no attention to the threats, the abuse and the colourful language. It was just a big noise dinning in my ears.

A realisation dawned. Inside I had a crystal-clear determination that I could never ever in my life spend another day with that noise ringing in my ears. I told him I was going out for the day with the children. I asked him if we could put any disagreement aside for the day and just go out as a family, have a good time. Life was too short for this. He refused and began bellowing again.

The loud shouting was the last thing I heard as I walked out to the car which was parked in the street. I had second thoughts once I reached the car. I sent my oldest son into the house to ask his father if he would change his mind and come out with us for the day. My little boy ran back saying his Daddy didn't want to come with us. On that day my child's words seemed symbolic. For me they symbolised the fact that Daddy never wanted to be with us. He wanted to be in charge of us, to dominate, to control. But just be with us; simply be a calm and loving presence in our lives? He wasn't capable of that. And I didn't believe that he ever would be. My little boy's words, for me, were the finish. They summed up everything about our lives. He was never with us. I got in the car and started up the engine. By the time I turned the key, I knew I was never coming back.

6

Escape

I turned up on my best friend's doorstep with four children and no luggage, not even a toothbrush or a pair of pyjamas. The first thing I said to Eva was 'I've left Jack', and then I burst into tears. It was an abrupt start to a new life.

The first night was scary. I had only moved around the corner after all, not any great distance from home. I was terrified, anticipating the moment when Jack would learn that we had fled. I expected him on the doorstep at any time, demanding our return. I waited for the hammering on the door. I made my friends promise not to let him in at any cost.

The knock came just as I had anticipated.

Eva's sister, Enya, answered the knock. Jack was forceful and aggressive outside the front door. I could hear him from inside the house. The children were cowering, white-faced, as quiet as mice, huddling up together in the sitting-room. I was terrified that Jack would push his way in and insist on us returning. Enya finally managed to persuade him to go away for the night.

He was back again the next day, and the day after, peering through the garden hedge, screaming and shouting. He bellowed at my friends in the street. It made me continually nervy and jumpy, fearing trouble.

However, we got our wish. We had that Easter breakfast with our friends after all, totally unexpectedly. That weekend started a fantastic feeling of freedom. It was the first time in years I had been able to do anything without permission from Jack. I could make my own decisions. I could go out without permission, choose when to come back without fear, live my life without the constant criticism and undermining that I had suffered on a daily basis. I could go to bed without fear of being kicked or hit in the night. No one was coming to wake me up any more. No more unreasonable punishments. No more counting out three sheets of loo roll when I went to the toilet, or having to answer intrusive questions like whether I'd cleared my bowels that day or not. No more hiding what I ate or what I watched on television.

The first taste of freedom in seven years was intoxicating. I needed that heady sense of freedom from oppression, that glimpse of what it felt like to be free, because there were black days ahead, some of them crushing.

At the first opportunity after the Easter weekend, when businesses and solicitors were open again, I found a solicitor. Eva and her mother Orla came with me for my initial appointment. I went along with my notepad and some handwritten notes. It was fortunate I had taken time over the Easter weekend to write things down about why I was seeking a divorce. I wasn't able to communicate once we reached the solicitor's office. I was lucky to have a pleasant female solicitor who was approachable, but I was unable to communicate in any meaningful way. The pages of notes had to speak for me, and my friends filled in the gaps.

Normally I have an excellent memory, but my concentration just went whenever I talked to the solicitor. Disorientation set in. When I got home, I could remember nothing that she had said. On occasions when she phoned me, a few seconds after she'd said something I forgot it. To my embarrassment I continually had to ask her to repeat things because I couldn't take them in. I needed my friends with me to remember all the things I couldn't absorb.

My solicitor used the phrase 'domestic violence'. I was taken aback. I had not thought of myself as a victim of domestic violence. No one had ever used those words to me before and I had never thought them to myself. It had not occurred to me that I was a survivor of domestic abuse. It was the first time I learned to think in such terms.

Since it was novel, I felt like a fraud at first. Didn't domestic violence apply to other people and other situations? I felt I didn't qualify. Wasn't domestic violence about extreme violence, strangling, knifing, burning, and breaking someone's limbs? I didn't know anyone like that. I had no idea there were other kinds of abuse. I certainly didn't know about emotional or psychological abuse. I hadn't even thought that being kicked in the back or being battered to the floor while holding my baby qualified as violence. Why not? Stupidly, I didn't think of it as violence because it had happened to me.

Domestic abuse happened somewhere else in the world and to other people. I don't know where I thought it was taking place. Sometimes when I used a public toilet I would see a sticker on the back of the door with a helpline number on it for anyone suffering domestic violence. It never occurred to me to write the number down. I used to wonder sometimes about the women who did jot down the number and ring for help. Who were they, what kind of a life did they lead?

One of the first things I realised after leaving was how ill-prepared for flight we had been. We had no money, no clothes. We were completely dependent on our friends. The only thing I had left from the marriage was the little Mini Metro which I had escaped in. I parked it in a different place every night, finding obscure parking spots in remote car parks and distant back streets, hoping my husband wouldn't come across it and drive it away. With four children all under age 6, the car was a godsend. It would have been very difficult to do without it. In the mornings I checked it was still in the same place and breathed a sigh of relief when I found it was.

Jack phoned me one time shortly after I left him. He told me I could come back home if I wanted. If I didn't, there would be 'a bloody battle'. I was 'crazy, a psychiatric case', and he would end up with the house and the children. I had better not fight him because I was going to lose. Orla put the phone on loudspeaker. There were half-a-dozen people in the room, all silent. We listened to his threats without speaking.

About a month or so after I had left, I was still struggling with very few clothes for the children. My friends had supplied me with some of their own children's clothes and we had scoured car boot fairs and charity shops to find others.

Nice clothes, some brand new, tended to find their way into the charity shops of affluent suburbs of London. Wealthy givers often donated clothes with the price labels still in them. One time I was shopping in a local store. I was wearing a beautiful leather jacket which I'd swooped on in Oxfam and bought for next to nothing. I had my hands full of bread and milk when I noticed a woman looking sideways at me. She came up and said, 'That jacket I gave to Oxfam looks better on you than it did on me. I'm glad it found a good home.'

Feeling some embarrassment, I thanked the stranger for the bargain of a beautiful jacket and paid for the milk at the counter with milk tokens. I was lucky in my local store. They exchanged the free milk tokens I got for the children for other goods as well as milk. They weren't supposed to, but sometimes it was really useful. We needed solid food a lot more than we needed milk.

I tried to get the children's clothes from Jack. I wanted access to our home when he wasn't in to get my own personal belongings and toys and clothes for the children. He wouldn't allow it. Instead I received an earful of abuse on the phone and the threat that he would see that I didn't receive a penny if I divorced him and that he would take the kids.

It was a month of bad luck. On the day my legal aid certificate came through to enable my solicitors to get to work on my divorce, the car was stolen. It was taken by joy riders who hotwired it and damaged the steering column. The thieves left it in the road, blocking the main highway. The RAC arrived to tow it away and take it to a repairer's. It was sad seeing it damaged up there on top of the truck. The kids and I stood on the pavement watching them take it away and I wondered how on earth I'd be able to get the money together to have it repaired.

I had to claim state benefits – Income Support. I found it a humiliating experience because I had to explain in what circumstances I'd left my husband and I had to prove I was no longer living with him. They sent someone from the Benefits Office to interview me and check I really was living where I said I was living. It took a whole month to get any money while they sorted out the forms and my application.

With no money, we had no prospect of finding a home. I was told there was a two-year waiting list for council housing. The best the local council could offer was bed and breakfast accommodation. We were very fortunate that our friends could house us. But it was a burden for my friend, who had a numerous family of her own and several members with significant health problems. There were just too many of us around the same house; we were all on top of each other.

My friends rented a flat around the corner. It was meant for Eva's sister and her carer. They decided that Eva's sister, who had health problems, should move in at home when she wasn't in hospital and the children and I could live in the flat. It wasn't really suitable but almost anything was better than the home we had fled from. There was no kitchen for one thing. I went to Orla's home around the corner for most meals and I relied on her garden for the children to play in.

The flat was above shops. We had to climb a rickety metal fire escape at the back of the shops to get up to the flat. At the top of the steps was the roof of an extension which we had to cross to get to the only door. The flat roof had no railings. I carried the baby up the stairs and down again, tucking her under one arm while I guided my two-year-old up the metal staircase with the other hand. I couldn't let the children out to play in case they fell off the roof. There was also the matter of the landlord, who didn't know we were in the flat. As far as he was concerned, Eva's sister was still in occupation.

The children and I shared a double bed in one room. I suffered awful backache for those months, sharing the bed with four children, two at the top and two at the bottom. I lay rigid at night, not daring to move my feet or legs for fear of kicking a child in the face.

Sometimes a child was sick or wet the bed and it was horrendous. I couldn't change the sheets without waking all the children and getting them out of bed in the night. At times I had to leave one of the children with sick on the sheet and just place a towel over it until morning because I felt I'd die from tiredness if I had to wake them all up and listen to them crying at being disturbed. If any of the children caught colds or coughs, the infections were immediately passed on to the others because we lived and slept in such close proximity.

I bought electricity by means of a key. I took the key to the post office and got them to put credit on it. If the electricity ran out in the evening or on a Sunday, there was nowhere else in the neighbourhood to get it topped up. We did without lights or heating until the post office opened. Living hand to mouth meant I barely put enough electricity on the key to last a week. It always seemed to be running out at inconvenient times. I hated it in the evenings when I had to sit in the dark with no way to boil a kettle and no light to read by.

The washing machine was not plumbed in. I had to remember to take the pipe at the back of the washing machine and put it out of the window into the drain.

'Please don't forget,' Eva asked. 'If you don't remember to put the pipe outside the window and into the drainpipe, the flat floods and the water leaks down into the shop below.' The shop beneath was a Londis.

Of course, I did forget. There was a knock at the door one afternoon. A frantic and dishevelled shop assistant demanded, 'Have you got the washing machine on?' This had evidently happened before. I was conscience-stricken and hurried to place the pipe through the window into the drain. I went downstairs to inspect the damage in the shop. I made a mental note not to buy packets of cereal, bags of sugar or anything that wasn't tinned when I saw the soapy water dripping through the sodden ceiling tiles on to the food shelves! And I was inwardly praying they wouldn't tell the landlord.

I did it again: forgot to put the pipe out of the window. My memory was not good for technical details like pipes and drains. I had so many other worries. I felt guilty whenever I shopped downstairs. The ceiling tiles remained stained due to my memory lapse with the washing machine. But the shop assistants were very kind. They enquired after the children and still let me exchange milk tokens for ingredients to make cakes for the kids.

We had an invasion of ants. We were on the second floor. There was a shop between us and the ground. Where did the ants come from? They trooped through the hallway in a long, orderly line and into the sitting-room. Hundreds, thousands of them, were creeping under the door which led out on to the flat roof. The kids screamed and danced about, scared to death in case they stepped on them. I hated ants: I was as scared as the children, but I had to look as though I wasn't for fear of giving them nightmares. I rushed out for ant powder and scattered it everywhere in a thick white blanket. It looked as though I'd covered the carpet in talcum powder. I gave the ants no chance to live.

We had no vacuum cleaner. There was nothing to hoover up the powder or the ants. Once they were dead in their thousands, littering the carpet in amongst the white powder, I swept up painstakingly with a dustpan and brush.

A bunch of firemen were living next door, across the flat roof. One of them banged on the door in the evening. He told me to keep all my windows closed because they had frightened a burglar in their own flat just minutes before. The thief had climbed in through their bathroom window and stolen a few items. The firemen surprised the thief and made him run off, but they hadn't managed to catch him.

Ben opened the sitting-room door after hearing the sound of voices and crept into the hall to listen. When I closed the door on the fireman, Ben was shivering in the hall with big eyes and a white face.

'Mummy, are the burglars going to come back?' I tried to reassure him but he had nightmares about it. He was frightened about thieves breaking in when we were asleep.

I reassured Ben that burglars only got into houses through open windows and I wasn't going to leave the windows open. Still, every noise made me nervous. I went around double-checking the windows just to be sure I'd closed them all. I peeped out the windows from time to time during the night. A noise and a shadow creeping over the flat roof made me start. I peered out anxiously. Not a burglar: just a rat creeping over the roof. I shrank against the wall. I couldn't bear rats; they were far worse than ants. They were common around the bins at the back of the shops. I'd also seen one washed out of the sewers in the rain, lying dead on the pavement in front of the shops. It lay there, dead on its back, until it was removed.

Then we had the loo backing up. The plumbing in the flat was ancient, connected up all wrongly. It was against current building regulations and contravened health and safety laws. The toilet and bath were connected, so if the loo got blocked, the sewage came back up through the bath plug hole.

Sewage in the bath! I was revolted. Worse, I had to call the owner about the blocked drains. But I wasn't supposed to be living in the flat; the landlord and landlady didn't even know I existed. They didn't know any children were resident in the flat either. I didn't make a good job of sounding like Eva. I relied on the fact that it was so unlikely that anyone would ring up and pretend to be Eva complaining about the plumbing that they probably wouldn't question it. I also held the phone at some distance from my face and coughed and sniffed, seeming to have a cold. If I sounded different from Eva, hopefully they would put it down to my having flu.

The landlady was incensed about the blocked drains. What a worry for her to have to get someone out to look at them, and how expensive it would be. I couldn't say, 'thanks but we're the ones who can't take a bath because we'd be swimming in sewage'. I wasn't supposed to be living there after all. I had to go out for the day with the children whenever I had notice from her or her husband that they were coming round to the property.

The landlady was one of those owners who just wanted to take an exorbitant rent for the property but not to have to maintain it properly or do anything to it. There were loads of such property owners in affluent areas of London. Too many people wanting to rent pushed the prices up, and because there were 20 people waiting to take your place in the queue for accommodation, you had no leverage to get the property owner to do any repairs. If you didn't like something, you could just get out. They would have no trouble finding other occupants.

The men who worked in the shop downstairs, kind though they were about swapping milk vouchers for food and giving the kids lollipops for free, wanted the flat themselves. When I shopped downstairs, they often asked me hopefully if there was any chance of us moving out because they had relatives lined up who wanted the flat.

Worse things followed. I was lying in bed one morning when I heard an enormous crash. I came cautiously down the stairs, not knowing what to expect, to find my way blocked by a huge pile of rubble and clouds of dust. The ceiling was down in the hallway at the bottom of the stairs. My heart turned over. It was a place my six-month-old baby regularly crawled about in. If she had been under the ceiling when it collapsed . . . The energy drained out of me. I don't know how I held up; it was one catastrophe after another.

7

The snatch and the recovery order

⚖

It was fortunate that I had engaged solicitors. I had done my best to keep out of reach and sight of my husband while I was living with my friends after the split. It wasn't easy; he lived close by. Sometimes I needed to go to the shops or to the doctor's. About a month after I left Jack, I encountered him in the high street. My mother and I were shopping. I had the two boys with me. Our friends were taking care of the girls at home. There was no quick or easy escape route with two infants in tow, a two-year-old and a four-year-old. We had walked to the high street, so I had no pushchair to bundle them into and walk away.

Jack gripped the hands of my two sons and took them. I tried pleading. It met with no response. My mother was in favour of screaming or asking passers-by for help. I was afraid of frightening the boys. Uncertain we followed my husband down the street, not knowing what to do. My boys looked back helplessly at me, bewildered. I felt sick with anxiety and fear, wondering what would happen. I phoned my friends. They immediately came to help and tried to persuade Jack to give the boys back. He merely shoved and shouldered away whichever of us tried to stand in the way. None of us felt able to make a scene that might have scared the boys.

Orla advised calling the police because there was no possibility of getting the boys back without a struggle which would have put them at risk. We hurried home and called the police.

The police came but could do nothing. Jack was refusing to return the boys. Without a court order there was no way of getting them back. I phoned my solicitors. Never was I as grateful for anything as for their speed in acting to get them back.

Originally, my solicitor had intended my divorce and the proceedings to be conducted in the magistrates' court. The snatch of the children put paid to that. We needed decisive action very quickly.

We were in the High Court, the Royal Courts of Justice on the Strand, the same day, within several hours. I found it difficult to get a grip on anything that was happening around me. Shocked, dazed, consumed with anxiety, I was going through the motions. I met the barrister who had been appointed to act for me at court in London. He wanted an account of events. It was difficult to keep my mind clear. I felt disorientated in the unfamiliar setting of this grand court building. Relevant facts slipped my mind. I couldn't convey anything much of what had happened. I was reliant on my mother and friends to supply the facts.

It was a very lonely experience. My friends were unable to come into the courtroom. I retain the image of the judge, who wanted to know why we were there so late in the day. My barrister explained our predicament. Anxiety about the boys' whereabouts and how they were feeling was uppermost in my mind. The recovery order we were asking for was granted and I now had the bit of paper which enabled me to seek their return.

The court police – known by the archaic name of the 'tipstaff' – asked me if I had any recent photographs of the boys to enable a search to take place. I didn't have any photos with me. I was asked to describe the children so the police would have an idea of how they looked. I looked at Eva for help in describing them. 'Both have blond hair and blue eyes,' she responded promptly. 'About two feet tall.' It was a horrendous situation but the 'two feet tall' made us dissolve into hysterical laughter. The police, normally hunting for villains, were being instructed to search for two angelic-looking kids only two feet high.

Armed with the court order for their return, I went back to my old home. Although I still had a key, it was no longer of any use. Jack had changed the locks. There was no sign of life at the house. We had been told to expect help from the police and the court tipstaff in locating the boys. I waited at the house for them.

There was a farcical scene when the tipstaff arrived to do his part but the police failed to turn up. A phone call elicited the fact that the police had been on their way when the tyres on their van had popped and they were stranded. It was a scene straight out of the *Wacky Races*. There was a further wait until the police eventually got there.

The court staff and the police tried to gain entry to the house but it was locked up and in darkness. A fire engine arrived. Fire officers went up ladders and peered through windows, trying to find out whether anyone was in the house. They used heat-seeking equipment. They finally assured me that no one was in there. It was difficult to accept. I wanted to seize a great stick, a branch from a tree I saw in the garden, and smash the glass in the door myself. They were reassuring but insistent; there was no point making the house insecure by breaking in. There was definitely no one on the premises.

I didn't tend to cry on these occasions. Dread seizes you. Your emotions dry up. Sometimes the anxiety is so great that you stop feeling anything at all and become an automaton, just doing what you know you have to. They are with that man whom you don't trust and all these thoughts about past incidents where he was willing to put them at risk without any compunction go through your mind.

Jack was furiously angry and determined. There were many times in the past when the kids had been in the way and he didn't care: like the times he tried to frighten me by screeching round blind corners on the wrong side of the road; or by deliberately speeding and then doing emergency stops. He didn't care that he scared us to death and left me fearing that we'd all be involved in an accident.

The tipstaff from the court went around knocking at neighbours' doors, looking for information about my husband and the boys, seeing whether anyone could shed light on where they might have gone. No one was able to help. Orla reported back snatches of conversation which she'd picked up on the doorsteps. Neighbours remembered having seen me in the garden on several occasions at night, locked out of the house in my nightdress.

I wondered why they admitted to having seen me. If I had seen someone in that state, I hope I would have intervened. Knowing what I do now, I wouldn't care if I was told to keep my nose out. It wouldn't stop me asking questions if I saw a woman in a state who looked as though she might need help.

Orla also reported a conversation taking place which upset me when I heard it: a discussion between the police and the court tipstaff about the difficulties on these occasions and how they sometimes sympathised with the men. Nearly faint with fear, it felt like a betrayal hearing such comments. It also scared me that perhaps they weren't going to put a hundred per cent effort into looking for the boys if, deep down, they sympathised with Jack.

Time and time again I have heard similar comments since: uncomprehending comments from people who think such controlling behaviour in a man is about love. It isn't love; it's a desire for power, a determination to control. I doubt anyone who thinks it is love when a man acts like that has experienced or understood real abuse.

Domestic abuse is like rape. It is about domination, power and control, not love. If a man wants his children so badly yet doesn't care that he puts them at physical and emotional risk, doesn't care that he denigrates their mother and beats her in front of their eyes, then he isn't capable of the selflessness and self-sacrifice of love. You have to be able to put your children before yourself. It's the essence of parenting. When he snatched them, it wasn't love and desire for their well-being that dictated his actions.

I had the images in my head all the time: mental pictures of the numerous nights I'd been deprived of sleep, bellowed at, and knocked about. I had the images of the hardness in his face, his complete lack of mercy when he was pinning me to a wall to ensure I got the point about something. The people who came into contact with us didn't know of the cruelty with which he could act. They didn't know that I lived in fear of his menace and bullying. But it still hurt when they made judgements about us, when they felt sorry for him for having lost his children. They didn't see the sadistic side that showed no conscience when he used the children to compel me to toe the line.

I wondered why people didn't see fit to question more. Why would a mother run away with four tiny children, putting herself at such disadvantage and ending up in poverty, if matters were not serious? It was hardly something you'd do lightly.

There seemed to be nothing more that the court officer, the police and the firemen could do that evening. The consensus seemed to be that they should clear off for the night and resume searching the next day. We had nothing to go on, no way of telling where Jack was. He didn't look like coming home that night. I didn't want them to go but there was nothing I could do to stop them. I had no idea where they should search or what they should do if they stayed.

Eva and I waited in her car further off once everyone else had gone. We parked in a side road, hoping that Jack and the boys would come back. The time ticked by. It was difficult to cope with a bellyful of anxiety and the sense of dread and foreboding.

It got dark and the street lights went on. We still sat there. Finally, late in the evening, around 11 p.m., a car passed us and turned into the cul-de-sac where I had once lived. I got out of Eva's car and walked in the middle of the road.

I wasn't sure whether it was Jack driving the car as the light was poor. The car began to turn at the end of the road. The headlights were shining in my eyes. I didn't recognise the car but instinct told me it was my husband driving.

Once the car was facing me, I could see Jack's face. I began to run towards the car. I was so anxious about the boys that I forgot my fear of my husband.

Instead of coming to a stop outside the house, Jack began to accelerate. Once he had seen me, he was obviously determined not to return home.

I was in the middle of the road and he was speeding up. I caught sight of his set, angry face. I knew him of old. In that split second I knew he would run me down if I stayed in his way. I leapt for the pavement and my husband tore past me in the car and screeched around the corner. I pelted after the car, yelling at him that there was a High Court order for the return of the boys. I might as well have shouted at the wind. The car disappeared at speed into the night.

I ran to Eva's car. She had used her common sense and taken down the registration number of the white car as Jack sped off in it. She started her car and we drove hurriedly to the next corner. Then we stopped and looked at each other. This wasn't a film, it wasn't cops and robbers. We weren't the Bill. No matter how desperate we were to recover the boys, sensible people didn't do car chases. It was senseless and dangerous chasing after him.

We went home. It was a terrible night. Madeleine had been asking repeatedly, 'Where are Ben and Jools? What happened to them? When are they coming back? Why aren't they here?' I couldn't cope with the questions. I couldn't even cry. I felt all dried up inside. I felt as though my jaw was clenched to breaking point. Where had they gone? Hadn't he heard about the court order? Why would he drive away from the house like that?

We had been talking of selling the house and moving abroad for ages. Suppose he disappeared with them and didn't come back? Were they miserable, missing their mother and sisters whom they had always been with? What were they thinking after being grabbed like that? Had they even been in the car? I hadn't seen them in the car. I'd only seen Jack.

The worries and fears went through my mind all night. I paced the room. I went to the loo innumerable times. I drank coffee. I walked down the road back to my old home repeatedly. I had lost my fear of my husband for that moment. I was too fearful over what had happened to the boys to care about what happened to me.

Morning came. I had not slept. And there was no sign of my husband or the boys. My friends had done as the court tipstaff suggested and rung around my husband's friends and relatives, trying to see whether we could get any information from them about his whereabouts. Either no one knew or they weren't telling.

8

The question of contact

⚖️

The recovery order for the boys had been granted on 25 April 2002. The following day we returned to the High Court to explain to a judge that we still hadn't managed to find the children. My husband's solicitors were ordered by the court to disclose Jack's whereabouts if they knew them.

I was given an interim residence order for the children, meaning that I had custody until the case could be considered in more detail at a later date, and a prohibited steps order, which was a court order prohibiting Jack from snatching the children in future. It was agreed at court between the judge and my legal representatives that we would apply for an occupation order and a non-molestation order against Jack. The occupation order would enable me and the children to move back into the family home and Jack to be removed. The non-molestation order was designed to prevent future violence or harassment from Jack.

It seemed that Jack's solicitors did have some communication with him because they put strong pressure on him to return the children. Finally he agreed to give them back.

When the boys returned, their behaviour was peculiar. My youngest son, Jools, only two years old, was very aggressive. Usually he was a real softy. His little face went red and angry when he saw me. He ran to the sofa and buried his head in it, repeating over and over, 'Daddy's not cross, Daddy's not cross.' We had to laugh even though it was alarming. The contrast between his red angry face and the stamping of his foot, and his assertions that no one was cross, was comical despite the seriousness of the matter.

My older son's behaviour was even more concerning. He kept

disappearing and hiding for lengthy periods over the next few weeks. There were several occasions when Orla's family had to help me search for him, our hearts in our mouths, thinking he'd been snatched again, only to find him secreted in some obscure hidey hole, silent and not speaking.

He had temper tantrums, which were disturbing because they were out of character and during them he would bang his head hard on the walls or floor.

Ben smeared his excrement over the walls and floor of the flat. I was horrified and clueless about how to handle this behaviour. What did it signify? I was sure this was down to his father's influence. Ben's father often singled him out from the other children for special attention. He was consistently favoured over the girls and Jools also took second place to his brother. Quite often, when I'd lived with Jack, Ben had been rewarded with approval for disobeying me and only paying attention to his father.

Somehow the boys had become imbued with hostility towards me during the time they had been snatched by their father. They came back with stories of how their mother and grandmother and friends were lying about their father and saying that they shouldn't believe it. This was all the more confusing for the boys since none of us ever talked in a derogatory way about their father in front of them.

W e had conscientiously always avoided scaring the children with our perceptions of the risk posed by their father, and all discussions about events took place between the adults in private. Their father was bringing the concept of bad mouthing and alienation in where it didn't belong. He was trying aggressively to counter something that didn't exist except in his mind, and it merely led the children to feel upset and confused.

I debated with my friends about whether or not we should tell my solicitor and the court the worst of the boys' behaviour. I was afraid that Ben's disturbed behaviour might be used against me by Jack to support his claims that I was a bad mother and that Ben didn't want to live with me. I wasn't confident that the court would attribute my son's behaviour to the correct causes: namely his father's influence and the fact that he was emotionally rewarded by his father for being rebellious or badly behaved with me. In the end I didn't tell anyone beyond Orla's family about the excrement.

We returned to court on 30 April for a directions hearing. At a directions hearing, a judge lays down his or her instructions for how the case should proceed in future. I was represented by a woman barrister who introduced herself in the long corridor that spanned the courtrooms. She had gleaming black hair, brown eyes, a smart black suit and a pleasant manner.

Naively, I was surprised that the issue of the children's contact with my husband appeared to be the highest item on the agenda. It was virtually the first question I was asked when I got to court: how much contact was I prepared to offer Jack? I didn't understand this approach. We were only a few days on from the snatch, during which I'd narrowly avoided being run over by Jack when he'd fled in his car. There was no discussion about whether contact handovers were safe for me and whether direct contact was physically and emotionally safe for the children.

Eva stepped forward. She explained to the barrister that she'd seen Jack drive the car at me only some days before. I recall the barrister's phrase in response. It was 'Oh my god!' But that was it. We had a bare few minutes' discussion outside court with this new barrister, in which I was expected to decide the future welfare of my children.

I wanted to jump in and say 'haven't you read my statement?' The abuse I had suffered had been documented by my solicitor and put into a statement for the court. It's true that the violence was described in a few lines here and there – it wasn't descriptive and didn't convey anything of the psychological impact it had carried at the time – but the control issues were well documented. On reading what I had to say, didn't the legal representatives and the judge see that my husband was seriously abusive and needed strict supervision when he was with the children? Evidently they didn't. It made the world of court seem unreal to me. In the outside world, anyone who knew about it was horrified. But here were people at court not taking it seriously.

Unfortunately I wasn't on the ball at this time. I was still numb with shock over the snatch, and lethargic with anxiety and sleeplessness. With hindsight I think the professionals involved may not have understood my state of mind. Mentally I was traumatised and barely present, but I had a quiet and reserved manner and didn't tend to show my inner turmoil; perhaps they didn't notice these effects. Possibly they were relying on me to say what I wanted and to give firm instructions. But I wasn't able to do this. These were the professionals and I was relying on them to ask the right questions and to do the right thing by my children.

Looking back I can see that, for whatever reason, there was a lamentable lack of communication between me and the professionals involved. Orla and Eva tried to help by speaking for me. This wasn't allowed. The barrister made clear that she would like to speak to me on her own and that she could only take instructions from me, even though I would have preferred Orla and Eva to speak for me. I was strained and I kept losing concentration. It was a very isolating experience and I wish the legal representatives had realised how badly I needed my friends' support to function. I am convinced, following my own long experience at court since then, that it would be very helpful for victims of domestic abuse to be allowed a friend with them in court as a source of emotional support.

I was handed Jack's first statement to read in the corridor at court. I have to say that it's a horrendous thing to be handed a statement by the opposing party just before one goes into the courtroom. This was the first occasion but it happened regularly at court from then on. Not only did it plunge me into emotional turmoil, reading the awful things which were written down about me, and distract me from the business in court ahead, but there was no time to digest the implications of his statement and formulate a response appropriate to the seriousness of the situation. There were complex issues here and they needed more than a few minutes' consideration given the possible consequences for the children's well-being and my own.

Jack's statement denoted his contemptuous attitude towards me. He thought it was all right to say that I was nuts, schizophrenic even. Didn't they see what a bad attitude it showed? When I read over the sheets of paper, it felt like the kick in the back I'd received when I was pregnant. It made my stomach churn. To this day when I read his statements, full of bile and denial of his abuse and violence, and full of accusations that I am unstable and mentally ill, they make me feel queasy. I find it difficult to get through them.

Jack repeated his allegations of my instability in the courtroom in front of the judge, Recorder U. The Judge had been a QC and was known as 'Recorder' because he was in the first stages of being a judge.

For some reason Jack had parted company with his solicitors and had turned up at court to represent himself. He was voluble and argumentative, heedless of court protocol. The judge told him that he was doing himself no favours and advised him to get legal representation.

Court and the concept of contact was a rude shock. Nothing in my experience had prepared me for anything like it. Previously I'd had little experience of judges or courts. I had no idea there were such things as family courts. I found it hard to get my head around it. Judges were for judging criminals, weren't they? What did they have to do with families? Why couldn't a mother just tell her ex to buzz off and get some therapy before he came pestering and demanding with threats to take the kids?

At first it seemed alien and outrageous. I was from a provincial northern background. I had grown up in a northern town with working-class parents and working-class values. Mums looked after the children and made the decisions about parenting. Dads went to work during the week and came home with a pay packet, cash in an envelope, on a Friday night.

If a couple split up, the kids always went with the mother who often got a new boyfriend. Sometimes the father stayed around, sometimes he didn't. Often he went off with a new girlfriend and eventually ended up with a second family. Either way the kids stayed with the mum, no question. And it was mum who decided how much the kids saw their dad.

It was pragmatic in all the cases I saw and it worked. It's not that there were no cases of domestic violence around. There were some on the council estate I grew up on. Mainly, however, the neighbours were respectable working-class folk, trying to better themselves.

During Mrs Thatcher's era many of them, my parents included, bought their council house and tried to improve their lot. They shared many of the material aspirations of the middle classes and wanted their kids to do better than they had. The rare family who didn't share these aspirations got well known. Such families were disapproved of. The children were pitied. Everyone knew who the odd feckless father was, who disappeared into the pub on a Friday evening after work and drank away all his wages without giving his wife her housekeeping first. These men were despised; a man should provide for his kids. My own mother worked full time, some mums worked part time, but it wasn't uncommon then for women to stay at home. I had many classmates with stay-at-home mums.

There were a few men on the estate who had drink problems and anger issues. I had a friend who regularly arrived at school with marks inflicted by her father when he was drunk. Her father hit my friend and her sister, as well as their mother, leaving them with black eyes or bruises. There was no social services involvement with the family; strangely no one reported it. My friend didn't seem unduly concerned by what was happening in her home. She accepted it as normal that her father regularly got drunk and hit them. I could not understand this acceptance of what I considered to be an appalling state of affairs.

I was a teenager but I really felt for this girl. I sometimes thought of reporting it myself. It crossed my mind, however, that it was not a hidden situation. It's not as if the sisters made efforts to conceal their bruises; they didn't show them off, but neither did they hide them. Because the girls weren't in crisis and everything else went on as normal, no one took steps to interfere.

I had a conflict about this situation even then. Although it was awful, I knew if someone had come along and suggested taking my friend and her sister away, they would have been devastated. It would not have been what they wanted. Their world was all they knew and anyone taking it away would have been regarded as an unwanted hostile intruder.

Adjusting to a different reality, in a children's home or with foster parents (and you couldn't assume that the quality of care in such a home would be any better), would have been utterly traumatic for them. Perhaps a move would have affected them more than the abuse did. Yes, they might be removed from an abusive situation if someone put them in care, but they would have a whole new set of problems and trauma to deal with. They loved their mother. They had friends. They were settled. How could you take children away in those circumstances?

The question arises: suppose the abused woman doesn't get rid of the man – because those involved, namely the abused, think the abuse is normal and they are used to it and possibly inured to it. Does that absolve an onlooker from interfering, trying to do something about it? It's a hard question and this was my dilemma. You want to step in and help when you see someone being hurt. But my friend did not want such help. If I had reported it, I might have hurt the family even more.

Taking control of a family which is unwilling to give over that control could itself be classified as patriarchal, unhelpful, disempowering, and abusive even. Families that have suffered at the hands of an abusive member need care and sensitivity, carefully managed offers of help, not reinforcement by outsiders of patterns of control.

What would have helped in this and in my own situation? Certainly not solutions imposed by outsiders that didn't take into account all the complex realities. A more victim-focused approach which required them to involve us in the solution would have helped.

I was running on two conflicting mentalities. Interestingly, when I look back now, I see that at the time when I was suffering domestic violence I made no connection between myself and the childhood friend in whose family female members were battered. The educated, feminist, rational side of me intellectually rejected such abuse. But when I was suffering it personally, I accepted it: emotionally, I seemed to be operating within the norms of my childhood – when women and girls just had to take hitting by fathers as a way of life and they couldn't expect outside help.

Now I was grown up and in court, here was a new concept and it was a shock. In this world of mainly middle-class, white, male judges, it was the judges who didn't understand that you should decide when and how their dad got to see the kids. This was novel. It seemed outrageous. Here was exactly my nightmare scenario of powerful strangers stepping in and imposing a solution on the victims that wasn't even tailored to meet their needs.

Here was a world where mums weren't powerful and they didn't make the most important decisions on behalf of the kids, as they had when I was a child. You couldn't get rid of an abuser because the court wouldn't let you. What sort of world with inverted values was this? It was a world to which I had to adjust. The adjustment was painful.

The fact that your ex was extremely abusive was largely irrelevant to the judge. The abuser apparently could still be a good parent. No connection was made between the two things. At first, I couldn't grasp the enormity of what was happening. I tried looking around. Didn't anyone else think the way I did? Barristers, solicitors, they all seemed to be toeing the official line as far as I could see. They seemed like a row of parrots on a perch, all saying the same thing.

Of course, I had been under my husband's thumb. He had made all the decisions for me. But although I had been browbeaten into putting up with this, all along I was intellectually at odds with it. I knew it was wrong; that I was in an undignified and morally compromising position. I had sold out any right to the feminist credentials that I'd previously tried to uphold. It was not what modern relationships should be: it was against the values I had grown up with and it was against the feminist values I had held as a university student. I sometimes used to feel shame. I wondered what had happened to the young women I had been educated with.

When I had been at university in the 1980s and early 1990s, we were expected to be independent, to make our own decisions. I felt I had sold out by capitulating to my husband, but I was trapped and had the children to think of. Opposition to my husband made it bad for the children. I felt I had to give in all the time.

I wasn't treated as a modern woman at court either. It seemed that they expected me to hand over my kids at a judge's behest without asking any questions about their safety. Seeing that safety was not an item on the agenda, at this first hearing, made me lose confidence in myself.

Picking up some of my reluctance about contact, my barrister asked if there were any relatives who might facilitate it. Lacking the courage to say that I really wanted contact to happen only in a safe and secure place, such as a contact centre, I agreed to a relative of Jack's hosting the contact sessions. The judge would be asked to make an order that instructed me to deliver the children to this relative's home in Hertfordshire, some miles from where we lived in London, for their contact once a week.

My barrister had another point to make. Jack was accusing me of mental instability; she thought I should disclose my medical records to prove that I was of sound mind. I didn't see any problem with that. I had suffered from some anxiety as a teenager but nothing after that for the last fifteen years. I wasn't mentally ill or unstable and had nothing to hide. Orla, who was with me, interjected to say that I shouldn't consider disclosing my medical records under any circumstances. There was nothing for me to answer. Jack could accuse me of mental instability all he liked, but he had no evidence to back this up and no witnesses because nothing had ever happened. I'd been a consistent parent with my children and I had nothing to prove. This was all about control and I shouldn't give in to his demands.

I didn't get Orla's point at the time. We argued in front of the barrister. 'There's nothing in my records that could harm my case. Wouldn't it just be easier to knock Jack's accusations on the head at the beginning by disclosing the facts?' I was persuaded by the barrister's view and she in turn put a stop to Orla's argument by putting her hand up as if she was stopping the traffic. 'I can only take instructions from my client.'

Orla was fuming. She was trying to do her best for me and giving me advice that later turned out to be right. I didn't get it at the time. I was naive and trusting. 'It's never good when someone gets hold of your medical records,' she told me. 'Even if there isn't anything in there, they'll find something.' This was before the days of the Roy Meadow affair and other scandals where medical experts had been trusted and had later turned out to be disastrously wrong. I finally compromised between the barrister's view and my friend's, and agreed to seek a letter from my GP saying I was not mentally ill, rather than fully disclosing my medical records.

The judge ordered a hearing to take place regarding interim residence and contact, on the first available date after 10 June. He ordered that these matters should be considered at the same time as our application for a non-molestation order and an occupation order. All this was to take place before a final hearing later in the year.

Unfortunately, the time needed to consider all these matters simultaneously meant that we couldn't get an early hearing because there was no room in the court calendar for a lengthy hearing in the near future. I argued the point with my solicitors. 'How long do we have to be out of our home? Isn't there a way to get an earlier hearing?' They said it couldn't be done. We couldn't split the issues up because a judge had ordered all the issues to be considered together at one hearing, and since my getting the house was linked to Jack's behaviour, which in turn linked to how much contact he should have, there was no way to hear the issues separately. We would just have to wait.

With no prospect of getting an early hearing, and knowing we were going to have to stick it out in unsatisfactory temporary accommodation, there was nothing to do but get on with things. There was a crumb of comfort about the car. It had been repaired at the time the boys had been snatched. The garage owner, seeing my distress over my missing boys, had practically repaired the car for nothing. I could have kissed him.

9

Charged with assault

⚖️

Contact sessions were supervised for some weeks by Jack's relative at her Hertfordshire home. It was possible to get there when I had the car. For a couple of weeks it was quite pleasant driving up the A1 and dropping the children off at their grown-up cousin's house in a pretty little village. Orla and Eva came along for the ride when they could, Orla treating us to breakfast in a quaint hotel with dark wooden beams, upholstered furniture and tables beautifully set with cloths, napkins and silverware.

Unfortunately, the little silver Metro which had survived one theft by joy riders was stolen again, crashed and abandoned by a bunch of teenagers who were seen running off.

There wasn't enough money to repair the car this time: I had to let it go. Contact was therefore up for grabs again because there was no way of delivering the children each week to rural Hertfordshire without the car. I hoped the legal representatives would be able to arrange sessions at a contact centre. Jack, however, opposed any kind of supervision and he applied for an extension to his contact time. There was a new hearing in June. It took place in front of someone I will call Judge T.

It was this June hearing which gave me a scary insight into the power politics involved in getting a good welfare outcome, or otherwise, for the kids.

I was very bad at standing my ground in court. The time spent at the Royal Courts of Justice so far seemed to consist of stressful and fruitless discussions about contact, most of which passed over my head. I was only conscious of developing migraines and feeling under terrible pressure. Outside the court, in the corridors where barristers and solicitors tried to pressure you into agreements about the children, I couldn't stand up to the stresses of disagreement.

Barristers used the levers of approval and disapproval, of power, to get you to agree: your legal funding could be removed, your kids could be taken away and given to your ex, and the judge will take a dim view of your case if you are not reasonable. They implied that the outcome would be worse if you didn't compromise. This approach made me feel I was gambling with my children's welfare and that the judge would be punitive if I didn't give way. I think it is very likely that the legal representatives didn't realise that battered women are incredibly vulnerable to pressure. It is easy to fall into the old patterns set by your abusive partner when you just went along with things because you were going to be punished if you didn't.

On this occasion I felt I didn't have a voice. I wanted to stand up in court and shout over my barrister's head at the judge: 'Actually I don't agree with what the barrister is saying. I was pressured into agreement. Please don't make my life hell by enforcing unsupervised contact.' But of course I didn't stand up. I kept silent, with my eyes down, feeling hopeless.

In the opinion of barristers and judges, agreement between the parties was a good thing. They reckoned that orders negotiated between parties held up better than solutions imposed by a judge. That may be true where both parties are confident and strong. If you have one party who is aggressive and determined and one who is weaker and more vulnerable to pressure, the result is a recipe for failure.

There is an uneven balance of power in these situations. Jack didn't have the kids and was unable to prioritise their welfare before his own needs; he could afford to be unreasonable, go for broke, and throw everything at me. He didn't have what he wanted – the children – and so he had nothing to lose. It made him unwilling to give any ground. You could afford to be reckless when you had nothing to lose.

I had everything to lose. I had the children, but the implications of the barrister's pressure on me to give more contact than I believed was right, were that if I didn't the judge would just order it anyway and he would like me the less for having to force it out of me. If this had been a card game, I would have been playing with a weak hand. Basically mothers were at a disadvantage in these negotiations. The more reasonable you were, the more likely you were to be done down in the wheeling and dealing. Seeing that the kids' welfare apparently depended on my correctly anticipating the judge's thought processes was a nightmare. Often the legal professionals couldn't properly anticipate a judge's thinking either, especially if they came before a judge they didn't know well. Judges had a wide range of discretion, and barristers could only tell you of the possible range of options in a particular case.

I was knocked for six when the barrister suggested that I was at a disadvantage on future residence issues because I didn't have a proper home for the kids. Jack was in a better position to offer the children a good home because he was in the house. The suggestion was that in leaving a violent home I had made myself worse off and might lose the children because of it.

There was no in-depth investigation at this June hearing. I had already been reduced to a nervous pulp by my barrister, who had done a good job in convincing me that I had to be 'reasonable' in front of this judge.

Judge T took one look at the previous court order from the time of the snatch and said that Jack wasn't getting enough contact time. His comment wasn't unkindly meant, but the judge lacked any knowledge of the bigger picture. He didn't even enquire whether there were good reasons for Jack's contact being so limited.

This crude guillotine method of case management – let's just cut off the past and start anew as though nothing had happened and there were no issues to resolve – finished me off. I didn't dare put up any more objections to unsupervised contact. With my barrister and the judge, I was between a rock and a hard place. I caved in and outwardly agreed to unsupervised contact even though inwardly I was dead against it.

In order to prevent their father from talking inappropriately to the children and running me down, I'd asked the court to make an order about this. Instead Judge T required Jack to give promises, called undertakings, not to talk to the children about the case. Jack refused to give undertakings to the court unless I gave them too.

I argued the point with my solicitor. 'I don't talk inappropriately to the children; I would never call him names or run him down to them: why should I have to give undertakings as well?' She argued back that it was the only way to get Jack to make the promises not to talk to the children, and since we wanted them, why didn't I just make the promises too? If I wasn't talking to the children about the case, there was no harm in my giving undertakings.

I didn't like this. 'If I give undertakings,' I reasoned with her, 'it will look later on as though I needed to give undertakings because I was talking to the children. No future judge who comes to the case fresh is going to know the undertakings were given only in order to persuade Jack to make them. He is going to think I had to give the promises for a reason, namely that I've been talking wrongly to the children.'

My solicitor disagreed with me. 'Judges don't think that way. They know things are often done to be even-handed, so that the reluctant party will cooperate and not be obstructive.'

I didn't like this kind of logic, although I encountered it regularly in the courts. It sends the wrong message to an abusive partner that they aren't fully responsible for their behaviour, that the court regards it as six of one and half a dozen of the other. Their idea of being even-handed was to treat both parties equally. It was like putting a flyweight in a boxing ring with a heavyweight and expecting the contest to be fair. It was a legalistic kind of reasoning done for convenience, but it wasn't based on the way people in the real world think and behave, and it is doomed to failure because it is based on false premises.

In domestic abuse cases, you are not talking about two reasonable parents who might be worked upon, reasoned, cajoled, argued into seeing sense. Most ordinary people will not shamelessly use and manipulate their children to a degree that is seriously damaging for them. Their logic might have worked with a relatively decent, normal parent. Here we were talking about one who was seriously emotionally abusive and who constantly tried to exercise power and control over the more vulnerable family members. The normal modes of reason and compromise didn't work with him.

It's a mistake to think you can persuade, coax, cajole an abusive man into behaving. For one thing, he probably has very little insight into his behaviour. Often tough consequences to force him into line are the only things he respects; something or someone more powerful than he is. The court hardly ever used its power to force him into line; instead the judges naively seemed to rely on a mix of good-humoured coaxing and persuasion, or, on occasion, banging our heads together as though that was going to sort the problem. The court was basically soft on abuse and violence, constantly minimising it.

They treated a woman trying to stop the abuse and to protect the children in exactly the same way as a perpetrator. There were no victims and perpetrators. He was treated as a normal father who would see reason. And of course he never did.

So now, after Judge T's involvement, we moved to contact handovers taking place in a public park. I used to deliver the kids, go away, and come back for them at the end of contact. Jack was supposed to stay in the park. It was in the contact order that he could not go back to the family home with the children. I had held out for that because I did not trust him to return the kids if he took them home. Possession was nine-tenths of the law in his eyes. If he took them home, I also saw it as much more likely that he would try to indoctrinate them; tell them that they wanted to stay with him. They would have been too little and too scared to resist.

At that time, while we were out of the house, I also thought it would have been cruel to remove them from the comfort of their own home at the end of each contact session. It would have led to endless trouble. And I would have been seen as the bad guy, removing them from the house twice a week only to bring them back to the disaster zone which was our flat.

We agreed that Jack would look after the children in the local park. It was a big park with cafés, a playground, sports activities and a garden centre. It wasn't explicitly phrased in the order that he could not take them away from the play area, but that was what I had meant when I agreed to it. We had agreed it verbally and because the order had been set up and phrased so that I would be the one taking and fetching them from the park, the order implied that he would stay there between the dropping off and picking up times. Naively I hoped this kind of agreement would work.

The sessions in the park happened for a few weeks without incident. Then I turned up to hand the children over as usual, only to find that Jack had brought along several relatives and was intending to leave in the car with the children. I was thrown by this. It was unexpected and not what I had agreed to. I didn't know then that there should have been an order specifically excluding him from leaving the park. I had assumed that a verbal agreement witnessed by solicitors at court would be binding.

I protested that it was against the court order. He disagreed. The court order did not exclude him from taking them away. I was getting panicky at this point. I had no means of physically keeping him in the place if he chose to leave. It didn't take much to make him angry. I could see the way things were going to go and my stomach was churning with the anxiety of it.

The added complication was his relatives. I felt vulnerable in the presence of my sister-in-law. This was a woman I had run to on a number of occasions when I had been badly treated, kept awake at night or locked out. I had told her of some of his abuse. I had run to her in emergencies. She had harboured me overnight one time when his behaviour had become unbearable. She had even promised to tackle him about it.

Now the same sister-in-law was acting as though nothing had ever happened; as though I was the person in the wrong. I really felt that. And I felt vulnerable because it was four members of the family I was facing and not one of them a friendly face.

I refused to let Jack leave the park with the children. I insisted he stay in the spot which we had agreed on at court. My husband's relatives were uncomfortable in the face of our disagreement and said they would go and have coffee and let us sort it out. They wandered off and I was left alone with Jack.

The children were all fretful by this time. I thought I had a solution. I suggested that we ring our respective solicitors and let them sort it out. It would be better to abide by what they said than to argue over it. He agreed to that. Unfortunately he managed to contact his solicitors straight away, who, of course, confirmed that he could take them away because it wasn't excluded in the court order.

I was upset and angry by what I saw as duplicity. I had no more thought to exclude Jack from taking the children away from the park than I had thought to exclude him from holding contact sessions in a pub. Not knowing better, I had trusted to our verbal agreements in court. I had not learned at that stage that court orders may not be worth the paper they are written on. They are incredibly difficult to frame. They tend to deal with one narrow issue and cannot cover all eventualities. A court order cannot consist of a long list of exclusions. They assume a degree of good will and honesty on the part of both parties. If that is missing, there is endless scope for conflict.

I was too upset to reason all this out with Jack and too anxious. He was not in a listening mood. He was never in a listening mood wherever I was concerned. He was just going to do what he pleased anyway. I could see the set of his jaw. I would not let him close the car door. It was the only chance I had of keeping him at the park until I had phoned my own solicitor. My solicitor had been at court; she had been party to what was agreed. She would know I was telling the truth, and if it meant going back to court to get the order reworded, I hoped she would be able to do it.

Unfortunately, my solicitor was out of the office. I had reached an impasse with Jack and he decided he wasn't going to wait any longer. He tried reversing out of the car park with the three older children in the car. I screamed at him because baby Mia was parked in the pushchair behind the car. My heart was racing. I had seen too much of Jack's reckless driving of cars in the past – his deliberate use of bad driving to scare the hell out of me.

Some men came running over. They had seen him reversing and the danger to the pushchair. I was crying now. They asked what was happening and whose children were in the car. Jack told them they were his children; that he had a court order enabling him to take them away; and that I was ill and needed a doctor.

To my horror, although I pleaded with one of the men to call the police, they left. They were classing it as a domestic quarrel and didn't see it as their business to get involved.

Jack was determined to leave. He tried to force the door of the car shut, trapping me painfully in it. I screamed and he squeezed harder. Then he got out of the car and forced me to the floor, scraping my knees and legs on the gravel and stones of the car park. He was gripping my shoulders brutally, digging his fingers in, and he twisted my arm and bent it upwards.

I was horrified that the children were witnessing this. Some of my emotions were taken up with the usual feelings of powerlessness. This had happened so many times before. Whenever he felt like it, he could do things like this. And I could do nothing. He was a strong man, tall and well built. I was small and slight. I stood no chance against him physically. I couldn't get free from his grip. I began to feel far away; as though this was happening to someone else and not to me at all.

My leg was bleeding. I was bruised and scratched. The following events merged into a jumble. At some point my in-laws returned from the café. They were unsympathetic. I phoned my solicitors. Miles away, they could do nothing immediate to help and advised me to call the police. I made a 999 call.

During the events which followed and for some time afterwards I had feelings of unreality. It was as though the chain of events, the pressure of my husband's abuse, and the strain of court all combined. The burden was beginning to get unbearable.

When the police arrived, I showed a woman police officer my injuries. I was placed in a big white police van, like a minibus, with all the children, and taken to the nearest police station. As we were driven away, I saw Jack up against his car with his hands behind his head while he was being frisked by a police officer.

I called Eva on my mobile from the police van. She promised to get in the car straight away and meet me at the police station. My solicitor phoned while I was in the van. I couldn't take in what she was saying. I asked her to repeat herself a number of times, but I was unable to absorb anything she said. I couldn't tell her what had happened. I said I'd call her back.

Eva and Orla arrived at the police station shortly after I did. I was questioned by a young woman police officer, who wrote down what I said in the form of a statement. Later another officer came and asked further questions. She said the statement should be more detailed. 'How did you feel when you were attacked?' I burst into tears at that point because I had experienced the feelings which generally predominated in any dealings with Jack: powerlessness and helplessness. 'Make it more personal, say how you felt,' she advised. A magistrate or a jury would respond to that.

The forensic examiner arrived to inspect my injuries. I found this embarrassing. I was grateful to have female friends with me. The police officer wrote her own account of my bruises, while the police doctor produced a separate account. He did it in a detached and clinical way, without comment, taking physical measurements of my bruises and using medical language to describe their location. I had bruising to my upper body. I was wearing a close-fitting top and had to remove it so that I could be examined. Jack's fingerprints were still visible on my shoulders.

I felt uncomfortable having my body stared at by a stranger in these circumstances. It was undignified. The doctor did his work quickly, however. While this had been going on, two or three kind officers had volunteered to take the children to their canteen for a drink. No one wanted the children to witness my bruising.

The police officers returned from the canteen chuckling. 'You've got a great little lad,' one of them said about Ben. On being asked what drink he would like, my four-year-old firmly requested 'a cappuccino please'. They explained they couldn't give hot drinks like coffee to infants but he could have orange juice instead if he liked.

Before I left the police station, the police officer who had gone through my statement with me said that she would be questioning Jack and making a decision about whether or not to charge him. I was told to come back in four days' time when my bruises had fully formed and they would photograph me. They said that bruises tended to show up better on photographs after a few days, when they went purple.

It had been a horrible day. I drove home with my friends. We tried to relax during the evening, although we were all on tenterhooks. A phone call from the police came late in the evening. I was told that Jack was going to be charged with 'common assault' for the attack in the park. There was going to be a criminal trial.

Two days after this there was another hearing in the family court, at the Royal Courts of Justice. Jack was asking for the contact order to be enforced. I opposed this and asked for contact to take place in a contact centre where he could be supervised. There wasn't time in the court schedule for a proper hearing on this day, so the whole thing was shelved until we could get a date in the court calendar. In the meantime, due to the assault charge, Jack's contact was completely suspended, which was a relief and the first respite I felt we'd had in ages.

Hearings were frequently shelved at court. You could turn up and your case might well not be heard. If your hearing was 'at risk', which it often was if you had applied at short notice, there was always a chance that you would be in court for a few minutes and the legal representatives and the judge would come to the conclusion that the issues were too complex to be heard in a few minutes. Then you got bumped off to another date and another judge.

Two days after the bumped hearing, I was still in pain from my injuries in the park. My arm was swelling. Dirt from the floor of the car park had got into a cut on my arm and it became infected. I went to the hospital to have it checked. Because it was the result of an assault, the doctor took out her pad and noted down the positioning of the bruises, just as the police doctor had. I was more comfortable with this female doctor, although none of it was pleasant. I felt like an exhibit.

At the beginning of August the first hearing in the magistrates' court took place. The police told me I wasn't required to be there; that they would handle everything. It appeared that nothing much happened, except that Jack was bailed and ordered to reappear on another occasion. One of the conditions of his bail was that he should not attempt to approach me.

10

A Few Good Men: giving evidence on the witness stand

⚖

On 5 August 2002 another family hearing was set to take place at the Royal Courts of Justice. This day stands out as one of the most stressful episodes in the whole series of court hearings. I asked my solicitor before the hearing whether we needed evidence regarding Jack's assault on me. She said that the fact of Jack's being charged by the police was enough evidence because the police didn't charge people for nothing.

The judge's face sticks in my mind vividly. I could pick Judge A out anywhere in a crowd if I had to; he made such an indelible impression. His behaviour when he entered the court was all bonhomie and affability. It was inappropriate; my husband was on police bail for assaulting me. The children and I were living in appalling accommodation with Jack refusing to move out of the family home in order to give them a place to live.

I could feel my jaw tighten with anxiety again. Why wasn't the judge taking this seriously? The last thing I wanted to do at that moment was to smile. Relaxing was impossible. The judge and my husband immediately seemed to strike a chord. Jack was representing himself and he had produced a statement that was all his own, with no advice from a legally qualified person. The judge commented that he liked statements like that – 'raw' and not sanitised by solicitors. I couldn't share the judge's enjoyment of Jack's statements; they were too laden with insults about me and denials of his violence to make comfortable listening.

Judge A bantered with Jack and quoted Milton. I felt I couldn't be myself in this court. I was hurt and defensive and I didn't come across well. But there was no way for any woman in my position to come across well. Friends aren't allowed into court. Often the judge is male, and many male judges have a forceful, rough-and-ready way of dealing with proceedings. Nothing in their backgrounds tends to give them the skills to deal with vulnerable or abused women. Many of them are public school or Oxbridge educated. They are highly paid, influential and powerful. It takes a great deal of imagination, empathy and skill for a man to put himself in the shoes of a woman who is completely in the opposite position: put upon, lacking in confidence and afraid to speak up. They are at opposite poles.

I toyed with a fantasy in my head where the judges in the courtroom consisted of a bunch of women from Women's Aid, people who would understand exactly what abuse is like. I imagined a furore; fathers' groups would be up in arms and cry foul – institutional bias against men. That's exactly what it felt like to be judged by a posh, privileged bloke who got chummy with the domestic abuser standing in front of him. I wasn't being judged by my peers, by people who had experienced or could understand psychological and emotional abuse and the mental scars it left.

Appearances didn't help. I kept being told by professionals and well-meaning people that I should dress smartly for court. The difficulty was that I was a stay-at-home mum; I no longer had work clothes. Jack had retained all my personal belongings at the house. I had no money to buy new clothes. I was stuck with cast-offs from friends and the charity shops.

I had arrived at court wearing a sky-blue sweater with flowers embroidered on it. It was too tight and revealing. I was conscious of the fact that it wasn't right, but I had been given it and I had nothing else more appropriate. With waist-length hair – I hadn't yet cut it short, the patterns of my marriage and not being allowed to cut my hair were still operating – I looked girlish, less serious than my husband. Older and with silver hair, a posh accent and wearing a beautiful suit, Jack was more likely to be taken to by the judge. I was reminded of the newspaper photograph taken at Westminster with my employer boxing another MP. Appearances can be deceptive. And the judge was totally deceived by superficial appearances. He fell for Jack hook, line and sinker.

I had a mild-mannered male barrister on this occasion. I was expected to give evidence on the witness stand in front of this judge. I was ill-prepared. It was at short notice and I had never given evidence before. I had only seen people give evidence in films and on television.

My solicitor had given me some advice beforehand about not saying too much in case I was tripped up or led into inconsistencies. She had obviously seen it happen before and she was giving me advice based on her experience. She gave me examples of the ways in which you could be tricked in the witness box.

I was scared. I'd seen the film *A Few Good Men* and I was basing my ideas of giving evidence on the scene between Tom Cruise and Jack Nicholson when Nicholson's character is cleverly led along a path of questioning into admitting that he did the deed. I knew how Tom Cruise could catch you out and make you say anything in the witness box! How you could make a fool of yourself.

In fact I took the buttoned-lip approach far too literally. I took it so far that I hardly said anything except yes or no. I had got it into my head that unless I answered in one word or two, I would be hammered into a pulp, humiliated, shown up as a complete idiot.

I laugh and cry now when I look back. I handled it completely the wrong way. It is not as though my barrister didn't give me opportunities. If I'd known then, what I know now, I would have done it completely differently. But I was that person then, and that's all I knew.

I came across as defensive in the witness box. I could have expanded about my husband's past abuse, why I was afraid of my husband's influence on the children, what had happened in the park. I did none of those things. Jack, by contrast, came across well. He came across as an educated, charming, intelligent man: which he was. But there was a whole other side which the judge wasn't getting.

I had got so used to defeat that I anticipated it and retreated into silent helplessness. And that's what I did now. I could sense that the judge was unsympathetic and I closed up. I needed a great deal of encouragement at that stage to speak up for myself and this sort of situation was guaranteed to freeze me into immobility. It was a disaster and I knew while it was happening that it was a disaster.

Jack got his unsupervised contact back. Judgment when it came was insulting. Not only had I not been believed about the assault, but Jack had got more than his original contact time, even though he was still on police bail. Sure, the judge thought a bit of shoving had probably taken place, but he seemed to think it was six of one and half a dozen of the other. Yes, if I had been a different person, confident, self-assured, I could have got my barrister to stand up and explain how we had previously agreed at court that Jack would stay in the park, but that we hadn't framed the court order specifically to show that. But I was not a different person. I was a scared, tongue-tied, frightened wreck.

The cut that went deepest was the part of the judgment which said that we were two parents who dearly loved their children and who only wanted what was best for them, but that we didn't agree on what was best for them. He said that we were caring and able parents who not long ago were capable of working together. He said that we should turn our backs on the court and try to solve our own problems because court time and public expense were better spent on families with much deeper problems. That was his grasp of the situation. He thought Jack was a normal, decent parent and that we could sort it out together!

I could feel the bewilderment, the sense of injustice, growing inside me. How was this happening? It was all out of control. I wanted to stand up and stop the proceedings, ask to speak to someone in charge, ask what was going so terribly wrong, but I didn't know how to do it. I was devastated because this judge was adding insult to injury. Not only had my children seen me assaulted, but I was being forced to hand over the children to my husband at the very park where the assault had taken place.

My friends telephoned the police and the social services for me after the hearing. Both the police and social services said that I should not put myself at risk by handing over the children at the park. I was advised to hand them over from my home, which was currently my friends' home. The injustice of having to hand them over at all to someone I believed should be supervised in his contact was hard enough, but the thought of going to the park sickened me. I couldn't do it.

I sent a note to Jack asking him to collect the children from outside my friends' home. He refused and sent a note back saying that he would only collect them from the park as per the court order.

I didn't go to the park on the following day, which was contact day. I had the children ready in case Jack should relent and pick them up from my friends' home. He didn't relent. He went to the park. And when I didn't turn up with the kids, he returned to court to complain that the contact order had been violated. It was the height of meanness. He knew I wasn't refusing contact; that I would comply with the court order for contact if he just picked the children up at Eva's house, but he wouldn't do it. He applied for a penal notice instead. In other words, he was asking for me to be committed to prison for not wanting to hand over the children in the place where I had been attacked.

The penal notice was not granted in my absence, but I was ordered to attend court the following day. I knew it was serious. I could be in big trouble for contempt of court. It was terrifying. I wrote another statement. I stated that the police and social services had each told me not to hand over the children in the park.

Eva had been unable to come to court with me on the previous disastrous court hearing, but she had been present while the police doctor had measured my bruises. She wrote a statement for me, detailing the extent of my injuries and the infected arm. She came to court prepared to be called as a witness. We tried very hard to get a statement from the police or some evidence from the hospital. None of it, thanks to bureaucracy, the Data Protection Act and official procedures was possible to get at short notice. It involved form-filling and waiting and red tape. I was really scared. I genuinely thought there might be a chance I would be sent to prison.

On the bench was the same Milton-quoting Judge A who had ordered me back to the park. Gone was the bonhomie and pretence of affability. He shouted at me when he saw me. 'What are you doing back here?' I was finished. Like a popped balloon I could not hold up any longer. I burst into tears.

I had a wonderful Irish woman barrister on that occasion. Like so many of the barristers who represented me, I only saw her that once. She was sympathetic and battled my cause with the judge whilst I was reduced to a mass of tears and despair. Pointing out that she hadn't represented me before, the barrister told the judge she didn't deserve being shouted at. He replied that he was shouting over her shoulder at me and that it wasn't directed at her. Refusing to move out of the way, she literally stood between me and the judge, telling him she was standing in front of me to shield me from his verbal wrath.

The judge would not hear any new evidence. He wouldn't hear my friend as a witness. He was completely unwilling to reconsider his earlier decision that Jack hadn't assaulted me. He was not humble or open-minded enough to admit that he might have made a mistake. Judge A said he'd give me one more chance. The implication was clear. Either I had to hand the children over for unsupervised contact or I'd end up in prison.

The tiny concession I got was that he rephrased the order so that the children could be handed over for contact from my friends' house; I no longer had to go to the park. He had little choice about that, since the police and social services were giving advice contradicting his instructions. He was clearly enraged about having to alter his order, however. The fact that it was a despicable thing to force a woman to hand the kids over where she'd been attacked was irrelevant to him. I had disobeyed him and I was in for it.

I was back in the old vulnerable mode, unable to speak or to defend myself; unable to explain anything of the mass of powerful emotions that were swilling around inside. When I looked at the judge's face, at that moment I couldn't see much difference between him and my husband. Here was just another angry, powerful man compelling me to do what I believed was wrong for my children and punishing me if I didn't do it. My god, how the judge resembled an angry, abusive husband: to a tee.

11

Cock-up by the Crown Prosecution Service

⚖️

That hearing of 5 August in front of Judge A led to depression. For weeks after it I was tired, lethargic and unenthusiastic. I felt beaten and humiliated. I could hardly attend to the children. Sometimes I couldn't eat because my throat seized up and my stomach churned. Other times I would not eat anything except sweets, chocolate and fatty foods because I wanted to comfort myself. I was going down. Yet there were moments of anger. I could hardly believe what had happened. I was left with an intolerable sense of injustice and disbelief. To find that I'd been assaulted and then been the one almost to end up in prison for it! My friends who had supported me were equally outraged. Nobody could believe what had happened.

Worse was to follow. The criminal charges against Jack were dropped. He attended the hearing at which he was due to be prosecuted and the case had fallen apart. I had no advance notice that the charges were being dropped; in fact I heard the news through Jack. He was gleeful, cock-a-hoop. He went around informing people and our legal representatives that the charges had been dismissed because there was no case to answer. I had falsely accused him of assault and he had been vindicated.

The news spread around our community. It was horrible. I was made to look like a liar, as though I had made it all up. I was devastated. I would rather he hadn't been charged at all than have to go through the mental trauma of preparing for a criminal trial only for it to be abandoned.

Orla urged me to look into matters. We were entitled to be

informed why the charges were being dropped, she said. She advised telephoning the Crown Prosecution Service to find out why he had not been prosecuted. Orla had just the right way of helping me. When it was necessary, she battled on my behalf with individuals and organisations. At other times she'd force me to do it, trying to ensure that I didn't develop a victim mentality. Sometimes she'd start a conversation, as with the CPS, and then force me to take the phone. My confidence increased gradually in some areas as she made me take the reins.

At first the CPS was defensive and high handed. They had in their possession a document from the family court. It was a copy of Judge A's judgment effectively saying that he thought my husband had not assaulted me. 'The judge said he didn't do it,' an officious voice from the CPS said at the other end of the phone.

The CPS read from this appalling judgment which had so devastated me when I had listened to it in the family court. What outraged me is that the document was legally confidential. How had Jack managed to give it to the CPS without permission from the family court, and why, given that it was not allowed outside the family court without the judge's permission, had the CPS accepted it?

Orla and I argued the point with the CPS. They had no idea they were not supposed to be in possession of documents from the family court. Even worse, it was the only evidence in their dossier. The police photographs showing my injuries, the police officer's statement, the forensic medical examiner's statement: none of them was present. The evidence that would have enabled them to prosecute wasn't even in their folder and they didn't know anything about it.

That same evidence had not been presented to the family court either. Judge A hadn't judged the case in the light of the evidence; he had judged in the absence of the evidence. And now, with completely closed circular logic, the CPS had dropped the charges because a judge in the High Court had decided the assault hadn't taken place. It was a blow. I was both devastated and angry. I was furious with Judge A for spoiling the criminal trial, especially since the police took the view that he had been unhelpful, saying that he could have picked up the phone and asked them for information about the evidence because, through no fault of my own, I hadn't been able to get it to the family court in time to be considered.

I was equally furious with the CPS for messing things up. In the beginning I wouldn't have cared whether my husband was charged or not; but I did mind the charges being dropped because of their mistake.

I was desperate to appeal in the family courts, no matter what it took. My solicitors refused to fund an appeal. They advised me that I had no grounds: We couldn't argue that Judge A had judged the evidence wrongly because he hadn't been presented with evidence of the assault. 'Precisely,' I argued. 'Shouldn't it be the responsibility of a judge in a family case, who is supposed to care about the welfare of my children, to make absolutely sure that he has all the evidence in front of him, and isn't it important that he goes the extra mile where our safety is concerned?'

Orla even offered to pay the costs of an appeal out of her own pocket. My solicitor explained that wouldn't do either. If she paid for a hearing in the middle of proceedings, the Legal Aid Commission would withdraw my funding and I'd also be liable for any subsequent proceedings.

Growing the courage of desperation, I considered acting as my own lawyer, disinstructing my solicitors and entering an application to appeal myself, since we were checkmated on the issue of paying for a barrister to do it. The reality check came when I realised I might also be stuck with conducting the financial hearings in relation to my divorce. It was hopeless. No way would I be able to find my way through the money and house issues without a solicitor to help. I couldn't gamble with our prospects for a future home.

This might have been law but it certainly wasn't justice. I couldn't understand the judge's lackadaisical approach. Fortunately, it was unnecessary to disinstruct my solicitors. Although they wouldn't fund an appeal, there was a big hearing coming up the following month at which the interim residence application, occupation order and non-molestation order were being heard. I could bring new evidence then in relation to the assault.

It was poor consolation for the travesty which had occurred, but it was something. Not everything was lost. I got to work assiduously with the help of my friends, trying to pin down the police and medical evidence in order to have it all ready for the next hearing, only a few weeks away.

We got in touch with the police officer who brought the original charges against Jack. She also tackled the CPS. The explanation they gave her regarding the dropping of the charges was that they considered it a waste of resources to hear the case both in the magistrates' court and in the family court.

That remained the official explanation, but it was not what I had been told on the phone, and I remained of the view that they had messed up but were refusing to accept responsibility for it. The new explanation did not sufficiently account for why they were in possession of a document they should not have had, or why the photographs were missing; nor did it cover the fact that they had broken their own code for prosecuting.

As the victim of the assault, I was entitled to be informed of a decision to drop the charges and I had not been contacted at any stage. If I had been consulted about it, I could have rectified some of their errors; I could have told them that the case had been heard in the family court without the evidence and brought the evidence to their attention, but their failure to let me know what was going on meant that their mistakes went unchallenged.

We do not know to this day whether the charges would have succeeded in a criminal trial if the evidence had been properly presented. But I was dismayed by the lack of an apology from the CPS for its shoddy handling of the case.

I was still cross that Jack had, in effect, stolen a family court document and used it without permission. How had he managed to get hold of a copy of the judgment so quickly? I didn't even have a copy myself yet. My fury was compounded when I found out from the police that Jack's family court solicitor had been the one to procure the document and that my husband was using it with his knowledge and consent.

There was nothing for it. I complained to the Office for the Supervision of Solicitors (OSS) about my husband's firm of solicitors. I was tearing my hair out. But it wasn't my fault. If official organisations supposed to deliver and act by the law broke their own codes and you suffered for it, weren't you entitled to complain? I was also disappointed. I quite liked Jack's solicitor and he had always been pleasant in manner towards me, but I didn't see how I could let it go. Such behaviour can lead to complete miscarriages of justice. And it had.

I was told by the OSS that although I had a complaint against one of its solicitors, the OSS could not consider the complaint itself because what he had done was not against its rules as such; it was a rule of the court. It was equivalent to contempt of court, they said. If the solicitor broke the rules of the court, I had to bring a court case against him.

Bring a court case against him! I was having trouble getting anywhere with anything in court, let alone trying to bring a solicitor to book. And where was the funding going to come from? I was already in a high-cost case. The legal costs for the children's matters and sorting out the finances were rising rapidly. They reached twenty thousand pounds and then thirty thousand pounds and they kept rising. Although I was getting legal aid because I was receiving state benefits, eventually I would receive a financial settlement upon my divorce and they would recoup all the money.

Also, I imagined my solicitor's face. Suing the opposing solicitor would have been ridiculously out of proportion. Was there really no other remedy for a solicitor breaking the rules than to sue him? Couldn't his own professional body discipline him? Seemingly not: I had to let it go.

The police officer volunteered to come and give evidence for me at the family court. She was a very knowledgeable and experienced officer from the domestic violence unit at the police station. She said that pieces of paper and cold facts were not much use in court cases. People needed photographs and images; they needed to hear a person speaking about what it was like to suffer an assault, to be a victim of domestic violence. She offered to bring the police photos and the forensic examiner's report to court. She was prepared to speak for me and put me in touch with other people who could help.

I was incredibly grateful for this sympathetic police officer's help, her genuine concern, going above and beyond the call of duty. She put me in touch with organisations and people who could help in all sorts of ways and continued to provide moral and practical support over the following year. It was in great contrast to some of the other officials in the system. My faith in the courts and in judges was rapidly eroding; this police officer was a shining light in the horrible dark morass of courts and officialdom.

12

See you in court:
the occupation order

⚖️

A major hearing early on in the proceedings, September 2002, was to hear the question of interim residence, an occupation order and an application for a non-molestation order.

Before the hearing took place, following my barrister's advice, I had asked my GP to provide me with a letter confirming that I was in sound mental health. I had never visited this GP with any anxiety or mental health issues, although I had seen him and other medical professionals regularly over the years. Due to the fact I'd had four pregnancies, I was almost never out from under the feet of doctors, midwives and health visitors for routine checks and visits. It must have been evident to him that I was in good health. I didn't even bother going to the surgery to request him to write me a letter; I merely rang him up, thinking it would be a simple matter. I thought no more about it after that: The GP had not raised any difficulties about giving me a letter saying I was in good mental health. Everything seemed well.

Orla brought the matter up before the hearing, asking if I'd instructed my GP to show me a copy of his letter before he sent it on to my solicitors to be filed at court. Stupidly, I hadn't asked for this to happen. I decided to ring the surgery to ask for a copy of the letter before it was sent to anyone. I was told the letter had already been posted. Taken aback, I asked the GP to read the letter to me.

My heart plummeted as he was reading. Instead of the brief positive letter I had expected him to write, and which he'd previously given me the impression he would write, confirming that I hadn't visited a doctor in the last fifteen years except for pregnancy-related matters; his epistle read in a very negative way. The anxiety I'd suffered as a teenager was documented in detail, including details of tranquillisers I'd been prescribed at the time. The whole emphasis was on an early part of my life with one small reference at the end to the fact that I had been seen regularly by doctors over the years at the practice who hadn't noted any mental health issues. That last small positive was completely outweighed by the GP's expression of concern that I might have some difficulties looking after the children, given my long-distant history of anxiety. He suggested that a consultant psychiatrist's opinion would clear matters up for the court.

I felt angry while I was listening to the GP read aloud. Where was the letter he had promised to write me? He knew I was in good health. I didn't understand his change of attitude. It didn't make sense. I knew while he was reading that I was going to have difficulty at court with this letter. My sense of anger was overlaid by a sense of bewilderment. I'd volunteered to disclose my medical past, I hadn't been compelled to do it, so why was the doctor being so cautious; not just refusing to back me against a husband who, as part of his general abuse, was determined to have me regarded as unstable and mentally ill, but actually undermining my case? I just wanted to get off the phone and process my feelings, come to terms with the sense of shock I was experiencing. I said something brief to the doctor and rang off before dropping the news on my friends. It was exactly what Orla had predicted.

'What do I do?' I turned to Orla. Now, along with the other complications to my case, I would have to fight a very negative view of me from a doctor I thought I could rely on. Orla was prompt in her suggestions. 'Complain to the GMC about the doctor and the letter. What he's done is unjustified.' I blanched at the word 'complaint' and my stomach lurched. I felt dizzy at the idea of yet another complaints process. Orla also told me to phone my solicitor to find out what could be done.

The solicitor had not yet received the letter. I told her the bad news that it wouldn't help my case and in fact might be harmful to it, and I asked if we could simply not file the letter. I was astonished to learn that we couldn't fail to produce the letter since it had been requested by the court. 'No judge requested a letter from my doctor,' I argued. 'It was voluntary on my part. Why can't I just discard a letter that is unhelpful?' As they hadn't yet received the letter, couldn't I just withdraw permission for the solicitor to consult my GP and pick up the letter, unopened, from their post room when it arrived? Apparently I couldn't since, voluntary or not, the letter had been mentioned in a court order, leaving us no choice. We were forced to disclose it once it had been requested.

It made my head ache going over and over the twist in events. I couldn't understand the doctor's change in manner and attitude since I had spoken to him on the telephone. I couldn't think of anything to account for it.

I woke up next day with a faint recollection of my father saying something on the phone about Jack talking to my doctor. My father had tried a spot of mediation between us in the beginning. He hadn't made any progress with Jack, who had mentioned that he was going to see the doctor. Jack and I shared the same GP. I hadn't given it any thought at the time when I asked the GP for the letter, since Jack rarely visited doctors. I had a growing suspicion that instead of approaching the doctor for help on his own behalf, as I'd previously assumed, Jack might have approached the doctor with made-up stories of my mental ill health, but I didn't know how I could prove it. It seemed the only explanation for what had occurred. I decided to take a stab in the dark. I telephoned the doctor and took him by surprise, asking him whether my husband had been telling him tales about me which had influenced his letter. Caught off-guard, the doctor began to stutter a reply, floundering, not knowing what to say. Significantly, he didn't deny it.

I immediately rang Jack and as soon as he picked up the phone I said, 'How dare you visit my doctor and impugn my mental health?' He didn't know I was guessing; he thought I knew. It surprised him into confession. He began to justify his actions.

I now had my answer. Jack had deliberately tried to influence what the GP wrote about me. And he had succeeded. The GP had been manipulated into his recent perceptions. In effect, both the GP and I had been set up. In pestering for something from my doctor, Jack must have intended from the beginning to have some input and influence on the doctor. I felt sick that I'd been so naive as to walk into it. On the other hand, when I thought it over in calmer moments, I also felt glad that I hadn't been suspicious. It would have required me to be suspicious almost to the degree of paranoia to predict and anticipate some of the sneaky things that my ex husband did. You couldn't protect yourself against that degree of deviousness without having a sneaky mind yourself which could anticipate such behaviour. On the whole, I thought I'd rather be handicapped with too much trust in people than lack faith in human nature.

I did complain to the GMC; more to have my theory confirmed than anything. I learned from the GMC, which searched the doctor's notes, that there had been an appointment between Jack and the GP between the time I requested the letter for the court and the court hearing. But there wasn't much the GMC could do – the doctor hadn't acted maliciously; he'd simply been manipulated. I was furious for a short period, but the GP offered me an apology, directly at the surgery and not through the GMC. He said he hadn't meant to hurt my case and that he'd been misled, and he was sorry. I was mollified. He was brave to face me in the circumstances and verbally apologise. I accepted his apology and let it go.

It wasn't the end of it. Jack seemed to have a thing for taking court papers and distributing them outside the court arena, even though doing so amounted to contempt of court. Since the GP wasn't going to help him with his case that I was unstable, he took the doctor's letter to a celebrity doctor who was a friend and asked him to write a commentary on it. The celebrity doctor, who regularly wrote a column for a national newspaper, but who had never met me, gave Jack the letter he wanted, implying that I had a personality disorder.

I was disbelieving at the turn of events. If this sort of thing appeared in fiction, you'd criticise it for being farfetched. It was like a Victorian melodrama where the man in the fiction has a woman certified as mad for his own purposes. The GMC was pretty useless in this situation, telling the celebrity doctor not to do it again, but had no power to make him withdraw it. Despite the doctor being reprimanded, Jack was still free to use the letter as he liked.

I reflected ruefully that the doctor concerned, often parodied by the satirical press as an 'utter fraud', had certainly lived up to his caricature this time. You couldn't imagine that such a throwback to an earlier century existed. As I pointed out to the GMC, a doctor might be the first port of call for a woman suffering domestic abuse. Doctors couldn't afford not to be clued up about domestic violence in this day and age. Women might well be put off trusting doctors if they thought the doctor would side with her abusive husband and not see through him.

It was a bit late in the day for Orla's approach, but I decided to adopt her earlier suggestions and laugh it off – adopt a scornful attitude where the two doctors were concerned. The evidence would speak for me; I had always been a totally committed and stable parent and they could produce no evidence to say otherwise. Let them do their worst. Although that was the stance I took and it worked, I still felt embarrassed and uncomfortable about it inwardly. No one likes their teenage self thrown in their face. It's a time when you're vulnerable and your personality is forming; who wants to be lumbered with reviewing all that, years later when you're a parent approaching middle age? There was no choice but to pick myself up from this setback with the GP and get on with things. A desperately important hearing was imminent.

I had a group of witnesses assembled for this crucial hearing which would decide whether I could move back into the house with the kids or not. Several of my witnesses had travelled long distances to be there. One flew in from Italy, arriving the night before the hearing. Another of my friends wished me good luck before everything started. 'I never ever thought I'd say this,' she said, 'but see you in court, kid.'

Orla mistakenly insisted on calling the witness box 'the dock', as though I were going to be on criminal trial. 'When are you in the dock?' she asked. The word 'dock' stuck. It amused us all to call it the dock and it took our minds off the impending outcome, which we were all hoping for/fearing in equal measure.

The case was heard by a courteous, painstaking and thorough judge, for whom I was grateful and relieved. He took the case at short notice and had to assimilate a heap of papers. The hearing was timetabled for four days.

I had a woman barrister; the same attractive dark-haired one who had represented me once before. It was not often I got a female barrister. I was told by one barrister that solicitors tended to get male barristers for female clients and female barristers for male clients, the psychology apparently being that a pair of aggressive men going for a mother looked brutal; and conversely that two women together attracted too much sympathy from any judge inclined to champion women. It was probably one of those myths designed to wrap their calling in a little mystique.

My husband was representing himself at this hearing. He had no solicitor or barrister. He did have several men with him from Families Need Fathers. I was familiar with two of them. They had previously accompanied Jack and the children on contact sessions. He wanted these two in court with him. In addition, he wished one of them to act for him and speak for him in court, much in the way a barrister would. The judge was not willing to allow this. My husband was highly educated and articulate, as able as any other litigant in person to conduct his own case.

There was an argument between my barrister and Jack as to whether the two members from Families Need Fathers should be present in court. My barrister argued that as they had acted as witnesses in the case and given statements, it wasn't appropriate for them to sit in court. The judge agreed with her, saying that there could be no objection to Jack, being a litigant in person, having a McKenzie friend, but that these two men were not appropriate court friends because they were also witnesses in the case.

Until that point I had not heard the term 'McKenzie friend'. It allows someone who is representing himself or herself in court to have a friend with them for support, as they do not have a solicitor on the case. However, Jack was refusing to take part in the hearing and was all set to head for the appeal court if he were not allowed to have these two men present as supporters.

The news that Jack would be prepared not to take part in the hearing didn't sound like dismal news to me! However, I took my barrister's advice that although he didn't have a legal leg to stand on, it would be more time consuming if Jack didn't have his way on this point. As she rightly pointed out, the children and I were in need of a home; we couldn't afford to delay on the occupation order. We had already been out of our home for six months. I gave way on this point and the two men were allowed in. They behaved like overgrown schoolboys for much of the time.

Official recordings of proceedings are made by the court. Transcripts can be obtained if needed. One of Jack's supporters was conscientiously writing down everything that was said in court in laborious longhand, since he lacked the ability to do shorthand. Unofficial recordings of proceedings are not allowed; you can write down what is said but not record it yourself on tape. At one point it was discovered that the trio were carrying tape-recorders with them. They were asked to stop recording. It drew some muttering and comments from the three men about unfairness and about judges being scared to have their comments heard by the general public.

The following day there were no tape recorders on the desk in front of them, but they were asked whether they had any recording equipment. It transpired that one of them at least did have a tape recorder on his person. I sympathised with anyone wanting a transcript of their own hearing; obtaining official transcripts was difficult and outrageously expensive. But the rules applied to all parties: Jack's crew seemed to think they were exempt from the rules which applied to everyone else. They were like naughty schoolboys being asked to turn out their pockets and were belligerent at being asked to behave according to the procedures.

The other member of Families Need Fathers, the one not transcribing, sat at Jack's elbow throughout and whispered advice in his ear. Jack refused to ask any question or make any comment unless he first consulted with his friends. The case was going unbearably slowly and the judge had to remonstrate with him about the length of time this consultation with his friend was taking.

My Italian friend Valentina, along with Eva and Enya, were subjected to unpleasant cross-examination by Jack, having to endure his attempts to impugn their veracity, their mental health or their standing in the community. The judge intervened at several points to restrain him. He had to be called to order when he tried to pursue a line of reasoning which implied that Eva and Enya were unreliable because they had a sister who suffered from schizophrenia. It was a crude, mean and childish way of attacking someone in the witness box, attempting to introduce an idea in the judge's mind that there was 'madness' in the family. He must have been watching too many films.

All of this was unpleasant but not harmful to my case; in fact it was the reverse. For one, he accused too many people of being unstable or morally bad. He was making himself appear in a very bad light, although I don't think the judge entirely understood what was going on with Jack. He seemed to be assuming that Jack was trying to smear and attack the other side in this dramatic way because he was not a lawyer and was untrained in cross-examination.

It was a mistake for the judge not to see Jack as someone to be taken seriously. This was a mistake judges always made. Sometimes in court Jack came across bumbling or eccentric in his manner. But there was a calculation and determination in his intentions that didn't necessarily show, and that led people to underestimate the lengths to which he would go if thwarted or challenged.

Those in the courtroom who didn't know Jack seemed to assume he was merely confused and not phrasing his questions properly when he implied that my friends had done a bad deed in taking me in. Their kind act in giving me a home had made it possible for me to leave Jack. He saw my leaving him as reprehensible and therefore my friends as morally wicked for facilitating it. His attempts to turn their kindness into wrongdoing met with puzzlement on the part of the judge, who referred to them as good Samaritans.

There was a constant failure by professionals in the court system to realise that these warped views were deeply ingrained and deadly serious, and that Jack had no respect for anyone who disagreed with him. If the whole world held a different moral viewpoint from his, it never made him reflect on his own views to see if he could possibly be wrong. Instead it made him believe that the world was decadent and wrong, and that he was right.

It really needed someone qualified, with psychological expertise, to explain this, but we hadn't reached that stage yet. The people dealing with him had no idea what they were dealing with and they never got his measure. It seemed so self-evident to me. But then, of course, I had lived with him. I knew him to be completely incapable of reflecting on his own abuse with any moral insight. I found it frustrating when they constantly explained away his extreme behaviour and views.

An alarming thought crossed my mind. Did judges and lawyers see so many men like this that they became desensitised towards them? I couldn't think of another explanation for it. Why couldn't they see what Jack was? Why didn't they regard him as very abusive? The professionals weren't brainwashed and downtrodden, as I was when I minimised his behaviour to myself. Were they impressed by his outward appearance – well spoken, cultured? What was it? When I felt uncharitable and angry towards these obtuse professionals I tried to remind myself that they hadn't lived with him and therefore couldn't really be expected to understand it. But then why did they have the power to take decisions about my life which could be so damaging for me and the children?

I had to undergo a lengthy cross-examination by Jack in the witness box. It was unpleasant. The judge intervened at various points when Jack's questioning was going off the point or, worse, becoming insulting. The GP's letter was dragged up as Jack tried to make out that I was a psychiatric case; however, this aspect of his attack had lost its power since he was accusing everyone who took the stand of being unstable. Since my witnesses, all female, were highly intelligent and articulate, displaying no signs of madness, it somewhat confounded his argument.

I was relieved on this occasion and on following ones that, although many judges were sadly lacking insight about domestic abuse, I didn't meet any who were daft about Jack's allegations of mental illness. He was generally given short shrift on that. It was outside of court that I had to bear the consequences of the behaviour of two ill-informed doctors. The letters were used out of the courtroom, passed around Jack's friends and acquaintances, to stir up support. The image he put about was that the courts were biased against men; that I was an unstable mother and the courts simply hadn't bothered to investigate it. Unfortunately, since one of the letter writers was a significant figure with an honour from the Queen, he tended to be believed by more credulous folks outside the courtroom.

Jack could use the anonymity and privacy of the family courts to put these things about unchallenged. Without resorting to the same tactics as he did, I had no way to counter them. I couldn't distribute the court papers as he was doing. I just had to put up with people's perceptions. Many of his accusations were also posted openly on the internet with his real name attached.

I couldn't avoid the fallout from the letters beyond the courtroom, but I did my best to put my distress over it to one side while I was taking part in the hearing. I'd had one bad experience on the witness stand where I had learned my lesson, so I was able to acquit myself well in the box this time. The two men from Families Need Fathers sniggered conspicuously and gave knowing looks at each other during my evidence. They were sitting just below the witness box in front of me, with my solicitor and barrister further back in the court, and several times they snorted disbelievingly, lolling against each other and laughing, when I was trying to explain my husband's past behaviour to the judge.

One of them pointedly took out a handkerchief and blew his nose with a loud trumpeting sound. It was infantile behaviour designed to throw me off balance. Several times they were threatened with being ejected from the courtroom for their contrived spoiling tactics. I tried to face the judge and speak to him rather than looking directly at these three hostile opponents.

If this had been the first time I'd given evidence, I would have made a mess of it. I had been defensive before, afraid of making a mistake, so I hadn't come across well. This time round I learned from my earlier mistakes and tried to give the judge as much information as I could about our home life and the way in which my husband had behaved.

As I was telling the truth, I could afford to be detailed. I told myself that I couldn't be tripped up because I was not lying about his violence. I did not get flustered by things I couldn't remember or by things which didn't quite add up. And I didn't berate myself for small inconsistencies. I was telling the truth on the bigger picture, and if I had forgotten or mistaken small details, I was ready to admit it.

I was grateful that the judge asked questions and that I wasn't left entirely at the mercy of Jack and his friends. The Families Need Fathers member kept whispering in Jack's ear, trying to direct the questioning. Jack didn't always pay attention to the instructions he was given on how to cross-examine. He was an over-enthusiastic cross-examiner, determined to make me incriminate myself. However, he often forgot the point he was trying to pursue and could not follow one scent. He was like a hound excited by the scent of three foxes at once and unable to decide which one to go after.

Jack was claiming to be the main carer for the children in order to bolster his application to have the children live with him. It was an outrageous lie. He had never changed a nappy in his life, never pushed a pram, never done a night feed, never even turned on the washing machine, plus he worked forty hours a week teaching; and then there were all his outside commitments and social activities. He did virtually nothing with the children. But he was peddling his usual line that I was mentally sick and that he frequently had to step in to take care of the children.

In the next moment he changed his line of attack because I had pointed out how reluctant he was around the children, how he never did a thing in the house, had never bathed a child or cooked a single meal. Suddenly he was defending himself: He had arduous work responsibilities, teaching commitments; they took up most of his time.

I agreed with him. He did work hard at teaching. And he was a good teacher; I couldn't fault him there. But he had just proved my point. He worked such long hours that it was impossible for him to spend time with the children. He appeared flummoxed here. In trying to prove the point that he worked hard at teaching he had lost sight of his main contention that he was the primary carer for the children. I did feel a twinge of pity for him at that moment. He was doing such a bad job of lawyering, he really needed a professional.

When Jack asked a question that backfired or when he got side-tracked into irrelevancies, his friend put his head in his hands and groaned. They appeared to be disagreeing on tactics and methods of cross-examining. One of Jack's friends left before the proceedings ended, as if unable to cope with the circus it was turning into.

This whole charade we were taking part in put me in mind of Crown Court, the television programme I'd watched as a child. It was on in the mornings. I enjoyed the times I was off school sick and had chance to watch it. This game we were taking part in was more like television than a serious attempt to elicit the truth in a complex situation.

It is pretty rough on the witness stand with a good cross-examiner battering you down, exposing any inconsistencies, tripping you up. I saw my first example of a really decent cross-examination, textbook style, of the kind Rumpole of the Bailey would be proud. When I watched Jack being reduced to a heap of inconsistencies and evasions by my barrister, I realised why my solicitor had previously been such a keen advocate of keeping quiet in the dock. If you said too much, you could really let yourself in for trouble.

One time after a beating up, Jack had pushed me outside the front door and locked it. He found it easy to deny that he'd ever locked me out. He didn't find it so easy when the barrister asked him how in that case I'd ended up on the other side of the door, forced to run to a neighbour for help. If you lied once, you had to think of a follow-up lie to back it up. Not so easy when an effective barrister is hounding you for answers. Hurried and flustered, Jack let slip the fact that he had been 'incensed'. He tried to withdraw the word afterwards when he realised he had implicated himself, but once you've said it, it sticks in people's memories and trying to withdraw or minimise what you've expressed merely reinforces it in their minds. Jack was clearly searching mentally for further evasions. It was embarrassing watching someone trip himself up.

Jack called his brother as a witness in the case. His brother owned a £5,000 share of our £400,000 house. It had been legally agreed that he would await his share if and until we ever decided to sell the house. Ownership of the house was relevant to the occupation order. My husband could not be put out of the house with the children and I being allowed back in unless I had matrimonial home rights.

My husband was objecting to my occupying the house on the grounds that the house was owned by his brother. His brother, Dr Charming, appeared in court to confirm his part ownership of the property. Neither of the two mentioned the actual sum of money which was owed to my brother-in-law, or the legal agreement that payment would only fall due if and when the house was sold.

Jack's ploy to keep me and the children out of the home was to make out that it was owned not by him, but by his brother and my husband's son by a previous relationship. Attempting to establish the amount owed to my brother-in-law provided a comic scene in court. Dr Charming's initial claim that he owned a 'substantial' share of the property was challenged by my barrister. He was asked if he owned a half share. Not wishing to perjure himself directly in court, he was forced to admit on the witness stand that it wasn't a half share. He was asked if he owned a quarter share.

A tortuous dialogue followed between my barrister and my brother-in-law, with her trying to get him to admit exactly how big his share of the house was, and him trying to avoid naming the actual sum. With each question the barrister reduced the suggested amount and asked if he was owed such an amount, or a lesser amount: an even lesser amount?

I instructed my barrister from behind that the exact amount was £5,000 and finally she put it to him. Cornered, he had ungraciously to admit that the amount was, yes, £5,000. He was owed £5,000 out of a £400,000 house. That was his share of the property and the extent of his ownership.

My barrister was very quick and effective in cross-examination. She had exactly the right tone of voice for the sceptical 'huh' she uttered in response to obvious evasions or transparent attempts to cover up facts. It was more effective in showing up a lie or half-truth than calling a witness a liar.

After Dr Charming's attempts to claim that he owned the house had been well and truly blown out of the water, she turned to me and raised her eyebrows, lifting her hands in amazement at the same time, before she sat down. 'He's such a liar,' she mouthed. 'And he's not even a very good one.'

Dr Charming was not only claiming to part own the house; he was claiming that he actually lived in it with Jack. On the second day of court, however, he turned up late. Jack had been on time. Judge K asked Dr Charming why he was late for court. In fact Dr Charming had gone to his real home for the night, travelling by train all the way from London to the south coast of England. No wonder he'd been late travelling to court the next day. He was tempting fate.

When asked to explain his lateness, he had to say his train had been delayed. 'Why didn't you travel on the same train as your brother?' the judge asked him. 'After all, you live with your brother. Why didn't you come to court together?'

If the judge was playing cat and mouse with the hapless Dr Charming, he kept a very straight face throughout. Dr Charming couldn't think of an answer to get off the hook. He muttered something about 'having business in the south of England'.

'You mean you had business in the south of England, where you live?' the judge asked drily.

Dr Charming had been made to look ridiculous and in a temper at being exposed as a fibber he began to bluster and rant. I was clearly after his brother's, my husband's, money, and he was going to help protect it by locking up the rooms in the house and letting them out to tenants if I were granted an occupation order. The children and I would be confined to one small room in the house.

Everyone in court listened in stunned silence. My barrister asked my brother-in-law, a doctor by profession, whether he was threatening to scupper the court order if the judge ordered my husband to move out and us to move in. It was clear from his answers that he was prepared to do just that. My husband and his brother stood united in their opposition to keep us out of the house. They referred to me in court as a 'gold digger'.

It took some discussions between my barrister and the judge and some consulting of weighty tomes to decide that, yes, I did have the right to reside in my home.

Then there was the question of a non-molestation order. Initially the judge had been in favour of merely asking Jack to make undertakings – promises to the court not to use violence or harassment towards me. More undertakings! I was dismayed. Jack had made promises before, in front of Judge T, and they weren't worth the paper they were written on.

The problem resolved itself when Jack made it clear that he would make no such promises, and threatened to keep returning to the matrimonial home if he was ousted. No one was left in any doubt that he meant what he said. The judge had no alternative but to make a non-molestation order with a power of arrest attached to it. The power of arrest meant that the order could be enforced by the police if necessary.

None of us knew what to expect when it came to the day of judgment. It was a long judgment, more than twenty pages, and it took a long time to deliver.

I was on tenterhooks for the earlier part because the judge reviewed and summed up the evidence and I couldn't tell at first which way it was going. The morning session of court was taken up with going over the evidence. When we broke for lunch I asked my solicitor if she knew which way the judge was leaning on the issue of the house. She couldn't tell either.

The judge didn't arrive at his conclusions until the afternoon. A bolt of relief hit me at the point at which the judge mentioned the children's contact with my husband. If he was talking about contact then clearly Jack wasn't being considered for residence. My husband picked up on that point as well. He told the judge he wasn't interested in contact, only in residence. I thought that was a telling comment. It summed up his whole attitude.

It was what my husband was all about. He wasn't interested in seeing the kids, giving them a great time because he is their dad and presumably loves them. He was only interested in residence. Substitute the word 'control' for residence and it says everything about him. I wished the judge had picked up on that sentence. It was so telling, entirely indicative of his attitude. Judges never seemed to pick up the throwaway line.

During the judge's long summary in the afternoon, my solicitor passed me a note in court. It said 'we've got it.' She meant the house. We had succeeded in gaining the occupation order.

Just as important to me as the house was the fact that the judge believed me about what had happened in the park when I had been assaulted. Judge A's dismissal of the incident had left an open wound which this hearing partially closed. The police officer who had originally brought charges against Jack was at court to give evidence for me and, on the basis of the new evidence, this judge was able to agree that Jack had caused the injuries in the photographs. The judge also found in my favour on all the other incidents of violence which my barrister put before him.

There was pathos in the degree to which I was grateful to this judge. I felt as though something had been restored to me. I felt I had got a bit of myself back, some of my dignity too.

So Jack would have to leave the family home. I was stunned and relieved after the judgment. I hugged my barrister outside court. My husband was given some days to move out. We had also got the non-molestation order which was necessary after Jack's threats to keep me out of the home and to return to it if he was ousted. I was scared, anticipating what he might do if he came back to the house, but I was so delighted to be returning home with the children that the thrill of that took my mind off the fear.

Jack left the trial early. He refused to stay until the end. Seeing which way the wind was blowing, he left, threatening to appeal the judge's order.

As I walked the length of the corridor at the Royal Courts of

Justice with Orla after the case was over, she gave an exclamation because she had seen someone she knew sitting in the corridor. She rushed over. 'What, are you involved in a court case too?' The litigant looked up. We had interrupted him in a conversation with his legal representatives. It was an embarrassing moment. The solicitor sitting by him was Jack's ex-solicitor, whom he'd sacked in order to represent himself; the same solicitor I'd reported to the OSS for his part in removing documents from the family court and giving them to the CPS.

Orla, never lost for words, greeted Jack's solicitor. 'Hello, how are you?' Disregarding any embarrassment, she told him why we were all so joyful. 'We've got the house.' The solicitor permitted himself a grin and held up his thumb. 'We heard you didn't get paid,' Orla went on fearlessly. 'You'll be lucky to get the money out of Jack.' The solicitor shrugged. 'C'est la vie.' It was a rare moment.

I had brought my group of witnesses to court in the morning. During the case, while evidence was being heard, I had not been able to talk to them. I was not allowed to have lunch with them. My barrister had an unfortunate experience at lunchtime, being screamed at in the corridor by one of Jack's witnesses, who had mistaken her for my Italian witness. It was a tribute to Valentina that her evidence was considered influential enough for the other side to attack her verbally for it.

After the case was finished, it called for a celebration. Our group headed along the road, looking for a bar. We found one that was empty and we crowded round a big table in the window. What did we all want? Requests ranged from double gin and tonic to chips.

I didn't need a drink. Just knowing that the kids and I would have a proper home again was enough. I was starving though. I'd suddenly got my appetite back. We had a scare when it came to paying. The pub wouldn't accept cards and none of us had much in the way of cash. We scraped enough together by going round the table gathering everyone's loose change. We needed every last copper.

Everyone exchanged notes and anecdotes after the trial. I'd kept to myself and gone off at lunchtime with Orla, the only one of us who hadn't been a witness in the case. We didn't know what was going on with the others during the day.

Afterwards they regaled us with tales of how an adviser from the men's organisation Families Need Fathers had come with advice and papers for Jack. They had seen him in the corridor outside court, giving my husband things to read and dispensing instructions to 'say this' from one paper if the case went one way and to 'say that' from another paper if it went a different way.

I was somewhat disgusted by Families Need Fathers. I had attempted to engage Jack's two mentors in conversation a couple of times in the past, trying to understand their mentality. I couldn't understand why someone would support a father simply because he was a father, on ideological grounds, especially when that father was a domestic abuser and was using the courts as a means of controlling me and the children.

Why were they so sceptical about the fact that he was abusive? They weren't long-standing friends of Jack's and they didn't know me from Adam. How could they judge the situation the way they did? I would have liked to talk to them, to understand the way they thought, but they would never engage in a proper conversation with me. They were hostile, unfriendly and evasive if I tried to approach them or ask questions.

I didn't understand their way of thinking. I supported women in similar circumstances to mine but not because they were women; only because they were victims of abuse. I wouldn't support a female perpetrator of violence against a male victim. I found violence abhorrent whichever sex perpetrated it and I thought that victims, female or male, should be supported.

Jack was refusing to take responsibility for his behaviour and he had a belligerent bunch of fathers around him saying just the same things that he was saying. These men were very vocal about their rights; they belonged to a fathers' group, they campaigned politically and tried to persuade people that they were victims of injustice. In many cases they gained political, judicial, media and public sympathy.

My husband was hiding his abuse amongst these men. Were there others like him? It was entirely possible that the fathers' group he was part of had other members like him, denying responsibility for abuse. Who knows? And who knows whether the sympathy they gain is deserved? Who knows what these men are like in the privacy of their homes? It would be interesting to ask their ex-partners before we are so certain that they are hard done by, cheated out of their parental responsibility as they so vehemently claim.

It transpired that Jack was paying one of these men from Families Need Fathers to help him with his case. It seems that one of his friends had experienced more success as a litigant in person than Jack and had even taken his case to the European Court of Human Rights. Jack was trying to emulate his methods in pursuing contact through the courts. Like Jack, this court mentor was claiming to be a victim of injustice. Identifying with Jack as he did, I suppose it was unrealistic to expect him to talk to me with any degree of openness.

I even tried writing to Matt O'Connor, the founder of Fathers 4 Justice, one time after I'd read an article of his in a newspaper which was very derogatory of his ex-partner, asking whether he thought that there might be perpetrators of domestic violence hiding themselves in his organisation, and whether he was concerned about this. I wasn't trying to score points; I was genuinely interested in the question. I didn't think it was right for litigants of either gender to avoid questioning themselves. However, I didn't get any response to my attempts to communicate.

I thought at the time that if some of these campaigning men, my ex included, put as much energy into improving their relationship with their ex-partner as they did into political campaigning, they might really do something worthwhile for their children's benefit.

Something else these men all had in common was how quick they were to denigrate the mother of their children. How easily they abused the mother's parenting; how ready they were to say she was a drunk or a depressive, unbalanced and unstable. In my case I had been depressed in response to the abuse; but my husband made out that he was long-suffering and patiently putting up with a depressive and sick personality: a complete distortion of the facts.

Often Jack made out that he had been driven to anger due to his difficulties in getting contact with the children. This wasn't true either. He had been angry, violent and controlling during the whole period the children and I had lived with him and before any questions regarding contact ever arose.

Like many people, I have read about and listened to aggrieved fathers who claim that the family courts are biased in favour of mothers. Some of them say that vengeful mothers get the kids and succeed in getting fathers' contact stopped or restricted by making false allegations. I don't buy it. In my experience judges are very sceptical about claims of domestic violence and regularly minimise the mental effects of it; women are not readily believed. I had gone through the mill to try to establish the truth of my allegations. In my experience, judges were not pushovers.

13

The Court of Appeal

⚖️

The process server, who catches up with people subject to court orders and serves the papers on them, went to the matrimonial home to serve Jack with the occupation order. He had a camcorder in his bag. He captured Jack threatening to come back and smash the windows if he were removed from the house. It was not reassuring.

The celebratory mood died a complete death a few days later. I received a phone call from my solicitor. Jack was going to appeal the occupation order. It looked as though we might have to wait longer for the home that we were all longing for. Although I had partly expected it, nevertheless it was a blow.

I plunged into a real low. After being elated at the prospect of returning home, it was like being dunked in cold water. I had no idea whether or not he would succeed in overturning the occupation order, but he had achieved a stay on the order and so until his plea for an appeal was heard we wouldn't be able to move back home. It put a damper on everything.

The day I received the news from my solicitor was a contact day. My younger son came back from his visit and announced, 'Daddy had a horrid judge.' My eldest daughter reported that 'Daddy had a horrid judge but he'll have a better one on Monday.'

My blood boiled when they came back with comments like these. My life was dominated by court proceedings, legal issues, solicitors, judges, but I had tried to protect the children as much as possible. I wanted them to be innocent and not involved in disputes. I didn't want them to take sides. I made the best of the way we had to live in the flat. I made light of what I could, attempting to shield them from the ugly realities of our situation.

The proceedings constantly preyed on my mind and I had to deal with a series of disasters. I tried to compartmentalise court in my mind so that I could cope with the stress of it. There were days when I was so lethargic that I sat all day under one of the great colourful sun parasols in my friends' garden and didn't want to move.

At least the garden was beautiful. I loved my friends' garden. There were masses of flowers in every conceivable size and shape of pot on the patio and wisteria growing round the door. I spent hours not really thinking, just looking at everything.

In spring, the vast wooden dining table, like one of those huge French rustic farmhouse tables, was placed on the patio for outdoor dining. It was outside for eight months of the year and taken in again during autumn. We had breakfast at it in the morning before those of the household who worked set off by train or car. And in the evening we dined until the moon came out; the table lit by candles and the coloured wall lights.

Eva's sister, Enya, prepared huge family feasts at the weekend. She was a fantastic cook. The table was loaded with plates of unusual foods, reflecting the family's mixed Irish and Arabic origins. Sometimes we talked all day. Sometimes we read books and newspapers in the garden: *The Times*, the *Independent*, the *Observer*, the *Guardian* and the *Daily Mail*. I grew to hate the *Mail* for its anti-women, anti-feminist stance and wouldn't touch it in the end.

We found ourselves drawn to miscarriages of justice. There were a lot around. Family cases made the headlines too. From that time onwards we followed cases in the news. We always seemed to be reading about controlling fathers who had run off with the kids or murdered them.

I read anything by Helena Kennedy. I was very influenced by her, especially her book *Eve Was Framed*. What she wrote about the legal system being stacked against women chimed with my own experiences and I began to collect articles about cases where women had got a raw deal in the courts. I soon built up a thick file.

It was horrible waiting for the appeal court hearing. The tension was building up unbearably, and I was going round again with a clenched jaw.

I turned up for the appeal with Eva and Orla. I was horrified to encounter Jack in the narrow corridor outside the courtroom with his old girlfriend there for support. There was nowhere to hide or retreat to. It was poky and narrow, unlike the newer building where our case was usually heard. This time round there was no sign of the men from Families Need Fathers. I was thankful for that at least. In fact they never showed their faces again: perhaps the cross-examination fiasco had an effect on their friendship!

The appeal court is open to the public. Ordinary members of the public could have come and sat in on the case, in contrast to the privacy ensured in the lower courts. My barrister wanted me to leave my two friends outside the courtroom. She said it looked bad to have friends or supporters in on family cases. However, once I saw that my husband's friend had no compunction about striding in and sitting in the public gallery, I insisted that my friends came in too. I felt for them, sitting in a small gallery alongside her.

Lord Justice Ward took the case. He came into the courtroom, a behemoth in full regalia, including scarlet gown and horsehair wig. The dais wasn't raised as high as in other courtrooms and the room was fairly small and homey. It was an improvement at least. One doesn't feel so intimidated in a smaller room. When the judge sits at a lectern, you can't help feeling you are being addressed by a headmaster. It does not make you feel like a responsible parent in the proceedings.

I was upset very early on in the hearing. Jack, as the applicant, opened the case. The Lord Justice said he was 'sympathetic' to him. I don't know what the sympathy was for. The judge did not elaborate. I expect he did not mean to hurt the respondent in the case, but I did feel hurt.

My first thought was, where is the sympathy for four babies out of their home? I also wondered if the judge would have been so sympathetic if he had been there to hear the threats Jack had made before Judge K at the occupation hearing – threats to keep his children out of their home, no matter if we ended up in some bed and breakfast place.

These kinds of casual comments thrown out by the odd judge really cut deep. They brought tears to my eyes and a feeling of desolation. This was the man who had callously marched up and down the room with my screaming daughter under his arm, refusing to let me breastfeed her, using her as a lever to punish me. What kind of sympathy did he deserve? It seemed like mocking all they had been through. There were no words of admonishment, no urgings to behave better. I felt utter despair.

The hearing didn't improve. Jack began a discussion with the judge about how children from broken homes went on to become delinquents. The Lord Justice pointed out that children remaining in relationships with two unhappy parents might do even worse; conflict was bad for children too. This was a valid point but then he spoiled it by referring to ours as 'a most unhappy marriage', with the parents always 'bickering'. Perhaps because I had been a student of English, I was very particular about the use of language. 'Bickering' was absolutely the wrong word to use. It implied a two-way fight. And I had been much too demoralised to fight.

Jack objected to being ejected from his home. The judge looked at the papers. He commented that Judge K had preferred my evidence to my husband's. He also referred cryptically to Jack's conduct, but said, 'We won't go into that.' He meant the findings of domestic violence, but he did not refer to them overtly, possibly because the hearing was being held in a court to which the public had access. And there were three members of the public at the back, albeit one friend of my husband's and two friends of mine.

I did not mind the evidence not being raked over. The four-day trial in front of Judge K had been more than sufficient without having to do it all again. However, it did make me wonder why judges were always cryptic and muted in their descriptions of men's violence towards women. They almost never actually referred to it as violence; they used the word 'findings' to describe a man's hitting or beating his wife. They skirted around the subject, using language that avoided exposing the horror of a woman living in fear of being battered.

Where violence was concerned, they had the same reluctance for the nitty-gritty of it that the Victorians had towards open discussion of sex. They needed to be better informed about the dynamics of abusive relationships and the mentality of perpetrators. Also their silence on the issue of a man's making reparation for what he had done spoke volumes. I began to feel a deep cynicism regarding the courts' ability to hear these cases.

I thought back to my university days and to the supervisor of my M. Phil thesis. 'The language is the man,' he would assert as he dismissed people who hadn't expressed themselves both with impeccable logic and properly reasoned prose. I wished I could do the same with these judges. I felt many of them played fast and loose with logic and language when they tried to make out there were no perpetrators and victims, merely parents in disagreement. And when language became detached from reality on ideological grounds, when it was used to serve a political purpose, it became dangerous.

I had no doubt by now that language was used at court in particular ways, to serve certain purposes. Judges wanted to keep a man in the family, even if he was doing his utmost to run that family off the rails. They weren't analysing their own language; they were just making it serve the purpose of forcing families together. No doubt this way of proceeding had started with laudable aims. They aimed to ensure that the non-resident parent didn't lose touch with their children. This was not a bad aim in itself, but it was a blanket approach which didn't work in cases involving ultra-controlling men. There were some families which should definitely not be together.

The judge's language did sting. I felt that, if he had cared to look beneath the surface, he might have read a definite lack of concern for the children on my husband's side. One of the revealing comments Jack made was that the children could continue to sleep in the same bed as me, in one room, because they were used to it. Lord Justice Ward's answer to this was 'Come, come, Mr Charming, we don't live in Victorian squalor these days.'

The cruelty of Jack's comment, the callousness of it, uncaring of what conditions the children were living in, unnerved me. My husband was a teacher. He had a university degree. He was entirely capable of saying what he meant. And he did mean what he said. Often I wondered why such comments passed over judges' heads. Were they inured to men showing such utter indifference to the material conditions of their children's lives?

I once heard the suggestion that legal professionals were reluctant to label certain types of behaviour as abusive since that would bring into the classification so much of the behaviour exhibited in the cases they dealt with. This immediately struck me as the wrong approach and attitude. It turns logic on its head. Instead of admitting that domestic abuse is widespread, they prefer to say that this behaviour is normal because a lot of men are doing it. It's a shocking fact to admit that the courts are failing women and children; it's easier to reclassify the less extreme ends of abuse and call them normal than to face the fact that we are not being very effective at putting a stop to it.

At the end of the hearing the Lord Justice asked for the tape to be switched off so that he could address us in an unofficial capacity. He urged us to 'stop quarrelling' and get on with things. Here the judge was equating my unwillingness to be controlled for any more years and my desire to protect the children from harm, with Jack's behaviour. He seemed to think they weighed the same in the scales of right and wrong.

I felt I was hitting my head on a brick wall. He thought the court dispute was a quarrel? Two people arguing? And if one of the most senior judges in the land saw it that way, was it any wonder that judges lower down in the courts saw it that way too? It was painful because such comments are a symbol of the struggle women still have to make domestic violence understood, even by those who deal with it year in, year out.

Jack's attempt to appeal was, however, turned down. He had no proper grounds for appeal. Making out that Judge K hadn't considered the evidence properly was useless, as the judge had been thorough and painstakingly careful in his considerations. Trying to pretend that his brother and son owned the house also fell on stony ground. It wasn't true and he could produce no evidence on that. The occupation order would stand.

My husband, seemingly gracious in defeat, pulled the house key from his pocket with a big flourish. With a grand gesture he handed it over to me in front of Lord Justice Ward. I pocketed it. I was astonished. Gracious in defeat? This was not like Jack. What lay behind it? I didn't find out until I tried the key in the door of the matrimonial home – and found out that he had changed the locks for a second time!

14

Arrest and an appearance in the Crown Court

⚖️

Jack had made a mockery of Lord Justice Ward. He had also bought himself more time. He wanted more time so that he could strip the house. The court order had stipulated that he must leave the furniture and take only his personal belongings. He used the four days that were left to him to empty the house.

Living nearby, I watched helplessly as van load after van load of household goods disappeared. When I was able to watch safely, peering with trepidation round the corner as my husband and his friends packed things into the van, I despaired. Even the frying pans, which he never used because he never cooked, were in there, swaying precariously on top of the tightly packed boxes of household goods. We would be lucky if there was a single kids' toy left in the place when we got the house back.

I phoned my solicitor. 'He's stripping the house. Can't you do something?' My solicitor replied, 'At least he's only removing the furniture. I've got another client whose husband is knocking the house down brick by brick to stop his wife getting it.'

The answer to the question was that we couldn't do anything until the four days were up. A letter from my solicitors elicited the response that a genuine key would be provided once the four days allowed by Lord Justice Ward were up. Meanwhile, we couldn't stop him in the act of stripping the house because there was still the possibility that he might put it all back. We could only do something about him breaking the court order once it was irrevocably broken, not while he was in the process of doing it.

My brother-in-law, Dr Charming, helped Jack to remove the furniture. He obviously wasn't going to stand around and let the 'gold digger' get her hands on it. I resigned myself. The furniture, including the children's toys and personal possessions, were gone.

The day for resuming occupancy of the house dawned warm and sunny. It looked auspicious but I didn't want to raise the kids' hopes too high. I had fears and misgivings. Would he leave today? He had put up such a fight on all fronts that I didn't really trust him to go. On the other hand, why would he strip the house of everything if he thought he would be able to stay put?

I stood with my friends, Orla and Eva, on the street outside their house. We felt we had to leave a decent amount of time after my husband was supposed to have vacated the property. It would have been unseemly to rush in the minute he was gone. Meeting on the threshold would have seemed like gloating, I reckoned, so we waited for time to pass, impatient to regain the home.

As we were standing there, my husband's friend, Don, passed us by in the street. He shook his head when he saw us. 'He's been driven to madness,' he said and went on. We looked at each other. Enigmatic words: what on earth did they mean? I had visions of my husband suffering a mental breakdown on the doorstep. But his friend would hardly abandon him if he had suffered a breakdown. It was much more likely to mean that he had been driven to some rash act, I deduced.

My nerves increased. Should I put off entering the house for today, leave it to another day? Orla and Eva had also anticipated something bad, but thought it would be putting off the evil hour to leave it. We voted for acting on the court order and occupying the house as I was meant to. My friends accompanied me but I didn't take the children initially. I wanted to check the place out before I risked taking them. I had the hard-won key in my hand. To my surprise I didn't need it. The front door was unlocked. That was suspicious in itself.

I put my head through the open door into the hallway. Quiet: empty of furniture. I stepped in with trepidation. I was the first to put my head through the sitting-room door and there he was, sitting cross-legged like a Buddha, with a strange smile on his face. I said one sentence: 'Does this mean you are not leaving?' He nodded. He had that look on his face. He was up for a fight.

I turned round, scooted out of the house fast and started to make my way back up the road. My friends followed, arguing with me.

What was the point of fighting so hard and then giving up at the last minute? Why was I fleeing? He was being pig-headed but it couldn't last. He couldn't defy a court order to leave.

I didn't want to call the police to enforce the court order and get him forcibly removed. It was horrible. I didn't want to fight. I wanted him out but I didn't want it this way. I just wanted a civilised divorce and somewhere decent to live with the children. But my friends' lease on the flat we were living in was coming to an end within a few weeks and we would have to get out. We had nowhere else to go except the matrimonial home.

We paced the street. I suggested calling my brother-in-law, Dr Charming, to see if he could persuade Jack to leave voluntarily so that it would be unnecessary to call the police. My friends rejected that idea. My brother-in-law had done everything he could, including making himself look foolish in court, to keep his brother in the home. What help would he be? I argued with them: 'Surely Dr Charming won't want to see his brother in prison for contempt? He's a professional man. He'd have more sense than that.'

We argued the pros and cons between us. 'Ring your solicitor,' they suggested. I did. She was sympathetic but she had anticipated this. 'Ring the police,' she told me. 'There is a power of arrest attached to the court order. They'll take him away.' My friends were cross with me. I had been weak on a number of occasions; this wasn't the time to vacillate.

I telephoned the police. They arrived in no time: a man and a woman police officer. They went into the house and didn't come out for ages. Finally the man, an outspoken Geordie, emerged. They were trying persuasion but Jack was resistant to their arguments. He had no plans to leave.

The police officer began chatting. In his Geordie accent he advised me to celebrate getting rid of an awful husband by painting the town red that night and going for a few bevies. It wasn't quite my style, although I appreciated the sentiment. Binge drinking hadn't then become the target for political and social opprobrium that it is now. Clearly the policeman didn't mind picking up drunks from pavements at night.

Orla decided to see if she could help the woman police officer in the house. She went in and tried to make Jack see reason, to offer an olive branch. He got furious at the sight of her and began shouting and blaming her. In no time the handcuffs were slapped on and the two police officers were practically carrying the resistant man from the house. They clapped him in the police van and drove away.

At least I was safe for the night, whatever happened on future nights. Jack would be detained under the power of arrest, kept overnight in the police cells and brought to the High Court on the Strand in the morning for failing to obey the court order.

I explored the house with my friends once Jack had been driven away by the police. The rooms had new locks on them; the sitting-room and each of the bedrooms had Yale locks. The doors were labelled with the names of my husband's relatives, including those of my brother-in-law and my stepson. Clearly Jack and Dr Charming had intended to carry out their threats to lock up the rooms if the children and I were allowed to move back in. It took another letter from my solicitor to Dr Charming, explaining the reality of the situation and the consequences of disobeying the court, to get the locks removed.

We were in court again following Jack's arrest and detention overnight. My barrister arrived. She was yet another new barrister. Apparently she practised a mix of criminal and family law. She had brought her wig with her, carefully unpacking it from its box. The wig was very expensive, she told me. She'd paid hundreds of pounds for it. No wonder she was treating it gently.

There was some discussion between legal representatives about which court the case should be heard in. Family court or crown court? Nobody was quite sure. They had a crown court judge on hand. Was she the appropriate judge to hear it? No one knew. The judge herself was consulted. There was a peremptory response. Of course she could hear it.

I went in with Orla and Eva. They were allowed in with me because it was a criminal court, not a family court, and it was open to the public. Boy, was it open to the public! While we were sitting there waiting for Jack to arrive, a troupe of A-level students on a day's tour of the law courts filed in. They filled up the public gallery and awaited the case with interest.

I wondered what those young men and women in the public gallery, probably too young to vote, were making of all this and what they would think of my husband when he came in. I didn't dare turn to look directly at any of them. I was too embarrassed. I wondered what they made of me.

Jack came in escorted by police officers. I wondered whether he had handcuffs on or not, but I didn't want to look. I didn't look at anyone except my legal representatives and the judge. The judge was a youngish and fairly attractive female. There was nothing soft about her. She was direct and to the point. 'Well, Mr Charming, why didn't you leave?'

He came out with some rigmarole about wanting to make a stand on behalf of his children, to prove to them that he loved them. I don't know how keeping them out of their home was meant to convey that point, but he wasn't given the chance to elaborate. He was given short shrift. 'Mr Charming, you have to promise not to go back to the house, or back to prison you go.'

I kept my eyes down. I was finding this incredibly embarrassing, and there was a public gallery full of people watching the exchange. The promise was unwillingly given, but it sounded genuine. I was only partially surprised to hear it. My husband was highly educated and cultured. I couldn't imagine him in prison; I was sure it would destroy him. It was impossible that he would hold out.

I was right. He was beaten on that one. Outside court my solicitor said she had looked at him as the judge said, 'Promise, or back to prison you go.' She said she saw a look of fear on his face. I don't think I have ever seen a look of fear on my husband's face. It is something I have yet to experience. I couldn't look at him throughout that horrible hearing. I just had to imagine the look of fear.

His fear did not, however, lessen his determination to push his luck as far as it could go. If he couldn't return to the house, he told the judge, he would like to be able to return to the garage. Our garage was not attached to our house; it was situated across the road and therefore not included in the order banning him from the house, he argued. It was splitting hairs; a cheekily defiant way of saying he would keep to the letter of the law but had no interest in the spirit of the order. The judge was not having it. He could not return either to the house or to the garage, she insisted.

He was lucky, the judge told Jack. We could have applied for his committal due to his contempt of court. My barrister interposed that we were planning to seek his committal over his defiance of the court in regard to the removal of the furniture. This sounded comical even to my ears. It looked as though I didn't care about my husband remaining in the house, but did care that he had removed the furniture.

Pursuing Jack for the furniture would have been too ridiculous. See someone in prison for removing his own furniture, even if it was in contempt of a court order. I felt I had to keep things in proportion.

No one was hurt. I would have felt a complete fool taking my husband to court over furniture. I couldn't do it. 'Let it drop,' I told my solicitor.

I expect she wasn't sorry. She saw too much of me as it was. That was a point in my life at which I talked to my solicitor, by phone or in her office, more than I talked to my own children. During that period when everything was happening, things had become very dramatic, and barely a day went by without the case requiring my attention.

A few days later it was my youngest son's third birthday. It was a double cause for celebration, being able to celebrate his birthday in his own home. Eva's father changed the locks for me on the same day. We couldn't prevent the windows being smashed if Jack chose to carry out his threat, but we could stop him coming in through the doors. I began painting the walls of the sitting room: new life, new décor. I decided on a cheerful apricot colour.

Regaining the house meant I could resume teaching with Eva. Working as a pair, we were often sent siblings to teach. It was convenient for parents to drop two children off at a time. It was fantastic being able to work in tandem and devising support strategies for some of our pupils who came with a range of difficulties, including dyslexia, Asperger's syndrome and ADD. I also found myself running a free homework service. The phone seemed to ring non-stop on evenings and weekends with pupils wanting help with assignments.

After my return home, one of my neighbours approached Orla and praised her for having taken me into her home for six months while we were awaiting the occupation order. She particularly applauded her generosity since I had apparently been suffering from post-natal depression. It was another of those nasty stories about my supposed mental illness that had got round.

Jack had thoroughly poisoned the wells in the neighbourhood before my return. I was constantly hearing rumours and false accusations about my supposed mental illness and post-natal depression. It made life difficult. It was a close-knit community. These things got back to me. I heard them repeated. I tried to ignore them, but they blighted our homecoming. There were people who showed hostility to me, especially in the beginning, because they had heard these rumours and obviously decided there was some truth in them. Never one for confrontation, I retreated into my own space with a small circle of friends, concentrating on my life with them and on the teaching, and tried to ignore hostility when I encountered it.

There were times I was shouted at in the street by my husband's friends, or when neighbours who had liked him but who didn't know me simply crossed the street or turned their heads away when I passed by. It was difficult at first. In the beginning I didn't want to stay.

My friends chivvied me along. 'Live it down, people will forget it. You'll be the centre of gossip for a couple of weeks and then it will all die down.' It never did die down entirely. There were always some people who remembered it. But I was grateful for the kindness of those nearer neighbours who had witnessed some of his bullying, who had heard him shouting at night and seen me locked out in the garden. It made up a little for the ignorance of the rest.

15

Facing the possibility of prison

⚖️

I had the misfortune to come before the same Judge A less than six months after the upheaval of the appeal and Jack's removal from the house. There had been constant difficulties with contact. Jack used every opportunity to indoctrinate the children about the court proceedings. He passed comment on the judges to them, whether he considered them good or bad; he told them about his 'rubbish solicitors' and how they weren't doing a good job for him. He told them how he was fighting to get them to live with him. He constantly ran me down and criticised my parenting, my friends and my lifestyle.

It was the same old rubbishing of me that I had to put up with when I lived with him. But now he was doing it to the children. My daughter grew to hate contact sessions and soon wanted to stop going at all. My eldest child was the one who had seen and heard the most abuse of me. She was afraid of her father.

Contact became fraught with difficulties. There were periods when some of the children didn't want to go, or none of them wanted to go. Jack made another contact application in February 2003. It was the same Milton-quoting Judge A whom I had come to dread. Of all the judges it would be him. I was terrified of him. I saw so many judges over the whole period – more than twenty up to that point – yet I rarely saw the same once twice; with the exception of Judge A. This was my third time in front of him.

I pleaded with my solicitor to try to find some way to avoid coming before him. She said it couldn't be done. I was sleepless and petrified the night before the hearing. And it was every bit as bad as I had expected. The judge, of course, remembered me. I was the mother he loved to hate. The hearing went all Jack's way. Not only was Madeleine ordered to attend contact sessions, despite her terror, but the judge made it impossible for her to refuse contact by ordering that she be collected direct from school by her father so that there was no chance of her refusing to go. There was no way for me to keep her at home if she was scared and unwilling to attend.

It was horrendous. It felt as though my life was in ruins. I minded this far more than the injustice done to me over the assault in the park. This concerned my daughter: my precious little girl who was only five years old. I had been pushed to the brink. The judge had gone too far this time. I felt such anger for my poor young daughter that I lost my fear and gained the courage of desperation.

I stood up in court and I addressed my husband. I told him he should be ashamed of himself for the fear he induced in our daughter and I left the court. The judge ordered my barrister to go after me. He was told to order my return to court. I refused.

At that moment I wouldn't have cared if he had ordered me to be locked up in prison. I had such a deep conviction that what he had done was completely wrong, and whether I won or failed I knew I had to do something about it. It was not possible any longer to take such unjust treatment.

The trouble is what do you do? I couldn't just demand the head judge and go and tap on his door. There were private corridors for judges which were separate from everyone else and there was security. You couldn't just walk up to them the way you could ordinary members of the public. Members of Parliament were much more accessible than judges.

The world had collapsed again. The following day I didn't want to get out of bed and face the ruins. Orla persuaded me to go and get help from a sympathetic doctor. She came with me and did the talking. I was prescribed anti-depressants and counselling. I had to function for the sake of the children, yet I was dogged with the pain and chaos resulting from the court hearings.

I made an official complaint about Judge A. Finding out the procedure for making a complaint was difficult. It took some phone calls and being sent around the houses before I ended up at the outlandishly named Judicial Correspondence Unit in the Department for Constitutional Affairs.

My initial complaint about Judge A was rejected. I didn't even know what role or official capacity the woman had who supposedly investigated the complaint. Her investigation had seemingly involved her asking the judge whether he had behaved incorrectly and him asserting that he hadn't. It made me hopping mad. How dare they call this a court service?

I wrote back to the woman who had rejected my complaint insisting that it hadn't been dealt with in a proper way, and I sent a copy of all the correspondence to my MP. Clearly we needed some outside help on this matter.

Eva and I attended the MP's surgery. We explained the predicament. He thought it was a pity that family courts were not open to the public, or at least to journalists. If the public or press could see the way it was possible to treat women behind closed doors, there might be a rethink on the way these cases were handled.

The sympathy was welcome but useless. The family courts are not open to the public. However, it did make me think. Part of me wanted privacy. I didn't want any Tom, Dick or Harry to know the unpleasant, intimate details of my marriage. I didn't want to provide fodder for nosy neighbours or to incite the twitching of net curtains. But after this I did want people to know the way judges could abuse women who had already suffered domestic abuse, and how they could get away with it with impunity because it was all done in private, with no one to hold them to account.

The secrecy of the family courts allowed the oppression of women and children; and it was that conversation with my MP which triggered my conversion to the belief that the press at least, people with accredited journalistic credentials, should be allowed into the courts. I thought there was also a case for allowing in other interested professionals to observe these difficult cases. There was too much at stake and too much could go wrong when justice took place behind closed doors. Justice should be seen to be done.

I was clear in my mind that there was a travesty of justice here. It didn't just involve me. I was acutely aware of that. How badly was this judge treating other women in similar situations? I'd had an inkling of this during the period when I had been sitting outside the courtroom waiting for Judge A to hear my case on one of those fateful occasions. I'd been accosted by a man in the corridor. 'Are you waiting for Judge A?' he enquired of me. I confirmed that I was. 'He's alright he is,' he chattily told me. 'He just told me to go home and not do it again.'

I found out what the 'it' consisted of a short time later when the man made a call on his mobile phone. He was laughing and talking to a friend at the other end: 'I only pulled her hair; she made such a fuss about it.' He was talking about his ex-partner. 'I only pulled her hair.' My God, he sounded just like Jack! It disgusted me and I moved my seat further away. I was obviously just another woman who had to put up with an assault by her ex, only to be told by Judge A that it was nothing. What messages was this awful judge sending to perpetrators? He was virtually patting them on the back.

My MP promised to write to the Lord Chancellor about my case. He was as good as his word and wrote straight away.

Naturally, the judge, in response to being challenged, tried to justify himself. I had been told by the police officer who charged Jack with an assault against me that Judge A could simply have telephoned the police station to find out what had happened that day. Judge A, in his response, dismissively said that it wasn't his business to chase evidence for me.

I was angered by the complete absence of an apology. I wanted the judge to know from me what his behaviour had felt like. I wanted my complaint to be personal. Thus I sent a letter directly to the judge answering his self-justifications. I found out from the court where the judge was currently sitting and I posted the letter to him at that court. It was twelve typed pages long!

When I wrote that letter I was too hurt and angry to be scared. Once I had sent it, some of the fear came back. I remained in terror of coming before Judge A for any contact applications. After I had complained about him, I didn't think it would be possible to receive a fair trial at his hands. I did not imagine for one minute that he would put his hands up and say sorry.

When I look at the letter with hindsight, I experience a mix of emotions. It is much more strongly worded than I realised at the time; stinging in fact: indicative of my state of mind. After all, it basically says the judge is incompetent at his job.

The part of me which admires feminists like Helena Kennedy thinks that I was right to send it because women should not have to plead and beg for justice or for protection from abusive men. Nor, when they come forward for help, should they be treated in such insulting and demeaning ways by judges. It is just another kind of abuse, but this time by the system. But the courage of desperation only lasts a certain time. The anger wore off once the initial shock and outrage was over and then I began to fear some come back for standing up to the judge.

I pleaded with my solicitor to do something to make sure that I never came before Judge A again. This time she took my view on the matter and contacted the court about it. I was informed that a note would be made on the file so that it would not come before the judge for a hearing while the complaint was being investigated. I was told in fact that it would have the words NOT TO COME BEFORE JUDGE A plastered all over it in big letters. I imagined that was a joke. It would be nice to think it was true, but I didn't believe it.

I had a very nice solicitor. I don't know what she made of me. Mine must have been a stressful case. She was younger than me, but I think I put some grey hairs in her head. My husband described her in one of his statements as having 'destroyed my family with incredible relish'. I interpreted this to mean that he thought she was doing a good job for me. Or did he mean that she had some warped personal interest in procuring divorces?

He probably thought she was sitting there with her notepad keeping a tally. Next year they had to improve their performance at divorces to hit new targets. Divorce-related profits down this year; bang goes the Christmas bonus. There were times you had to take refuge in humour just to keep your sanity.

I couldn't hold out against Judge A's order. Jack had tried to seek my committal several times. If I disobeyed the judge, I feared I would end up in prison. The fear of ending up behind bars took a huge toll. My mental health began to suffer. I suffered headaches and sleeplessness, and had severe outbreaks of eczema due to stress.

Protracted adversarial court proceedings, as anyone who has been through court will testify, really take it out of you and bring you very low. At the same time, I suspect that women feel that they can't complain of the stress of proceedings affecting their mental health. In my case any hint of such things was used by Jack as an offensive weapon, as if to say: 'Look, she shouldn't have the children because she can't cope with them. She can't get out of bed in the mornings; she can't be taking care of the children. She always was neurotic, incapable; I would be a much better carer than she is.'

This sort of attack made me avoid seeking help and support when I needed it because I knew it would be used against me and I couldn't take the stress of fighting more than I had to. One repugnant aspect of the family courts is that instead of attributing blame where it lies, and considering the impact which abuse and adversarial proceedings would have on the victim, judges sometimes appear to give credence to the man's claims that the woman is mentally ill. From talking to other women in the same situation, it appears to be a classic form of abuse to accuse the woman of mental illness.

It is, of course, repellent in this day and age that mental health should be grounds to attack anyone with. It never fails to amaze me, however, that women are questioned and examined about their mental health, but men are not held to account for their abuse or violence. Given that there is an obvious linkage between abuse and consequences in terms of poorer mental health for women, one would hope that the courts would be more enlightened and give a man short shrift if he accused a woman of being crazy. Listening to such abuse gives a dignity to the accusations which they don't deserve, and it leads to a vicious circle of a woman feeling unable to seek help for the emotional and psychological scars of abuse in case she is accused of not being able to cope.

If I couldn't hold out against Judge A, my daughter felt she could. She was six but she had a strong fear of her father because of what she had witnessed and experienced in the past. His fear and deep resentment of women had made him unable to form a close bond with her. Contact was miserable for her because she had to listen to constant criticism of me and to her father's complaints about his failure to get custody of her through the courts. The failings of solicitors and judges and their refusal to give him justice were dinned in at her ears during contact sessions.

Knowing full well that her father would never be satisfied unless he gained residence was a perpetual strain for a little girl of six. I could not refuse for her, but she did begin to refuse contact for herself. She spoke to her teacher at school about her fear of contact. The school's support for my daughter led to the court taking it more seriously.

In the meantime, the climate of conflict was increased by the fact that the financial proceedings had begun to run parallel to the family courts. The courts do not order a financial settlement until it is decided whom the children will live with.

Jack wanted the matrimonial home sold because he wanted his share of the assets. Although the children and I had needed the house temporarily because we no longer had the flat, I agreed with selling the home. I thought it would help us both to move on; and I didn't want to live permanently in the neighbourhood I had lived in during my marriage.

One motive I had for agreeing to the sale is that Jack made my life difficult when I was in close proximity. The harassment continued for the whole period I was in London. There were frequent malicious complaints made about me to social services, the police and other people, saying that I wasn't taking care of the children properly.

Also, had I stayed, a charge for the legal proceedings would have been placed on the house. You have to pay interest on the legal charge. I couldn't have afforded to pay off the interest, so by the time the children were grown up, there would have been no equity left in the house.

The first financial hearing was a waste of time because Jack failed to disclose his financial position. Costs were awarded against him and the hearing was rescheduled. My barrister, the same who had coped with the snatch and the recovery order on my very first occasion at court, resigned from the case during the financial hearings and advised me to seek a more senior barrister.

Jack had gone for a barrister with a mean persona. From his manner, my husband's barrister might have been better suited to a post as a nightclub bouncer. He was a real bruiser. My polite, well-mannered barrister was insulted and taunted outside the court by the other side in the preliminary discussions and jeeringly asked how many years he'd been doing the job, implying that he was green about the gills.

The other side were going to play rough and my barrister didn't fancy the job. I don't know about green around the gills; he was green in the face. I didn't blame him. I felt green and sick whenever I had to deal with my ex or his representatives. He always seemed to pick the aggressive types to represent him.

The whole thing felt like a jungle. But you are tied in with children. If it had been just me, I could have walked away and gone back to work. But there was no prospect of working with four tiny children. There was no choice but to fight, if only in order to provide them with a roof over their heads.

Finally, a year after court proceedings had first started, I was given residence of the children. Final residence when it came was an anti-climax. It was conceded by Jack. I couldn't understand it. He had fought in every dirty way possible to get the children; why wasn't he fighting dirty to the end?

It emerged later that Jack had been advised he stood little chance of getting residence, since I was recommended for residence by the Cafcass report. His legal representatives couldn't justify giving him legal funding to fight for residence. As it was public money, the Legal Aid Commission would only agree to pay if an application stood a chance of success. Evidently Jack's representatives felt that it didn't in this instance.

It left me with a court order on paper, although Jack did not emotionally accept it one iota. He told me privately that he still intended to wage a war to get the kids and that he would not give up until all the assets were wasted if he had to.

It was a final hearing in terms of residence – it gave me permanent custody of the children – but there would be further hearings. In line with a recommendation from Cafcass, Jack was referred to the Domestic Violence Intervention Project, an organisation which would assess the safety of future contact. A review hearing was ordered to take place later which would consider the DVIP report once it had been produced.

16

Cafcass

There were a number of interviews at the Cafcass offices during the year after I left Jack. A Cafcass officer is the person who decides what she or he thinks is in the best interests of the children and then writes a report about it for the court, when the parents disagree about whom the children should live with and when they cannot agree contact arrangements.

At the four-day interim residence/occupation/non-molestation hearing in front of Judge K in September 2002, the judge had requested Cafcass to produce a report on our case in time for the final hearing. It was this report which persuaded the judge at the final hearing to give me residence of the children.

I had no idea what to expect at the initial meeting. I went on my own the first time, without the children. Cafcass in Finchley operated from a large old house. Inside it was not terribly welcoming; there was nothing friendly or homely about it. It had mainly bare white walls. A lick of paint and a few flowers or ornaments wouldn't have gone amiss.

I never do well with strangers. Being expected immediately to delve into the most personal and intimate details of my marriage with a complete stranger was incredibly unpleasant and stressful. I resented it. I was a totally committed and conscientious parent but in these offices I felt I was expected to prove myself. It is something that in the normal course of things parents aren't expected to do. Most people take their authority and right to parent unquestioningly. In court proceedings it is questioned. You are expected to show that you are a good parent. It is a most unnatural and demeaning process.

I had been the main carer for my children all their lives. Although

I had been criticised and denigrated by their other parent, still I had been the one to put in the time. My husband never entered this world of practical child care. He was old fashioned and refused even to push a pram because he considered it unmanly. He didn't cook, he didn't clean. He didn't crawl around on the floor playing with bricks and balls; he always wore a suit and kept his dignity. He refused to change nappies on principle because he regarded it as women's work and he never got sticky and dirty caring for the children. I did all this as a matter of course but having to demonstrate this at the Cafcass office felt like being an actor on stage. What else did they think a resident parent did? I wasn't on the social services at-risk register; clearly I was a normal parent.

I hated Cafcass interviews. At the back of my mind was the fear that Jack would fool the officer and persuade her that he was a great fellow, as he did with so many people. I also felt unnatural and stilted. Maybe I could have talked if I had been asked straight off about my concerns, but when you go to Cafcass you are questioned by rote, according to a specific welfare checklist.

On the first occasion I was interviewed, I had no idea what the welfare checklist consisted of. I was working blind, not knowing what she was looking for or what was expected of me. Nothing was explained. I expected her to interview me, but no one explained what the purpose of the questions was or where they were leading.

The questions the Cafcass officer asked at that first interview didn't seem to cover the things I was worried about. I wasn't asked specific detailed questions about violence or abuse, and most of what I had experienced went unsaid because there didn't seem a point at which I could bring it into the conversation. One or two things came out, but it was unsatisfactory. By the end of the interview I was left feeling: is that it? Was this exercise designed to elicit a true picture of our lives?

After that first interview on my own I was expected, as all parents are, to take my children along for interview and observation. I dressed them with a sinking feeling in my heart on the appointed morning. I made an extra effort with their clothes. I lined them up in a row to look at them once they were dressed and I realised that the children all toned and matched. They were all in shades of blue. Matching the clothes to the mood? I'd even found a blue flower for my daughter's ponytail. I felt proud of them. They looked sweet and tiny.

The Cafcass officer looked on with an expression of dismay when she saw them all: four of them. Not an easy interview with four. One of them was crawling, another was a toddler. 'They are very small,' she said.

It was like play acting in front of her, something I was not very good at because I was far too embarrassed and self-conscious. I could handle the children effortlessly at home with no one looking, but being asked to demonstrate what I would otherwise do quite naturally was something I felt awkward about. What was she looking for? I felt I must be perspiring with the stress; it certainly seemed very hot in the room. I felt as though I had to pass a test. How was I doing? Would I get good marks?

So much with children was a matter of luck too, especially with tiny children who could be unpredictable. Even normally placid children, which mine were, could have an off-day. The two littlest ones might quarrel over a toy and one of them might start crying.

I started to panic. What if one of them had a tantrum? What if they all came to blows in the Wendy house? Was I doing the right thing letting the baby crawl about the floor; maybe I should pick her up, look more interested? Was I going to be marked down if the children were too loud or too noisy? Perhaps if they were too quiet they would be seen as unnaturally withdrawn. It was a horrible self-conscious hour, spent like a Woody Allen film with a constant inner neurotic monologue.

The Cafcass officer was also required to observe Jack with the children. I went away and found somewhere to have coffee while she did so. I felt dismal at the prospect of her observing the children with my ex and of her interviews with him. He always turned on the charm with outsiders. And he was charming; intelligent and an excellent conversationalist. Who was going to believe me against him?

Acting was Jack's profession before he turned to teaching and he was wonderful at putting on a show and making small talk. I was sure that if this was a contest to appear well, he would be bound to win it. But it would be a hollow sham, I also knew that.

How could you possibly tell from seeing someone once whether they were abusive or violent or not? If it was so easy to tell who the abusers are, children wouldn't be killed or harmed by their parents so regularly. If social workers couldn't tell in the easy cases, in Haringey and other places, how on earth could they make judgements in less obvious situations which involved emotional and psychological abuse?

Jack was a teacher and he could certainly handle kids and keep them in order. But this observation of him with the kids wouldn't tell her whether Jack was likely to use the children as levers to control me; or whether he was likely to attack me again at contact handovers; it wouldn't tell her how he could verbally abuse at the top of his voice and then switch to charm mode again in a second. None of his abuse would show, so what was the point of it? I felt very dispirited.

I sometimes asked these questions of barristers but they didn't seem to understand the situation either. If a child is unhappy with a parent, it will show up, they would argue. I didn't buy that argument. You can't simply look at an abused child and know it is an abused child. Children who suffer abuse or witness abuse against their mother don't look morose and unhappy all the time. It is not nearly as simple as that. If it were that easy, we wouldn't need specially trained people who are skilled at picking up abuse and we wouldn't need child psychologists and child psychiatrists.

There is an alternative point to consider: that a child, not knowing it is being treated in an abusive way, simply accepts the situation – just as my friend from secondary school had. This doesn't mean that we should deliberately expose young children to harmful relationships.

I felt that Cafcass to some extent operates on pretence. With cases like ours it really needed a psychologist to ask the right questions; someone skilled, with expertise in domestic violence, to understand the whole complex family dynamic, not a woman with a clipboard and an hour to spare.

To be fair to the first Cafcass officer who assessed us, she did not try to assume the role of an expert in domestic violence. She asked the court to make findings about the 'cross allegations of domestic violence', since Jack had made allegations about me. And she was also responsible for referring us to the Domestic Violence Intervention Project. She thus proved herself to be thorough enough and fair minded in her work. Our disastrous experiences as a family with Cafcass came later on and in a different place, but I wasn't convinced that the observation of us was an exercise in anything except futility.

The Cafcass officer's report when it came was a puzzle to me. I didn't know how to interpret it. I was dismayed on the first reading and I telephoned my solicitor. 'I've got a bad report from Cafcass.' My solicitor, who'd read many of these reports before, assured me that in fact it wasn't a bad report at all; it recommended that I should have residence of the children (be the custodial parent, in other words) and it said I was a good mother. 'Where does it say that?' I was meant to read between the lines it seemed; to understand Cafcass-speak.

There seemed a lot of inconsequential detail in the Cafcass reports which I couldn't see the point of, such as Jools playing with the toy letters in the Cafcass play room and the children all looking at things out of the office's windows.

I learned from the Cafcass report that Jack had brought a picnic with him to the office. Apparently he made the children sit down on the floor and eat the meal. Clever of him, I thought. He'd certainly planned it all beforehand if he'd come ready prepared with a picnic. Part of me was amused, wishing I'd thought of food. It was a brilliant way of making sure the children would keep still and quiet and be no trouble.

I was somewhat annoyed by the officer's writing that he made them eat in an orderly and tidy way with good manners. Such details, along with what toys the children chose to play with, were superficial. It was pretence to think you could tell enough from these mundane details to decide a family's future on. What did they say about Jack? They might say to an outsider that he could keep children in order and was teaching them polite manners. If you knew the children better, it might appear that they were so used to close control by their father that they would never risk putting a foot wrong because the consequences would be serious. You can't watch children without a context and a history.

On the occasion when the Cafcass officer came to visit me and the children in the matrimonial home, once we had been able to reoccupy it, Ben wandered around the house with a damp cloth trying to clean the windows, and even this found its way into one of the reports. My solicitor received the reports before I did and she always telephoned me and read them out. Even she had to laugh when she got to the part about the damp cloth and Ben window cleaning. I just couldn't see the relevance. Perhaps it meant that Ben wanted to be a window-cleaner when he grew up!

17

The Domestic Violence Intervention Project

⚖️

Following the recommendation from Cafcass, Jack and I attended the Domestic Violence Intervention Project (DVIP), which involved assessment by a psychologist with expertise in the field of domestic violence. Jack would undergo a risk assessment and I would also be interviewed by the psychologist.

The DVIP has been cited by the Home Office as a best practice project and it offers a 32-week group programme designed to hold men accountable for violence to their partners and to address the attitudes and beliefs that underlie their abusive behaviour. The programme addresses a wide range of abusive behaviours including physical abuse, emotional abuse, sexual abuse, stalking and harassing, jealousy and parenting issues. It aims to inculcate greater awareness and understanding of domestic violence in men and to help them develop better ways of relating. Partners and ex-partners of abusive men are also offered support services.

I was told that sometimes the motivation for these men to attend was that their wives or girlfriends had refused them access to their children unless they got help for their behaviour. I was astonished. It had never been suggested to me at any point over that horrendous year that I had any say over contact matters. Contact was determined by the court and it seemed I had no right to refuse my husband access to the children on the grounds of his abuse. Where were these women who were able to tell the man to go away unless he behaved? If there were such men being denied access, they presumably hadn't been referred to the DVIP via the courts because statistics don't back up the perception that violent or abusive fathers are being refused contact.

In reality, the courts are only too ready to bend over backwards to give contact to almost any kind of father, even if he deliberately destabilises the mother and children. Anyone who comes with a 'father' label is acceptable if you look at the figures, which show that barely any contact applications are turned down.

I never came across a single woman myself who had been able to tell a man to get therapy before he had contact. I came across women who complained that the courts enforced a man's contact no matter what he had done, even if the children hated going. That was the pattern I saw. Despite the myths and rumours you see in the newspapers that there are vengeful women out there fooling judges and keeping fathers away from children for no good reason, I did not meet a single mother who fell into that stereotype.

The ones I met were in the same situation as me. Demoralised, living in difficult circumstances, frustrated with judges who dictated the terms of contact without having any real understanding of the problems and issues these women were facing. I saw mothers who were angrier than I was; who were more aggressive, less educated and less articulate. But these were no reasons why a mother who had genuine concerns about her children should be distrusted or treated with scepticism.

The fear, anxiety, anger, helplessness that disempowering women in this way causes is doing no good to the welfare of the children either. Little girls are getting the message that this is how relationships function. Love and violence go together. Daddy treats Mummy like that and no one in authority says it is wrong.

I was worried about my own sons. Jack was their role model for manhood. They were being taught to preserve appearances, to be cultured and well educated, to speak the Queen's English, but they weren't being taught good relationship skills for life. In the very area which was most important to their welfare, they were being let down badly.

I didn't want my sons to grow up thinking it was all right to treat women in this way. I worried about learned habits and patterns of behaviour but I felt helpless on this score because it was not an argument which ever persuaded a judge. They were much more focused on immediate welfare. Unless a man was actually belting the kids, there was no way to get supervised contact.

I felt this was short-sighted, neglecting the attitudes which would affect their whole lives in the future. Perhaps they would grow up unable to form equal and loving relationships. How were they going to develop the skills and emotions which would enable them to be successful spouses and parents through the years ahead? If the court wanted to put an end to the repetitive cycle of violence, it seemed to me they had to take a strong line with perpetrators. They must change if they wanted contact.

The Domestic Violence Intervention Project was the one place I found in the whole process of court proceedings, lasting eight years to date, which seemed to grasp the issues and the damaging emotional consequences of abuse. I had gone with low expectations. After the horrible events I'd experienced in court, I didn't expect anything good from this programme. I dreaded the whole prospect of having to go over past abuse in detail with strangers. I dissolved into tears at the door when I arrived and nearly went away again.

It turned out to be an interlude which I could look back upon with relief and hope: where the psychological and emotional issues relating to abuse were properly understood and explained; where I didn't feel helpless in the face of scepticism when I described the crushing impact of constant belittling and menace. At least they understood control – that it wasn't love which led a man to try to keep control over his children's lives; it was sheer bloody-mindedness. For a while the DVIP restored some of my confidence.

18

An abusive judge

⚖️

There was another upset with contact. Incidents were continually happening and upsetting the contact arrangements. My son Ben had been frightened by his father shouting and being aggressive towards him. This time Jack was angry about my solicitor. I saw her so often that her presence had become a normal part of life. My five-year-old had made an innocent comment about my solicitor helping us, and he had been bellowed at and told that my solicitor was 'a horrible woman who only takes the money and just cares about herself'.

His father had driven the car with his knees so that he could lean into the back seat and frighten him. It was a recognisable pattern. It was exactly the kind of attack which I had got used to, but which would scare a small child to death. He came back saying, 'Daddy fighted (*sic*) me and I don't want to go again.'

My son's rejection of contact led to a torrent of abuse and anger directed towards me by his father. Apparently I was to blame for it. I was alienating his son, turning him against his father. Jack took no responsibility at all for his own anger. In his view, he had a right to be angry and to show it. The kids should just accept it. My husband showed no insight into this attitude. He had a right to express any emotion he liked, to act out any angry feeling he liked, just because it was him.

Only a month after the supposed final hearing at which I had been granted residence, Jack applied for another penal notice. He wanted his contact back with his son and he wanted me committed to prison if I didn't go along with it. We had what my barrister described as a 'grumpy and lazy' judge. It was another of those seemingly interminable hearings where nothing is decided. The judge was very rude. He appeared to have no humanity, no respect for people and no manners. If they hoped to inculcate reasonableness in the parties, they might take a look at their own attitude in court.

Another two months passed. A review hearing took place to look at the case in the light of the Domestic Violence Intervention Project report. Unfortunately, the report at that stage had not been filed.

I wanted to wait for the report to come in before anything regarding unsupervised contact was decided. The judge who looked at the case before the report was filed thought differently. The hearing which dealt with my son's refusal of contact stands out in my mind along with the hearing in front of Judge A in which I had left the court in disgust. This one was equally appalling. They are not easy memories to live with.

I gave evidence in front of Judge C. The judge kept telling me, irritably, to speak up. I had a quiet voice but I did my best to speak loudly for his benefit. I think his irritation probably had nothing to do with the tone or pitch of my voice; he just did not like my case. He did not hear my husband speak. The phrases which dinned themselves into my ears from that hearing were that I was 'neurotic' in my fears for the children – 'that's what fathers do – they shout at children' – that there had been a 'low level of violence' in the marriage and that he 'couldn't see that my husband posed any risk' to the children.

It feels horrendous to be insulted in front of the husband who has abused you in the past and who is determined to control you in the present. I felt my legs go weak in the witness box. To my immense frustration, my voice broke and I became tearful. I hated showing weakness.

I felt at the mercy of two powerful men in the courtroom: my husband and the judge. I knew tears wouldn't gain me anything. Men who were in control tended to despise you for tears. They regarded them as weak, manipulative, crocodile tears. I didn't want to do it. I tried to get control of myself. The judge's face was hard and unsympathetic.

Judge C gave instant judgment. It was little more than a paragraph. He said that I was implacable and hostile to contact. He uttered the words, 'I am sure I am right.' I was sitting beside my solicitor while he was giving his verdict. If he'd taken a hammer to my head and smashed it, I don't think I could have felt more dazed and disorientated by what was happening. It felt as though every single time I tried to explain that I had real fears and concerns for my children and that my children too were afraid, I was treated sceptically. On this occasion I was 'neurotic'.

Unfortunately at the time I couldn't brush these things off. They went deep. I was so used to being called names, to being belittled and demeaned, that I internalised it. I retreated into feeling bad about myself, imagining that I invited this treatment, instead of feeling outrage at the inhumanity, the stark chauvinism and the outdated attitudes of an ignorant judge, which I do now

I took responsibility upon myself for this judge's appalling attitude, when clearly I should have told myself that I wasn't going to win a case with a man who believed it was a normal mode of relating to shout at your children and that smashing a glass light over a child's eyes was low-level violence.

My friends tried to rally me after this hearing. They were angrier than I was at how I'd been treated. Orla tried to push me, 'You can't stand for this; you have to complain.'

I was beginning to feel like a serial complainer. How many complaints had I made? The worst of it was that I wasn't a complainer by nature. I loathed confrontation. My nature was pretty compliant. I could get angry when injustice was done to other people but not when it was done to me.

There was a residue in me, however, that felt as though I must fight back. I felt in my gut that this could not be happening only to me. It must be happening to other women too. Judges like Judge A and Judge C didn't exist in a vacuum. They were the worst of a bunch, but nevertheless the system allowed them to flourish. They weren't interested in abuse or its effects. Basically they were blokey with the types who did it. And the secrecy of the family court allowed them to behave like this. I was convinced that such treatment of women couldn't flourish in an open court system.

I had constantly to try to detach myself from my own bad self-image. I tried to look at it objectively. If a woman I didn't know had been treated this way, what would I have thought? I had no doubt. I'd think that judges like Judge A and Judge C should be sacked, or moved to some position in which they can't do any more harm to women and children. But because it was me, I felt continuous self-doubt.

I don't think retraining these judges would have done any good. They were lacking the empathy which might have substituted for a more formal knowledge of the issues surrounding domestic abuse. Some judges just did not have what it takes to understand the issues from a victim's viewpoint. They shared one thing in common with Jack: they despised you if they thought you were weak and were more likely to walk on you for it.

What is it about vulnerability that we feel the need to attack it when we see it? It was something I had noticed regularly since leaving Jack. Faced with a battered woman, people were often hostile. If they weren't going to respond to the woman with sympathy, very likely they were going to respond with anger, hostility and rejection.

I often wondered about the feelings lying behind that rejection. Certainly there was embarrassment in some cases. Really listening to someone who is vulnerable is a hard thing to do. It requires you to be understanding and it brings you closer to someone. That's a difficult challenge to rise to. It's much easier to brush a vulnerable woman off than respond to her. The extreme reaction I got from Judge C, and to Judge A before him, suggested a kind of hatred which was presumably rooted at some level in a fear of relating to and communicating with women.

After these episodes I became further convinced that the system should change and that a proper mechanism should be put in place for choosing family court judges. Personally I would be in favour of psychological testing for anyone wanting to be a judge in family matters. There are plenty of professions which require psychological profiling of applicants because of the risks involved in employing the wrong people. I think becoming a judge should be included among those professions. The consequences for individual families and for society in getting it wrong in family cases can be devastating.

I have on several occasions heard such bullying behaviour by judges described by more senior judges as 'robustness'. The aptness of such a term depends on which side of the room one happens to be sitting in. From a victim's viewpoint, such aggressive behaviour could be construed as bullying. If one is vulnerable, the same behaviour that a strong person might describe as robust can appear as being abusive and bullying. It's a matter of perspective.

I decided that I would complain about Judge C. I knew the risk. I had already complained about Judge A and had experienced a small degree of success. The Lord Chancellor had written back through my MP offering his sympathy because I had been a victim of domestic violence. He had spoken to Judge A about showing more awareness in future when faced with such victims of abuse.

I was aware I could spoil it by complaining about Judge C too. I was well aware how it would be regarded. Those in authority might be prepared to believe there was one aberrant judge with unacceptable attitudes, but two? I would be regarded as an unreasonable person, a serial complainer. They would begin to blame me and not the judges.

And so it was. My complaint against Judge C was rejected. I was told rather waspishly in a letter by the Lord Chancellor that he wasn't a line manager; he couldn't stand over the judges and interfere in their cases.

I had expected him to wash his hands of it and he did. I knew that they could probably bear criticism of one judge and might even believe it was justified, but two judges began to look like a fault in the system, and that they wouldn't countenance. No one likes to be told they are part of a flawed system, or that powerful and privileged men are not well placed to judge cases involving vulnerable women. They didn't want to be told that judges were routinely failing victims of domestic abuse.

Part of me didn't care. There was a principle at stake here which was vital and I felt it was part of a bigger war. I had expected to lose the battle. I didn't regret making the point even though I knew they probably now doubted my original complaint because they had classed me as an unreasonable customer. Any systemic injustice takes time to dismantle and there were layers of complacency and denial about the system which I couldn't hope to challenge in one complaint or two. It would take a lot more than that to change things.

The psychologist's report from the Domestic Violence Intervention Project eventually came back. The report's structure was extremely thorough, assessing perpetrators under several headings including: denial of culpability, understanding and insight into perpetrated violence and abuse, victim empathy, remorse, belief in male dominance, exposure of children to domestic violence, indirect risk of injury, ability to talk responsibly about abuse to the children, motivation for wanting contact, and motivation to attend treatment programme, amongst others. These were all the issues which I had repeatedly tried to put before the courts and which I had never succeeded in getting a judge to factor into the equation.

At last here was an organisation which considered that these were serious and significant issues that needed addressing. The irony that the psychologist's report followed shortly after Judge C had called me neurotic for raising these same issues was not lost on me.

The DVIP report was soundly rooted in the CASC guidelines,

which were supposed to apply in cases of domestic violence. The impossibly titled Guidelines for good practice proposed by the Children Act Sub-Committee of the Advisory Board on Family Law lists psychological abuse, including but not limited to intimidation, harassment and threats of abuse, under the heading of domestic violence. The guidelines also recognise that abuse may consist of one act or of a number of acts which may appear to be minor or trivial when viewed in isolation, but which may form part of a pattern. They recommend using a broad definition of domestic violence.

My experience was not limited; I had been in dozens of courtrooms before dozens of judges and not one had considered domestic violence in its broadest forms as defined by the CASC guidelines. On two or three occasions the violence was referred to as 'low level' and perhaps it was if you used a very narrow definition, such as whether I had been hospitalised or not, as one barrister suggested to me. But when you looked at the overall picture, it was clear that the psychological abuse perpetrated by my ex-husband fell well within the broad definition of domestic violence and indeed was quite extreme if you considered the degree of control he exercised within our marriage and the length of time he had tried to exercise control after I left him.

The CASC report quotes a number of respected authorities that had contributed to its findings, including Professor Mary Hayes of the Department of Law at Sheffield University, who wrote that 'Judicial certainty that contact will virtually always promote a child's welfare sits uneasily with research into the effects of domestic violence on children'. ChildLine was also quoted as saying that it was 'concerned that the emphasis often appears to be on the separated person's rights to maintain contact with the children (which could be for questionable motives) rather than the children's interests in being safely looked after and protected'. The overwhelming response from those who submitted answers to the questions raised by the report considered that, in cases involving domestic violence, contact should only be ordered if it could be made safe before, during and afterwards.

The guidelines are sound and sensible, but it seemed to me that judges needed a great deal more understanding and training before they could make them work in practice. My own experience suggested that we were a very long way away from what was intended by the guidelines.

The system was failing women because it assumed contact; and the threshold at which domestic abuse was considered serious enough to put the blocks on contact was raised so impossibly high that practically no family could reach it.

It is interesting to note from the CASC report that the judiciary, unlike women's organisations, was heavily against legislative change in this area of domestic violence. The judges clearly think they are doing enough to protect women and children. It is the victims of that abuse who are saying differently. Is it right that those in power, with little experience of what it is like to be on the receiving end of abuse, should have greater say than the victims? The voices should surely be more equally balanced.

The Children's Society emphasised the need for perpetrators to address their violence and seek therapy, and it saw this as crucial to the question of whether contact should be awarded or not. In my experience, this question was regularly overlooked in the family court system.

Jack did not come well out of the DVIP report. He was reported as greatly minimising his abuse and having very little insight and awareness into it, as well as virtually no empathy for the children or me. An important point also raised was that he seemed to be using the courts as a way of getting back at me for his perceived wrongs. He was considered to be a high risk both to the children and to me; and it was recommended that he should have no unsupervised contact. If contact were to take place at all, it was suggested that we should be referred to the Coram Child Contact Centre in London, which offered highly supervised contact.

Jack rejected the findings of the report outright and refused to take part in any perpetrator programme. We thus reached an impasse. Although we were referred to Coram, they had no space to offer us the twice-a-year highly supervised contact which they suggested was appropriate for our family. Rather than being found other facilities or ordered to have indirect contact, we were back at square one again, with everything once more up for grabs.

19

The Royal Courts of Justice

⚖

All the court hearings so far had taken place at the Royal Courts of Justice (RCJ) in London. When you are waiting for your case to be heard at the RCJ, you sit in a very long corridor with recesses housing big tables, around which litigants and their legal representatives talk.

Sometimes the area is bustling and it is an effort to negotiate a way through the teeming crowds of suited and gowned barristers, solicitors pulling trolleys laden with boxes and legal papers, and the host of witnesses, friends, relatives and supporters accompanying litigants.

When you turn up not knowing what your barrister looks like, trying to locate him or her in the crowd can be daunting. You have to look for a person who is looking for someone. Quite often you go up to someone who is looking, but you are not the person they are looking for! Once you've introduced yourselves, it becomes evident that the wrong litigant and barrister are matched. Eventually you find your legal 'someone' in the crowd.

There are rare occasions when the corridor is quiet. I turned up one time to find myself alone in the long corridor with my ex-husband before any of the legal representatives arrived. It was horrible hearing the tap, tap, tap of my shoes down the corridor and then finally, in the last recess, finding my ex-husband sitting at the table with a sour grin on his face.

I went to the café. The café at the RCJ became a haven. When you know you are going to have a stressful day ahead, at least you can reckon on a couple of decent moments in the midst of it. You can retire to the café with your friends and let off steam, reduce the pressure, by moaning about judges who seem to have complete power in your little world and yet no means of seeing what it is really like for you. Laughing at them is a coping mechanism: the only one available to you.

If you joke about the judge, you can fantasise about putting him in the same situation that he quite happily put you in: I move a motion that says all male judges should be removed from cases and the Women's Aid Federation drafted in to hear all disputes involving domestic violence. Discuss. Or, all judges' children under the age of 12 should be forcibly removed from their parents, placed in the care of domestic abusers and made to report back. All judges' wives are to be compelled to take part in a reality TV wife swap programme, being given a domestic abuser in place of her husband; non-compliance will be considered contempt of court and a penal notice issued. Playing the see-how-they-like-it game while drinking hot mocha with a cinnamon topping was about the only consolation available to us.

In the middle of a rotten day, the café seemed something to look forward to. I went there with every person who accompanied me to court. On the train in the morning, Eva and I looked forward to the avocado pear, tomato and mozzarella sandwich, with mayo, on French bread that we were going to buy at lunchtime. We always had mocha coffees, sweet and chocolaty; comfort food. It was an antidote to the acid stomach, butterflies and churning feelings you otherwise had on court days.

Sometimes I got tranquillisers for court. The trouble is, they didn't work, not unless I took a large sedative dose that was more likely to make me fall asleep than to calm my nerves.

All kinds of things caused the nerves: the build-up of stress in the months, days, hours before court; the waiting – sometimes for hours – outside in the corridor for your case to be called; fear that you might get another indifferent or bullying judge. The usher in her black gown came out into the corridor with her clipboard shouting 'Matter of Charming', and all the parties connected with Charming made their way into court.

One time Jack brought a witness with him to court who thought the usher wasn't shouting loudly enough. To the usher's annoyance the witness insisted on relaying the command 'Matter of Charming' in stentorian tones up and down the corridor.

Most of the courtrooms were old fashioned, with the judge up on a platform at the front behind a piece of wood that looked like a palisade. He looked well fortified, surrounded by minions with papers and jugs of water, scurrying to minister to him if he so much as raised an eyebrow.

The seats, wooden like school benches or pews, creaked. If you were uncomfortable and shifted your posture, it produced peremptory sounds. You were afraid of seeming defiant by producing any noise at all. You generally had to be told where to sit. I always got it wrong. Was it applicant on the right and respondent on the left, or the other way round? Was I the applicant this time or the respondent? Barristers sat in the front row; you sat in the row behind, next to your solicitor.

Once a clerk in the courtroom passed round a bag of sherbet lemons. She said it was the court staff's Friday ritual – celebrating the end of the week. To my surprise Jack took one. He hated sweets. They had been banned from our household, particularly sticky coloured sweets of the kind the court clerk was passing round. I watched as he put it in his mouth. He was probably retching inwardly. But he was doing his usual buttering up of officials.

I did like sweets, particularly sticky yellow ones. But I didn't want a court sweet, even at the risk of seeming churlish. I didn't feel like smiling and taking a sweet from the bag. Attending court felt like an exercise in mental survival. Sherbet lemons trivialised that somehow.

Aside from eating, we tried to lighten the days at court by going around the courtrooms and watching other cases. They don't let you sit in on family cases, of course, but there were generally other interesting things going on. We used to scan the notice boards to see whether we recognised any of the parties or if there were any interesting cases. Bing and Hurley were listed one day. We were there when the case took place of Michael Douglas/Catherine Zeta Jones and the magazine that had allegedly taken unauthorised photos of their wedding day. Of course we kept a lookout, hoping to see the Hollywood stars. We didn't see anyone except a band of people from the press.

When they had big cases going on or celebrities present, there was increased security. I got used to checking through my handbag and removing embarrassing items before setting off for the train, in case they searched my handbag at the security point.

Even if security didn't rifle through the contents, you had to put your bag through a scanner which showed up the contents on a screen. I had padlocks and tools, which were my young son's. He's mad about locks and keys and gadgets. With my usual collection of tools I would probably have appeared equipped for a night of crime.

My friend Eva carries a vast bag. It is bigger on the inside than on the outside. Like Mary Poppins she carries every conceivable useful household item about in it, including a wine corkscrew that was once picked up by the scanner. She had to remove it from her bag and leave it at the desk. I suppose it's conceivable that someone deranged might use a corkscrew as a weapon. I tried to imagine an aggrieved parent, unhappy at the outcome of their case, jabbing the sharp end at a judge.

We wandered into an appeal case one hot day and squashed ourselves on to the creaky wooden bench at the back. The heat in some of those old courtrooms is intense, horrible in summer. There was a youngish lawyer with an extravagant turn of phrase who liked long convoluted sentences. He seemed to be enjoying himself; he was wearing a flashy ring which kept catching a ray of sun coming through a high window. Half-mesmerised by this glinting ring, I was falling asleep until I heard what was presumably the prosecution side talking about a man who'd been found guilty of killing his wife. But the body had never been found. I looked round for the murderer. Disappointingly he wasn't present. I don't know what kind of a man I expected to see: probably someone who looked guilty. Of course, if you could pick out guilty people just by looking at them, you wouldn't need trials.

Over the years, in the spare time we had, we used to observe the collection of fancy court clothes donned by judges. The fine wigs, robes, gowns, scarlet and ermine are impressive. When you see them it is hard to remember that beneath the fancy costume stands an ordinary person like you or me, who may or may not be a good spouse or parent.

The point about the costumes is that they didn't look out of place in the seventeenth century. A judge in those days would not have stood out by wearing such a costume; in fact, he would very much have fitted in because he would have been wearing what his peers wore. But these days the costume appears designed to impress and overawe.

If you saw judges without the trappings, it might make you wonder how they are qualified to judge. No doubt they are intelligent. But passing the bar exam doesn't qualify you as an expert in human relations. In fact, power and privilege can deaden you to empathy and sympathy. It's harder to put yourself in someone else's shoes if you are powerful and they are not.

I've never been one for pomp and circumstance, and the sight of wigs and gowns tends to lessen my respect rather than increase it. I felt that cloistered precincts and hiding behind seventeenth-century court dress put these people apart, allowed them to stay in an old-fashioned mentality. Not only their costumes but their attitudes towards women were a throwback to less enlightened times.

It would improve the situation if senior judges wore suits and brought themselves into line with twenty-first-century dress. It would be better if someone opened the door and allowed a fresh wind to blow through those cobwebbed corridors, sweeping away quaint costumes and old attitudes that have no place in a modern society. Without the fine extras they might be held more accountable and it would make it easier to say, when it's true, that the emperor has no clothes.

Institutions and organisations can easily become cluttered and laden with language, practices and extras that obscure realities. In some respects the law resembles the church, with those in charge wearing fancy dress and carrying honourable titles. To lay perceptions there can be an enormous difference between the essential dogmas – laws – and how they are practised. Challenge to established practices often carries the risk of meeting outright hostility, fury and rejection.

It didn't lighten the atmosphere surrounding my court case that the tragic miscarriages of justice involving Sally Clark, Angela Cannings and Trupti Patel were in the news. To a lay person, it just appeared that the court system was biased against women. If you can't find an obvious medical cause for a child's death, rather than cite lack of knowledge – the fact that we don't know because medical knowledge hasn't advanced far enough – you must find someone to blame, and it must be the woman. I cut articles out of the newspaper about these cases. They made painful reading. It's impossible not to feel deeply troubled by them. People suffer enormously when judges get it wrong Lives are wrecked by it.

I also felt sick when I read the case of the father who'd murdered his four boys in north Wales by gassing them in the car. One of the little boys had spoken to his mother on a mobile phone just before he died and told her that the car was all smoky. They were found too late. It just broke your heart.

It struck me that in cases where fathers had harmed their children, allegations of domestic violence and classic signs of abuse, such as jealousy and threats, often accompanied mothers' descriptions of their relationships. And yet, friends and neighbours of such fathers regularly described them as loving, doting dads. There were clearly two sides to these men; just as there were with Jack.

20

The guardian ad litem

We were at impasse after the psychologist's report. It recommended a perpetrator's programme for Jack. He refused to accept it. We had been recommended for a highly supervised contact centre which in the event proved unable to take us due to lack of space. You'd think these two factors might be a block to contact. No, the emphasis on contact always took precedence over anything else. If he wouldn't change, I came under pressure to give way, not him. I would have to be the one who moved my position since he wouldn't and we had to make what the judge called 'progress'.

The judge thought differently from me. Her idea of progress was merely getting contact restarted. My idea of progress was for my ex-husband to make some effort towards changing his abusive behaviour.

It was a female judge this time. Before we went into court, my barrister advised me that this was 'a man's judge'. I often heard judges divided up like this by barristers. Apparently there are certain judges whom barristers representing men hope to get; and certain judges whom barristers representing women hope to get. On this occasion we weren't lucky enough to be getting the judge who was known jocularly as the 'housewife's choice'.

My barrister related an anecdote about this particular female judge: that she had committed a mother to prison for refusing contact. He had been representing the father on that occasion. He was gleeful that he had won the case. The opposing party had been sent to jail.

Orla stepped forward. 'In my opinion,' she said, 'there is never a case for sending a mother to prison who is trying to protect the interests of her child.' I wanted to cheer, but I was too cowardly. It was an awkward moment and I hated awkward moments. Orla was the type of person who could bear awkward moments when she was concerned with a matter of principle. With me, the traitorous impulse to tidy things up, smooth over, retreat from uncomfortable truths always rises up. I could have kicked myself for my own cowardice. My barrister looked awkward and embarrassed. He swallowed. You could hear the swallow in the silence. 'Well, she got sent to prison anyway.'

The lawyers always had these stories, about mothers being sent to prison for defying contact orders. I never heard stories about any men being sent down for abuse. Perhaps there were stories. Maybe the lawyers saved the stories of men being jailed to scare difficult fathers, to persuade them to back down outside court. It made a lawyer's life easier if he or she could get the client to agree outside court. They just went in then and presented the judge with a court order to sign. They liked the fait accompli. They didn't have to argue it out in court, see who was the best debater and risk the wrath of a pro-woman or pro-man judge, depending on who was on the bench.

I went in front of this fierce pro-man judge who according to legend sent women to prison. I was shaking in my shoes. She didn't even look at me. I stared at her, wondering what sort of person could send a woman to prison in these circumstances. I received not so much as a glance in return. I wanted to stand up and attract her attention. Hello, I'm here. I'm human. You can look at me.

The hearing was incredibly short. I don't know whether she had read the psychologist's report. She gave no indication that she had, or that she was concerned with any of the issues in it. Her idea of progress was to restart contact. We were going to have a guardian ad litem.

This was a new one on me. A guardian?

The judge apparently expected me to agree to this, although I had no idea what any of it meant. We were to go out of court and my barrister was expected to apply pressure on me to agree to a guardian being appointed.

We shuffled outside into the corridor. My barrister explained to me that a guardian was someone who was appointed to speak on the children's behalf; to represent their wishes and feelings to the judge.

But I was representing the children's wishes and feelings. Not only that, I had good cause to mistrust Jack. He had written a lengthy refutation of the psychologist's report and he was refusing to accept that he had been abusive in any way.

I wasn't going to agree to a guardian. I told my barrister I wanted to stand on the Domestic Violence Intervention Project report. I didn't see why we should suffer because there were no facilities to implement the highly supervised contact which had been recommended by independent experts, or why we should be forced to continue with court proceedings because Jack was refusing to go for therapy. I felt there was something fundamentally wrong in the court's attitude here. What had happened to perpetrator programmes and taking abuse seriously?

I expected some discussion in court, some challenge by my barrister, some attempts at negotiation; pressure on Jack to go for counselling. There was nothing. The judge made an order to appoint a guardian and that was that.

It felt surreal, as though I'd been watching an execution through plate glass. I could do nothing, say nothing. It was over in minutes.

Cafcass Legal was invited to provide a guardian for my children. They wrote back and declined. They couldn't see what more could be achieved in the case. They didn't see any grounds for appointing a guardian. And if my ex-husband needed to undertake a course for the perpetrators of domestic violence, they didn't have the funding to see that it happened.

We were back to square one. Did this mean we didn't have to have a guardian, I enquired of my solicitors? They didn't know what would happen. They hadn't been in this position before. With hindsight I think it might have been worth an appeal. Here was an authority saying there was no reason to have a guardian. If I had been legally savvy, I might have seen an opportunity to appeal the order which had led to the psychologist's report being ignored and to Jack escaping the requirement to undertake therapy. But I was worn down, depressed, court weary and compliant.

My solicitors persuaded me that having a guardian was in my best interests as well as the children's. They argued that judges more readily believed independent persons, Cafcass officers and guardians, than warring parents. It made sense to have a guardian to put the children's views forward because when the guardian said that the children didn't want to go to contact, it would protect me from having to face sceptical judges again.

With the psychologist's report behind us, they also felt confident about any inquiry by a guardian. The guardian would be bound to take the report seriously and could put pressure on Jack to undertake any necessary programme. I talked to several solicitors in the firm who quelled my worries and persuaded me that guardians were really in everyone's best interests. One solicitor told me she always breathed a sigh of relief when a guardian was appointed because it made it unnecessary for the resident parent to fight over contact issues; the judge always believed a guardian.

The theory was well and good. I was persuaded. I have no doubt they meant it all and were well meaning, but the reality was a far cry from the picture they had painted.

It took months before finally a National Youth Advisory Service (NYAS) guardian was found. But to my astonishment, it seemed as though we were starting from scratch again. The psychologist's report carried no weight at all with the guardian. And it appeared that she was starting from the Families Need Fathers' premise that it's always good for children to have a relationship with their father. That's fine if there's no coercion, no denigrating of the resident parent. If all that was the matter was that I was a hostile mother putting obstacles in the way, she would have worked beautifully as a guardian. As it was, Jack managed to charm her, as he did with so many people.

By this time the children had not seen their father for over a year; the court processes and time between hearings were so lengthy. My littlest child did not even remember her father. She had not seen him since she was a baby and had no memories of him.

Just one or two supervised visits to the park when Jack was on his best behaviour and trying to make a good impression led to the NYAS guardian forming the view that he was a wonderful parent.

I deflated like a child's balloon. I had fought over so many issues that I had no fight left in me. It was incredibly difficult when someone found him charming and showed no recognition of the underlying issues. It drained all my confidence.

The appointment of a guardian coincided with the conclusion of the financial settlement after the divorce. I had become passionately interested in law during the court proceedings. I had always been interested in politics and social justice. I became very interested in family law. When I wasn't dwelling on the personal aspect of it and how I felt my case had spiralled out of control, I was interested in law generally.

I began to collect a virtual law library at home, cutting out newspaper articles on cases, following trials with avid interest. I sat in on cases at court whenever I could between my own hearings. I felt strongly that the family justice system was stacked against women. I was interested in working with women who had experienced domestic violence. But I felt that the law needed to change; that it didn't sufficiently protect women and children. I really wanted to help women in the same situation as me, but I felt I needed a proper qualification to do it.

I decided to apply to Cambridge University to do a Law degree. I passed the entrance exam and was offered a place to read Law. I had spent ages on the application and preparing for the exam and interviews. The day before the interviews I was so nervous about getting everything right and arriving on time that I drove from London to Cambridge and parked in the college car park just to make sure I knew the route inside out before I did it for real next day. I was thrilled to get in. Passing the exam revived my self-confidence, which had been sorely lacking; but the degree wasn't to be.

Jack indicated that he would be seeking residence of the children again if I returned to full-time studying. Not only that, the guardian supported him. She wanted me to defer my course. Deferring was not a possibility. I had to enter that year, or give up and apply again in the future.

I had been desperate to do something for other women in the legal arena. I felt then and I feel now that patching up is not enough. Rescuing women who have been abused was one thing, but where was the protection for women which would have made abuse unacceptable in the first place? The attitudes of some judges towards women almost lent approval to the men who perpetrated abuse. I felt there needed to be new legislation because the existing law couldn't protect women and children. It was clear to me that there also needed to be political and social changes as regards domestic violence.

However, I was under pressure not to take up my place, and all the fight had gone out of me at that time. Rather than face down my ex-husband and the guardian, I gave in and resigned my place at Cambridge.

I decided then that I wanted to go back up north, where I felt comfortable and at home. I wasn't a Londoner and my neighbourhood was not happy because Jack had poisoned the atmosphere. There wasn't enough money after selling the matrimonial home and dividing the assets to stay in the same affluent area. In addition, there were huge legal bills to pay.

I decided to return to Wales. I had been at the University of Wales for five years and gained both my degrees there. I knew the area I wanted to live in. I had been warned that my ex would fight for residence again if I tried to move to Wales. But there was nothing I could do; all my options had been cut off.

I felt I was buying Jack off by offering him more contact in return for being allowed to move to Wales. It was a kind of barter: I would give him more contact if he would agree not to go to court to prevent me from moving there. This arrangement was negotiated through the guardian.

I was glad to be leaving London. The guardian was London based. She would pass out of our lives if we moved to Wales, and I was glad of this. She hadn't made herself welcome in the family, except by Jack. None of the children liked her. They were strangely reticent about contact and about their guardian. I was too anxious and stressful about the prospect of moving and the uncertainties of entering a new life, and too depressed about court, to enquire into it.

The guardian seemed glad to wrap matters up and to bow out of our lives. She seemed to think that her job was done now that she had got contact going again. Her reports for the courts did not reflect the reality of the situation, but I had to weigh up the possible consequences of challenging her. If I challenged her perceptions of Jack, who flattered her and buttered her up at every opportunity, and fought for the psychologist's recommendations to be implemented, it would mean another interminable round of court hearings. The toll they were taking on my health was great. It exposed the children to greater conflict. The financial costs were enormous. Between us my ex and I had given over one hundred thousand pounds to lawyers. It had to stop somewhere.

I weighed up the options. How much damage could their father do to them if his contact was limited to a few weeks a year in the holidays? He would do some damage, I was sure of that. He was critical of me and controlling in his behaviour towards them. But, on the other hand, I had to balance that against the damage that was being done to our family by legal proceedings.

We had endured an endless procession of police, social workers and health visitors, people from Cafcass and NYAS, as well as solicitors in our lives. There was constant intrusion and lack of privacy. Jack missed no opportunity to report me to the authorities. He once reported me to social services for not taking care of the children. Social services were obliged to investigate the complaint, although fortunately we were seen by an enlightened social worker who accepted that the complaint was malicious.

This social worker, like the police, told me that I should talk to the children and explain to them that their father's behaviour was wrong. She said it was important that the right messages were given to children about domestic abuse, and she asked my permission to talk to the children about this. I agreed with her approach but I felt unable to carry it out because I was afraid I would be punished by the court. Jack and I had given undertakings in front of Judge T not to talk to the children about the case. Unlike the police and social workers, judges did not appear to distinguish between telling children that abuse was wrong and telling the kids that their father was bad. According to them, a mother had to present a father in a positive light no matter what.

We were continually being investigated, and although it was always accepted that I was a good parent, the strain of the investigations was considerable. I never felt at ease; I always felt on show, as though I had to be on my best behaviour.

I had strained to be the perfect wife and mother in my marriage and now I had to strain to be the perfect mother and carer because any tiny mistake was seized on by Jack and exploited in court. I constantly had to explain myself to any Tom, Dick or Harry with an official badge who came across the threshold. Even if they were nice, sympathetic people, and some of them were, the intrusion was wearing. I just wanted to close the door and let our home be our home. Instead people walked through our lives as though it was a corridor. And people less competent, less intelligent and less committed than I was, were regularly making decisions for me and treating me as though I wasn't competent to make them myself.

I regularly gave way in the face of more aggressive or assertive personalities. I could see myself doing it. I felt frustrated, angry with myself, but I kept repeating that pattern. I desperately wanted to recover my old chipper self, the person I'd been before I married. Then I'd felt I could do and achieve anything I wanted. I hadn't held on to the life I had then because I hadn't known it was under threat. I'd let it go and I didn't know how to get it back.

I got angry sometimes. I wanted to wrest control back from the court and my ex-husband; but I couldn't do it because I had the children. They were always the lever used to compel you to do what other people wanted. The only solution seemed to be for them to grow up. I couldn't see myself getting my freedom back until they did.

After we moved to Wales in August 2004, I had to send my children to London for staying contact. My smallest child hated leaving me. She had screaming fits beforehand, not wanting to be sent. I had to cajole, persuade and trick her into going. My eldest daughter withdrew into herself. She said nothing, either good or bad, about contact. This was a surprise to me. Only the boys seemed to enjoy going. But sometimes they returned from their father with hostile, critical comments about their home. According to the guardian, they voiced those comments to her. To me they spoke of their father's influence. They were picking up hostility towards me. She apparently interpreted it as meaning that they preferred their father to me.

I felt it was hopeless challenging the guardian. She had come in with the fixed opinion that mothers stopped fathers from seeing their children. She was an assertive, somewhat impatient, personality. There was no subtlety in her approach. She did not even make the effort to come and visit the children's home in Wales. Not one single visit.

The guardian and I held opposing views. Due to my own hard experiences, I had come to believe that it was possible for abusive fathers to do more damage by being around than by simply going away. She worked from the premise that the children would be emotionally destabilised if their father was off the scene. She started from that basis with no particular expertise or knowledge of child psychology, no expertise in the area of domestic abuse, no research background and without even looking carefully at our family to understand its dynamics and the personality of each child. From two or three meetings, snapshot portraits of my children, she felt she could assess the situation better than a properly qualified expert psychologist.

The NYAS guardian's reports and conclusions were directly opposite to those of the court appointed psychologist. It alarmed me and made me deeply cynical that no questions were asked at any stage by anyone connected with court how contradictory conclusions could be reached about the same case and the same man. This had implications for every case. It spoke volumes about the inconsistencies and complacency in handling family cases. No one made any connections or drew any inferences from the differences in the reports. I doubt if anyone even noticed. We were on a conveyor belt and only the latest report counted. There was no mechanism in the family courts for considering the bigger picture.

Very rarely do the courts consider whether contact from an abusive father is good for the children. There are some famous cases.

Several cases heard together in the Court of Appeal in the year 2000, which involved the issue of domestic violence, were supposed to set a precedent. In Re L and other cases, the fathers' attempts to appeal orders which limited them to indirect contact rather than direct contact with their children were turned down. Perhaps the Lords Justices hoped that good practice would filter down through the courts; it seems not to have done so.

The trouble with landmark cases is that no two cases are exactly alike. And it is difficult to extract the relevant principles from one case and apply it to another. Very often the similarities are not recognised and the parallels are not drawn. Judges are not experts at recognising the varied forms of abuse. Very often domestic violence is considered only as the problem of hitting, and not under its broadest CASC definition. Such cases fail to be classed as ones involving domestic violence and the legal principles involving Re L are not applied.

It was all very well the Lords Justices, guided by eminent psychiatrists Sturge and Glaser, saying that this was how domestic abuse cases should be handled; but how is a case classified as involving domestic violence? There was the rub. The threshold for domestic violence was regularly set so high that almost no one met the criteria; and since they weren't counting emotional harm as violence because they either couldn't recognise it or discounted it, domestic violence cases just slipped through the net.

The issues defined by the psychologist in our case were never discussed at court. The report was not even opened in the courtroom. It was a lengthy document, exceedingly well prepared, with sound conclusions in line with the best practice supposedly set in 2000, but the guardian who had been appointed to safeguard the welfare of my children made one brief reference to it in her reports. She noted that my ex-husband had been upset by the report and had sought to clear his name in relation to it. She said that he was to be commended for his perseverance.

The monumental stupidity of this comment provoked my anger and roused all my defences. I was rarely provoked to anger, but there were only two possibilities here: either the guardian couldn't string sentences together properly or else she was commending Jack for denying his past violence.

At one of the review hearings, I objected strongly to the wording of the guardian's report. I said it was outrageous that a man should be encouraged to deny findings of abuse and violence, let alone be praised for doing so. That was how her report read. Unless it was changed I was going to fight the report all the way. My barrister put on his boxing gloves. He recognised the depth of my determination.

However, the point was conceded by the guardian at once. She agreed to change the wording so that her report commended my ex-husband for continuing to seek contact with the children. I grumbled a bit behind the scenes about that. The psychologist had specifically made the point that Jack was using the court as a means of control, for paying me back. You couldn't judge the quality of an act without looking at the motivation behind it. A man who has abused power in the past was likely to do so again. However, at least the report no longer suggested that Jack should be commended for trying to deny hitting me.

I noted that under the welfare heading asking whether a child had suffered any harm, the guardian made no reference to the DVIP conclusions and there wasn't a single mention of the harm they had been exposed to in being minutely controlled by their father and seeing their mother subjected to denigration and beating. The only harm mentioned was the potential harmful effect of losing their relationship with their father.

I could see the harmful effects of Jack's behaviour on the children, however. Some children show the effects of emotional abuse in overt ways. Some children show it by behaving in an anti-social manner. My children showed it in fear and anxiety; the effects tended to be internalised. Tummy upsets, headaches, sickness and toileting problems were frequent occurrences.

The senior law lords in Re L and the other three cases heard in 2000 had said that domestic violence should not be the only factor in the equation regarding whether contact should be allowed; but they hadn't intended domestic violence not to count at all. It should weigh somewhere in the balance and was one of a range of factors to be considered, they said. But in my case domestic abuse was routinely being ignored.

There was no questioning of Jack's motives by anyone other than the psychologist. His monomania about having the children was interpreted as a commitment to them, love for them. When I tried to point out that a man who was genuinely concerned for the welfare of the children would have vacated the family home so that they could have somewhere decent to live; that he wouldn't have locked up the rooms or threatened to smash the windows; and that a man who loved his children would provide for them, whereas he had not paid a single penny towards their upkeep since the day I left him, I was regarded as spiteful or vengeful.

I don't think I was either. I was not interested in doing my ex down. I had moved on emotionally and had no regrets about leaving my marriage. I was fulfilled in other ways and looking forwards, not backwards. Neither was I motivated by bitterness or revenge.

I was intelligent enough to work out for myself that a bitter, vengeful woman would not be an attractive person. And I wanted to be attractive to my children. I didn't want to ruin their childhood by dwelling on past hurts. I wanted to move forward with them into a life free from fear, anxiety or brooding on the past. I wanted my children to grow up feeling they had experienced a loving childhood with their mother. I didn't want to influence my children's views of their father because I knew they would remember it and think less of me as they grew older. I wanted them to know that abuse was wrong, but I did not want them to hate their father.

My intentions were difficult to achieve, however. Their father constantly nagged them about their new lives. He spoke of me with contempt and anger as someone who had turned him out of his house, who had stolen his money, who had lying and perjuring friends who had conspired to make it go badly for him in court. Nothing that the children did with me was approved of. The clothes I bought for them, the haircut my daughter chose, the pets we had, the PlayStation I bought for my son's birthday, my son's handwriting; nothing escaped his notice or his criticism. He was still going on in exactly the same way he had when we all lived together.

Not only did Jack complain at court about me, but he allowed his anger towards me to seep into all his dealings with the children. No wonder I was constantly anxious about contact. It was never used solely to give the kids a good time. They were made to feel guilty for having a good time with their mother and as though they should be feeling sorry for their father living alone and kicked out of his home. They were made to take on a burden of guilt about the occupation order and the divorce that they should not have had to bear.

Sometimes their father's anger scared them. He was unpredictable and could have huge outbursts for no apparent reason or for very trivial reasons. They had to tread on egg shells, just as I always had in the past. Basically his controlling behaviour was switched from me to them.

The trouble with control is that it is very hard to spot. It can easily disguise itself as over-protectiveness or concern. Jack's control extended to the minute details of life. I knew about this, but it was hard to explain it to other people or to have it taken seriously. If I told people my husband made me count out three sheets of toilet paper when I went to the loo, they laughed. They thought it was funny.

My objection to this behaviour had led Judge C previously to call me neurotic. He referred to Jack as a 'control freak' and left it at that; as though it wasn't serious. He's a control freak. So what! That was the attitude.

It was serious, however. The imposition of a vast set of rules, deviating from which in the smallest particular will result in you being punished, should be taken seriously as abuse. Each thing by itself may seem petty, but it amounted to a stranglehold on our lives. How can children grow up to be independent, fully formed adults if they are subjected to this kind of control? I was abysmally stunted by this control and I was an adult. If I had fallen prey to the effects of such behaviour, how could children cope with it?

I tried to cocoon them in response. I made the mistake of not being open with the children about court and what was happening to us because I was trying to protect them. Jack was talking constantly to the children in inappropriate ways about their mother and legal issues, and in an attempt to balance that, I did the opposite by not talking about it at all. I simply tried to create a space in which we could be happy: a kind of bubble in which we read books, went to the park, visited the cinema and theatre, played games, stayed with friends, went on outings and took advantage of as many cultural opportunities and social invitations as we could.

Looking back, I should have explained more. Not talking about things and trying to protect them too much was counterproductive. It created anxiety because they could sense that things were going on but didn't know what they were. It must have seemed that we had a no-go area, something we didn't talk about at home. However, for the moment issues were not dealt with.

Once contact was up and running again, as I had expected the NYAS guardian felt she had accomplished her task. She was not interested in any of these wider welfare issues or the children's Welsh life. She signed herself off from our case and was gone.

21

The set-up

Predictably, after the guardian had gone, problems with Jack resurfaced. Jack could perform for the occasion and behave charmingly when he was being supervised, but the minute we were left alone again, things turned bad.

My eldest daughter and youngest son came back nervous and anxious after spending part of the summer holiday with Jack. Madeleine began suffering blinding headaches. They lasted for days and weeks on end. The weeks of headaches turned into months. I began to get seriously scared. With a non-stop headache that wouldn't go away even after weeks of medication, I began to think about brain tumours or something terrible. She was also remote, unwilling to talk. The headaches got so bad that she was referred for a brain scan.

Jools started refusing school. He was anxious and disturbed about things which had not bothered him before. Crippling stomach aches were the order of the day. Day after day he was doubled up in pain. There were endless trips to doctors, referrals to consultants. After a period of months, no physical causes could be discerned for Madeleine's headaches or for Jools's tummy aches. Anxiety was diagnosed.

I wasn't sure what was going on, but I instinctively felt it might help if the children didn't have to travel to London for their contact. I offered Jack my house in Wales for some of his contact with the children, and I moved out while he stayed there. I'd hoped, naively, that their dad would prove to be less controlling if he was staying in their home, rather than them being in his.

The children spent Christmas 2005 with their father in London.

After the holiday I was supposed to collect them. I turned up to find the children not ready to come home. They weren't packed.

Almost as soon as I arrived at the door, Jack began haranguing me about the children's education, saying that they would never amount to anything if they stayed in Wales to be educated. It was the kind of inappropriate talking in front of the children which I hated. I tried to pacify him, saying that I would talk to him about it if he phoned me once I reached home, but we had a long drive in front of us from London to Wales and I wanted to set off.

It became clear that I was not going to be allowed to leave with the children. A split developed. It seemed that I was going to be able to take three of the children home if I left my older son. Ben was giving me cause for concern. He was lying down on the floor, clinging to the radiator.

This was not my sunny, affectionate, equable child who had gone away at the start of his holiday. This was a strange child. He was unnaturally remote, uncommunicative. He wouldn't speak or meet my eyes. I had never experienced anything as extreme as this before with Ben. He had been strange after the snatch in 2002 but this was something new. He seemed to be brainwashed in some way. He was acting like an autistic child.

What had happened? I was seriously alarmed. And I didn't see a way to get out of Jack's home. I had ordered the three other children into the car and they had gone. But my ex was not willing to let my older son go. He had established such a hold over his mind in the week or so that Ben had been away that he was unable to behave like a normal child.

I tried to chivvy Ben up, speaking in a brisk, no-nonsense way about needing to set off because we had a long drive in front of us, telling him not to be so silly. Inside I was in turmoil. I had no idea how to handle this situation. I was in my ex-husband's home and I did not know how to leave and take my son with me. There was no way I could leave him in this dangerous state of mind, brainwashed into hostility.

Jack hovered around. When I tried to edge Ben towards the exit, Jack began to cling to him, tearful, upsetting the child, making him feel guilty for leaving, playing on his feelings. I fell into the old useless patterns, attempting to plead. Why did I always do that? It had no effect. He seemed to feel his power when I pleaded; it was more likely to make him worse than to persuade him to show mercy.

When I tried to take Ben with me, Jack attacked me, twisting my arm up my back. He hung on to me, refusing to let me go. I felt a familiar sense of horror. I was so used to this. These were the old patterns of our home life. I felt complete revulsion that this could be happening to me again, so long after I had left him.

I had my mobile phone in my pocket and I managed to call the police from Jack's hallway. Jack began to bellow insults at me, telling me that I was a liar and a perjurer and that I had stolen his money. At one instant I saw an opportunity to run for the car and I bundled my son out of the door in front of me and hurried him to the vehicle. Jack followed. I shoved Ben into the car through the front passenger door because it was nearest the kerb and I shot into the vehicle after him. The other children were huddling, petrified in the back seat. All of us were crying and terrified.

Jack had run out after us and was holding on to the car door, stopping me from shutting it. He carried on bellowing and shouting at the top of his voice. A knot of people began to gather, strangers, neighbours, looking at what was going on.

Strangely, there were no friendly faces, only hostile ones. The back hatch to the car was open. I asked one of the passers-by standing on the pavement to shut it. It would have offered some privacy from the staring strangers and Jack's enraged insults. The stranger refused to shut the car at the back or to get involved. I had already called the police, but several neighbours said they were going to call them because the children were so distressed.

I was perplexed by Jack's behaviour. Usually he kept his aggression hidden and put on a charming persona when others were present. Something strange was going on. I could not understand the neighbours either: why nobody offered any help or seemed friendly. They appeared hostile towards me and yet I was on the receiving end of the abuse. I hadn't done or said anything to my ex that was remotely confrontational.

The police were taking an inordinate amount of time to come. I telephoned my friends who lived nearby for help. Orla and Eva arrived in their car to offer support sooner than the police did. Finally the police arrived. I told them I had been attacked. One of the police officers began her official speech and took out a notepad. I recognised this part. I had been through this before at the park. I was being asked if I wanted to make an official complaint. I knew what would happen if I said yes. We would all have to go to the police station and I would have to give a statement. I could not face going down that route again. I just wanted to go home. I asked the police if I could leave.

My ex had been questioned separately by police officers at the scene. To my surprise, Jack had told the police and the neighbours that the children were crying because they didn't want to come home with me. This explained the neighbours' hostility towards me at least. I must have appeared like a wicked witch coming to take the children away against their will. None of them had witnessed the scene that led up to this, or seen Jack's manipulation of events.

It took time to piece everything together. It took my daughter months of confidence building to come out with the fact that the whole thing had been a set-up. She was so terrified that she would have to go back to her father and that he would punish her, she wasn't able to tell the truth for a long time.

Finally I understood Jack's behaviour. At the time it was as if he wanted to be seen bellowing in the street. He had gone on for so long that it appeared he wanted witnesses at the scene. For a man who denied he had ever been violent towards me, he had gone a long way to knocking his credibility on the head. Why had he been so public with his temper?

Madeleine's account made sense of everything. He wanted witnesses. He had instructed the children before I turned up that they must behave badly towards me and say they didn't want to come home. Three of the children had merely been distressed by the whole set-up, but Ben had actually carried his instructions through.

Madeleine was absolutely terrified of her father. I stopped contact again after this, but she had to be reassured by months of no contact and having her fears calmed that he couldn't come and get her if she told what had happened. She referred to it as 'Daddy's big plan', and she was scared to be truthful. She was also angry with her brother for his part in it. She was furious that Ben had been a 'traitor', as she called it.

It was sad. I hated the relationship between my two eldest children turning sour because my son's loyalties had been torn in that way. His father was to blame. He was the adult and he had put the child in that position. It wasn't my son's responsibility and he couldn't be blamed for his father's behaviour. What else could he do when his father had leaned on him so heavily? I knew all about being leaned on, being pressured to do things I believed were wrong. I understood how you could be forced to give up your independence and autonomy; how you could be brainwashed.

But I had some hard thinking to do. This was a turning point for me. Mr Charming's behaviour had reached an intolerable level. I came to the realisation that both of us could not parent. He could not accept that I was the residential parent and he would never leave us alone, never stop trying to split our family. It had to be either him or me who was the residential parent, with virtually no input from the other. The perpetual conflict – trying to make contact work when my ex-husband really didn't want contact, he only wanted it as a means to residence – had to stop.

I decided that, while I was the residential parent, unsupervised contact would never happen again. If the court was going to push me back into an impossible and abusive situation by forcing direct contact, it would have to take the children from me. It was only my conviction that the damage being done to the children in this situation was worse than their doing without one parent that forced me into this drastic decision. The evidence of my own eyes was compelling. Direct contact always led to disaster. It had to be all or nothing in these circumstances.

I had some tough decisions to make regarding my son. I told myself that I could not make a major decision which would have life-changing implications for him on a whim or in a short period of time; neither could I make a decision while he was in his brainwashed state.

It took a month or more to re-establish a normal relationship with Ben. He could not hold a proper, relaxed, uninhibited conversation with me for weeks after Christmas. I was seriously worried about him. In the meantime, I consulted friends and family members. I wanted to be as objective as possible about my coming decisions and I wanted as much input as I could get, aware that whatever I decided would have serious consequences. There were two possibilities. Either he would go to live with his father and I would not seek contact with him; or he would live with me and have no unsupervised contact again during his childhood.

I decided to give Ben time to recover and then I would make the decision about whom he should live with. It was teetering in the balance at that stage. I was leaning towards giving him up, thinking that it might be in his best interests. I had no doubt that living with his dad would cause him some damage. His father was abusive and could not provide a proper adult role-model for him. But if he wanted to be with his dad, and it made him unhappy to be with me, I reasoned, perhaps I would cause him more damage by forcing him to stay with me than if he went to his father. They were two different kinds of damage. It was a question of weighing evils. Which was the least bad option?

Ben's father had always usurped my authority with Ben when we lived together and had taught him hostility during contact. I had no doubt that if he had residence, there was no point in my seeking contact with him. His father would do his best to make him reject me. At least Ben would be saved from the kind of emotional abuse which would pressure him to hate his mother if I didn't seek contact. I was clear in my mind that if I let him go, it would be a complete letting go for his own good. I could at least exonerate myself on that count. I wasn't dependent on Ben. I could let him go if I thought it was for his own good.

My friends and family were split fifty-fifty. Half of them believed I should let Ben go to his father if it was what he wanted because Ben's unhappiness at being forced to stay with me might outweigh the harm his father could do if he had residence. One friend presented me with the view that Mr Charming should not have residence, even if Ben wanted to live with him, because it was not in Ben's long-term interest, in terms of the development of his personality, to be with him. The friend suggested I should overlook Ben's short-term unhappiness and ensure he stayed with me. I hesitated between these opposing views, weighing, considering, wanting to make the best decision but not being sure what the right view was.

I decided to give Ben a year. If he still felt the same way, if he showed an insuperable preference for his father in a year's time, I would let him go. I had three other children to think of too. Having Ben as a reluctant family member, whose presence with us incited his father to harassing us as a family, impacted severely on them. They had no doubts about wanting to live with me and not wanting to be with their father. I had to think about what was best for them. If Ben went to his father, it might give them some respite from court proceedings and endless conflict because it was likely that Mr Charming would be content with the child whom he had consistently favoured over the others.

Time passed. I worked preternaturally hard on building up our family life, wanting to give Ben every chance of settling back into our family before giving up on that option. We adopted the rather corny practice of family conferences, where we would deliberately set aside a period of time and gather to discuss any issue affecting us, with everyone allowed a say and no one making any judgements. I tried really hard to listen and to provide a non-judgemental environment.

Once Ben and I could relate more normally again, he was unable to talk about his complicity in his father's scheme. He evidently felt ashamed about everything. However, it was a turning point for my son as it had been for me. He came to see that he had been manipulated and he began to resent his father for that. It gave me no pleasure because, accurate or not, it did his welfare no good to see his father in such a poor light. I blamed the courts too, for forcing us into this position. The guardian who had so congratulated herself on getting contact up and running again was not around to take responsibility for her misconceptions when it fell down so predictably. The judge who had acted with such self-confidence in appointing her and who had rejected Cafcass Legal's advice that a guardian wouldn't achieve anything in our case was no longer around to see the consequences of her orders either.

It sickened me. I felt angry, let down, betrayed by the system and the way it always put fathers' rights before children's safety and well-being. If judges were going to march into your lives, making decisions which could make or break you as a family, they should be 100% sure they had got it right. Incessant meddling, pushing, forcing, had driven our family to breaking point and not one court official who had helped to bring this about was now around to take the rap for it.

No contact took place for several months. The time approached all too quickly for the next school holiday. Jack emailed, demanding his contact back. I decided that this time he must be made to understand the consequences of his actions, and I insisted that he go on the perpetrator programme recommended by the DVIP psychologist.

Predictably my ex rejected the counselling/therapy suggestions and took me back to court. I was back in the bullring again. I consulted with friends and relatives. What should I do? A life of continuous court cases – it was now five years of hearings – was becoming intolerable.

22

Being a litigant in person

The series of court hearings began again, this time in Wales where I was resident, rather than in London. We had a couple of hearings in front of one judge. I turned up at court on my own, without a solicitor or barrister to help. I was so sick of my stomach churning at the sight of official letters on my doormat and the sleepless nights after I read them, that I decided to manage without a solicitor and represent myself.

In addition, I detested the impersonal way hearings were conducted when you had a barrister in the case. I hated the way people talked over your head as though you weren't there. Often the judge didn't even bother to look at you if you had a legal representative standing in front of you. At least they'd be forced to speak to you directly if you went to court on your own. It brought some humanity into the situation.

Jack's barrister met me at the court door. She was tapping her watch exaggeratedly, indicating that I was late. I was late, by five minutes, having had to organise four children before I set off to court. They hated me going to court and they felt anxious seeing my stress.

'Mrs Charming, it's very serious,' she said. She meant it was serious for me, disobeying a court order which gave Jack contact. She had obviously decided to go on the attack, overawe the litigant in person and put her on the defensive. I had seen too many of these tactics by barristers to take any notice of this blustering. In fact, I was annoyed by it. Why did they always put the responsibility for Jack's violent behaviour on to me? Why did they never ask him: why were you violent? why did you behave that way? Why did they instead always ask me: why don't you give him contact? why don't you put up with being attacked?

I deliberately misunderstood Jack's barrister. 'Yes, it is very serious. Mr Charming has been violent and abusive again; he has behaved very badly.' I did myself no favours with this barrister. I got the impression she disliked me because I refused to back down. She couldn't see the toll that long years of court proceedings had taken on me already. I perceived that after this she couldn't resist digs about me in front of the judges.

The courtroom was better than normal: the hearing took place in the judge's chambers, so everyone sat round a big table with the judge at the head of it. It was less intimidating than previous courtrooms where the judge sat miles away up on a dais. However, the hearing was still unpleasant. I asked to have a friend in the room with me, as a McKenzie friend, but this was refused. They evidently weren't used to McKenzie friends in Wales. I didn't have the confidence to argue the point as Jack had done over his McKenzie friends from Families Need Fathers.

I took a pen and pad to jot down notes as the hearing went on. There was a horrible moment when I dropped my pen and it rolled under the table. It came to rest by Jack's foot. He saw it and could have picked it up, but he didn't. Neither did his barrister. I could have asked for my pen back, but I couldn't face asking Jack. Or I could crawl under the table and grovel at his feet. That would have been too much like times in the past when I had had to grovel at his feet in order to pick up shopping money thrown at me.

I searched my bag for another pen. I didn't have one. The judge had observed all this. Without saying anything, he leaned over and gave me his own pen. The judge was decent and human. Once, when my parking time was nearly up, he allowed me to go and move my car from a parking space. The Cafcass officer who was on duty at court was less than sympathetic about my parking dilemma. She wanted me to talk to her about contact, regardless of the meter ticking. I tried to explain that a parking fine would be a large chunk out of the week's food money if I incurred one. Fortunately the judge stepped in and urged me to go and move the car.

As was always the case when you got a judge who didn't seem so bad, you got moved on. The judge transferred us upwards to a more senior judge in light of the fact that we had been involved in protracted and complex proceedings for some years. I was disappointed to find that he wasn't going to be hearing our case in the future.

I hated starting from scratch with any new judge. The papers by this time filled two lever arch files. Our new judge, Judge F, initially took the view that there was no need to appoint a guardian for the children. I believed this to be the correct decision, but Jack and his barrister pushed so hard and made such a fuss about it that the judge agreed to send the court papers to the local Cafcass office to let them decide whether we needed a guardian or not.

This was the beginning of a trend which became very noticeable with this judge. He often said one thing and then ended up doing another. He let the professionals run loose in the case without giving them proper directions, and the case went up and down like a seesaw, as he veered between one decision and the opposite.

The children were set against having another guardian. Madeleine told me she had been very upset when her NYAS guardian had dismissed her when she told the guardian she didn't like contact. Apparently she had been scolded and told she had 'a wonderful father'.

Unfortunately, the local Cafcass office didn't even bother to see the children and ascertain their views before recommending to Judge F that one of its officers should be the children's next guardian. From reading the NYAS guardian's written reports, they had come to the conclusion that there was nothing wrong with Jack's parenting and behaviour; that the real problem in this case was a quarrel between the parents. They had prejudged the case without even getting the children's views. These early prejudices and assumptions were to cause us no end of trouble over the following two years which we spent in front of Judge F.

Notwithstanding his earlier view about not needing a guardian, Judge F took the decision to appoint a guardian from Cafcass. I was angry and dejected at the thought of being subjected to yet more intrusion which would probably not accomplish anything. It had not accomplished anything to date, except to make me and the children hostile and suspicious of court and of court officials.

I did try to challenge the views of Cafcass, since they didn't match the kids' perceptions of their first guardian or of their father. I pointed out that the NYAS reports contradicted the DVIP report. Why should a poorly trained and unsympathetic guardian's views trump those of an expert psychologist? The mere fact of my challenging the opinions of Cafcass seemed to annoy them. I got the feeling that the judge and the children's new representatives were digging themselves in and resisting me because they didn't like my opposition to what they were doing.

At an early hearing in front of Judge F, I tried to argue the point about a guardian not being of much use in our case. 'I am arguing that the children are being subjected to psychological and emotional harm,' I told the judge, 'and you are offering me a guardian. It needs an expert to assess Mr Charming.' I didn't get anywhere with this argument. I found Judge F to be one of the most frustrating judges I had to deal with because when I made a valid and logical point which required an answer, he simply ignored it.

I pointed out that Cafcass Legal, earlier in the case, had said there were no grounds to appoint a guardian. I was told somewhat waspishly by Judge F and by the solicitor appointed to represent the children that a guardian had been appointed on perfectly proper grounds this time. The children's solicitor said that each individual ground on which a guardian might be appointed actually applied in our case.

'Where are these grounds?' I argued, from my place in the court where a barrister normally stood. 'None of these grounds has been spelled out or gone over.' I asked for a copy of the rules under which they could appoint a guardian. They fussed around and eventually came out with a copy.

Looking down the page, I immediately found several grounds which didn't apply to our case and I started to argue them. The judge cut me off arbitrarily. 'A guardian has been appointed perfectly properly.' I wasn't allowed to speak on the point any longer. We had run out of available time, it seemed.

I tried to pursue the issue of appointing a second guardian both by writing to the children's solicitor and in statements for the judge. The children had disliked their previous NYAS guardian and she had succeeded in making matters worse, not better. They couldn't understand why I couldn't speak for them at court and why they had to have a stranger talk for them. Neither did they understand when I explained to them that the judge wasn't accepting what I said on their behalf. I argued this point in court. I asked the judge whether he thought I was leaning on the children and putting words into their mouths.

The judge responded that 'in case after case mothers are found to be influencing the children against contact'. I was shocked at the time by this blatant admission of prejudice. Did he really think that in every single case mothers were dishonest and manipulative, and that there couldn't be any genuine reasons for children refusing to see their father?

Such a comment also reveals a peculiar and unbalanced perspective. The logic of it says that the violent father's actions and witnessing his abuse have no effect at all on the children – they are immune to it; that the mother's attitude is the sole negative influence on children. Not only is this against the whole body of research which shows domestic violence to have very negative effects upon children; but it is the antithesis of Re L.

Did the judge really expect children who had witnessed beatings and heard constant denigration of their mother not to be afraid of the perpetrator and not to be mixed up and confused in their attitudes towards him? Did he really think that it was only the opposition of a bitter woman that was preventing the children from seeing their father; that they really couldn't be afraid of him after all he had done?

Finally, because I pressed the point so hard, the judge agreed that if the children could say to the new guardian he had appointed that they didn't want her, he would consider their request.

I thought it was unreasonable for the judge to expect children of their age to have to say directly to the guardian, Mrs Hall, that they didn't want her. They were polite, well-mannered, sensitive children and she was in a position of authority. It was very unfair to expect children to sack their guardian directly and not through a third party.

Again, this last argument didn't even merit a response. I thought Judge F's mode of proceeding was heavy-handed and inept. Family proceedings are supposed to place the wishes and feelings of the child centrally, but no real effort was made to take their wishes into account or even to investigate in a thorough and sensitive way. I felt they had just determined to deal with the case in the usual manner they dealt with these cases.

On top of the children's unhappiness with the way things were turning out, I was disbelieving and incredibly cross when the judge decided to hold a telephone conference with only the professionals in the case allowed to take part. Instead of a proper hearing which Jack and I would be able to attend, he was going to hold a private telephone conference to decide how the case should proceed. It seemed like third world justice; you couldn't even know what they were going to say about you because you couldn't take part.

In addition, I realised at this time what a mistake I'd made in letting the previous NYAS guardian go unchallenged in her reports, and not making a fuss at the time about the DVIP report being neglected. The professionals had only bothered to look at the guardian's report, not the earlier papers in the case, and they were assuming that her reports were correct, that the kids had a great relationship with their dad; that Jack and I had simply had a quarrel in London which we could move on from because it was six of one and half a dozen of the other. When I saw this, I rued the day I hadn't raised a storm over the psychologist's report. It was time to do something about the chaos this case had fallen into.

23

The Court of Appeal a second time

⚖️

According to the American journalist and writer F. P. Dunne, an appeal is when you ask one court to show its contempt for another court.

I tried to get the Court of Appeal to show its contempt for Judge F's court and to cut through the necessity of having to undergo yet another useless round of court hearings by appealing against the appointment of a second guardian. Something had changed in me. I had been pushed so far that I had decided at last to stand up for myself.

You have to ask permission to appeal. I requested permission first of all from Judge F, as is the proper procedure. Of course, he wasn't going to agree to my appealing his order, so I had to ask permission directly from the Court of Appeal.

I didn't know how to appeal. I asked at the court office. They didn't know either. One clerk said they'd never had an appeal in a family case before. It meant looking up the rules. The downside of conducting your own appeal is the papers. They have to be arranged correctly according to procedures. It was a nightmare of typing and photocopying, and trying to put together grounds for appeal. The court clerks were very courteous and helpful, but I felt embarrassed and conspicuous as the first litigant to be appealing against the judge. The court was small and parochial; there was no privacy and everybody seemed to know everybody else's business.

I had to go back and forth from my home to the court office a number of times to ask about appeal procedures and to file papers. I tried to go when it was quiet because at the court on Anglesey you had to stand at the counter in the public waiting area and talk to the clerk behind her glass window, close to where the parties in other cases await their hearings.

I was surprised one time by the children's solicitor standing at my elbow while I was trying to file appeal papers, demanding to talk to me about the case. It wasn't a family court day; I was on my day off, in effect. Her manner was imperious and it annoyed me. I felt I was experiencing this attitude a lot from the judge, the children's solicitor and Cafcass in Wales. They seemed to forget they were offering a service; their attitude conveyed the impression that I had just better do as I was told. I bristled. I was an intelligent, caring parent and I wasn't going to be talked down to. I insisted on finishing my business at the counter first. In the background I could sense the children's solicitor fuming that I wasn't dropping everything as she wanted. I got a moment's amusement from spinning my business out as long as I could at the counter, until she tired of standing and had to leave for another appointment.

They were petty here, uncooperative simply because I insisted on my children being treated as individuals and because I demanded respect from them. They made my life difficult in a number of ways. On the day the children and I moved house from Anglesey to mainland Wales, they forced me to attend court. It made the day stressful for the kids because I had to abandon them to a babysitter while I raced fifty miles to court in one direction, hared back home to supervise the removers, and then raced another fifty miles in a different direction, attempting to get to our new house before the furniture van arrived. Some of our belongings got left behind in the process because I didn't have enough time to deal with everything – all because the children's solicitor and Jack's solicitor, both of whom detested me, wouldn't allow me to postpone the court hearing for two days. If they had been child focused, as they claimed, they could have done a lot more to make the children's lives less stressful.

The legal professionals' meanness over our removal merely rubbed salt in the wound because the reason we were moving was the huge legal charge they were about to slap on my house for past legal fees. Over the years, the legal fees which had been taken, despite my and the children's wishes not to be involved in endless litigation, directly impacted on the kids' standard of living. They had far fewer expectations and opportunities, and a lower standard of living, thanks to the cost of lawyers, than they would have had otherwise.

The charge on my house was made worse by the fact that they added interest at the rate of £10 per day. If we stayed where we were, the value of the house would be eaten away before the kids grew up. It was the same dilemma which I had faced in London. With a legal charge on your house comes interest. It seemed better to sell the house, clear the charge and start again debt free.

It was Lord Justice Scott-Baker who heard my request for an appeal at the appeal court in London. It was back to the old familiar RCJ on the Strand; but it was a hearing to leave one cold, like all the others. I caught the train to the capital and stayed the night before with my friends.

Orla and Eva came with me to the appeal court. We were dismayed to encounter Jack in the corridor. He had the legal right to be there, but there was no necessity for it since I was merely asking leave to appeal. His being there at the back of the court threw me. I was conscious of his presence even without being able to see him, and I knew that Orla was forced to sit with him in the public gallery, which must have been unpleasant for her.

Eva was able to sit beside me in the court for support, as a McKenzie friend, although she was of course unable to say anything. I was glad to have her at my elbow because my throat went dry and I lost confidence part way through, when I saw how unresponsive the judge was being to my case. He was clearly unmoved by it.

I put the question directly to the Lord Justice: 'What is the role and function of a guardian?' The courts say they are child focused, but if a child doesn't want a guardian and would rather have a person of his own choosing to speak for him, or the other possible alternatives of bringing proceedings to a halt or taking part in them personally, then foisting a guardian on him is clearly not child centred. Can a guardian take the stance: you will have me to represent you, whether you like it or not? It is a contradiction in terms to say to a child we are giving you a voice, but then only to allow that child to express wishes in terms of what the adult wants for him. Why give him a say at all? Why not follow the logic of their stance and say: we are taking decisions out of your hands and those of your resident parent; all decisions will be made independently by a guardian. In effect, that's what was happening where my older son and daughter were concerned.

I also posed the question: was the court asking a guardian to perform the role of an expert psychologist? Why were we making do with an untrained substitute here?

These were legitimate and serious questions. It seems to me that we do need a proper study and discussion of the role of guardians in these cases. The Lord Justice didn't answer my question. Like Judge F, he obviously found it more convenient not to reply.

I could hear from the judge's tone and see from his expression before the hearing was concluded what the outcome was going to be. When you have sat through dozens of hearings in front of different judges, you get a sense of this. You pick up tone and nuance. I could tell from the judge's tone as he began his brief judgment that I was going to be refused leave to appeal. And so it was. I was told basically that I should have waited to appeal the final outcome of matters if that turned out to be unsatisfactory, rather than appealing on the grounds I had. I'd tried to bring up the Re L aspect of the case and the need for the CASC guidelines to be properly adhered to.

I suppose to the appeal court judge I must have seemed naïve, using the method of appealing against a guardian to achieve my ends of having them consider the judge's case management. But it seemed to me that we were always waiting for the case to go wrong first, in order to put it right afterwards. And trying to unravel things when they had gone wrong in the past generally turned out to be nigh on impossible. My hope was to prevent things from going wrong before they went too far down the wrong route.

I had hoped to have Mr Charming re-referred for a risk assessment and the DVIP report properly aired this time round, or else a new assessment undertaken, since we were now some time away from the original report. And I hoped to have Judge F directed along the right path because I had no confidence in him. It was an exercise in futility, however. The whole thing had taken 35 minutes from beginning to end. And that was that.

Perhaps it was naïve, but I had hoped for more; that a judge, for once, might be willing to consider the bigger picture, not a narrow range of legal issues. Yes, on the face of it and in theory there was a good case for a guardian; but there was a lot more to our case – issues which had never been dealt with – and I wanted to appeal to the judge, as a human being, to understand the big picture.

I observed the appeal judge in his wig and gown, with his carefully enunciated speech, and wondered whether he ever gave a thought to anyone who came before him; whether he remembered them when he went home and felt concerned about them. In my case, the answer turned out to be no.

After I lost the right to appeal, I decided to write a personal letter to the judge as I had done once before, setting out all the issues and our family's experience of court.

Lord Justice Scott-Baker replied through an administrative official. He didn't remember me from the appeal. Obviously judges don't suffer from sleepless nights after hearing cases. I was thanked for my letter and the issues it raised; however, he was not going to be involved in family cases for some time, since he was involved in the inquiry surrounding the death of Diana, Princess of Wales, and he had therefore passed my letter on to the head of the family division, Sir Mark Potter.

Ironically, I had to collect Lord Justice Scott-Baker's reply from the sorting office some miles away because whoever had posted it had failed to pay enough postage. I saw it as symbolic. Not only did I have to go miles out of the way to collect a reply that wasn't helpful, but I had to pay a pound postage for the privilege!

The head of the family division, Sir Mark Potter, had his own response to my letter which had been passed on to him. The response was well meaning but inadequate. He seemed to be saying, maybe we got it slightly wrong in the past, perhaps we didn't pay enough attention to domestic abuse and its effects, but we've got it more or less right now. Sorry you had an unfortunate experience, but you are the exception and while we feel sorry for your unhappiness, we are getting it right in pretty much all cases now.

There is a real Victorian complacency among judges that we are at the pinnacle of civilisation. We can show the world a thing or two. But that doesn't accord with my experiences – and I have experienced the family courts for eight years to date – or with those of the hundreds of women I have talked to since I began campaigning on these issues. An awful lot of work and education is needed before they should feel a minute's complacency about the system. It is still riddled with failings, with lack of understanding, with sheer horrific ignorance, with sloppy law and judicial insensitivity. A slight sense of shame wouldn't be out of place; but, no, the judicial system is full of people thinking they are getting it right.

Appeal lost, I was back in front of Judge F. I felt sick at the thought of returning to the same judge after appealing against his decisions. It is an unpleasant fact of the system; if you appeal against a judge's order and lose, you end up back in front of the same judge.

I missed the next court hearing that was scheduled to take place. From my home it took three buses and two and a half hours to get to the court at Caernarfon where the hearing was scheduled. I made the journey and got almost to the doors of the court. I was within sight of the building when I realised I couldn't go in, that I was nearly at breaking point. I turned around and got straight back on the bus. The journey home was terrible. A big part of me didn't want to get off the bus and go home; I wanted to keep going, to disappear somewhere, walk out of this life which was not my own and get another life. I was inches away from walking out.

The hearing took place without me. I didn't care. My presence or absence never seemed to affect the court orders that were made. I realised that I'd reached rock bottom.

Out of despair something dawned that day which took a while to develop. I began to realise that the fear itself was worse than the worst thing that could happen in reality. For years I'd been terrified that if I held out over the issue of supervised contact, the children would be taken away. I was living that fear every day anyway. It seemed to me I had nothing to lose any longer by holding out for no unsupervised contact ever again. The worst that could happen would be that the children would be taken and given to Jack. And yes, that would be terrible, but I was already feeling as badly as if it had happened. I couldn't feel any worse.

If I had a breakdown, I would be no use as a mother to my children and so I might as well hold out. If I refused any more unsupervised contact, at least I'd be free of the perpetual anxiety, the ever-present 'what if?' feelings.

Although things didn't change at once, it was the beginning of a new phase. I became aware that not only was the court allowing my ex-husband to control me, but I was allowing him to control me too. I was giving in to the despair and the control just the way he wanted me to. He still had control of my emotions and I was allowing him to make my life miserable. I decided that I was going to take back that control. The court might try to impose horrible consequences, but I could refuse to allow it to take away my dignity. I was taking back my life.

Additionally, I felt I had responsibilities towards my children. I was particularly worried about my daughters, since I was their role model for womanhood. I had begun to worry that I was not giving them a proper example of strength in difficult circumstances. It would be much better for their welfare if they had a strong, competent mother. I didn't want my daughters feeling despair or powerlessness. I wanted them to feel they could make choices in life and they didn't just have to accept control and abuse from a man or anyone else. It crossed my mind that if my sons could learn bad attitudes from their father, so my daughters could pick up the wrong messages from me if I wasn't careful. Suppose they learnt to be victims and not strong, assertive women? I had to do the right thing by showing them the way, teaching them to be self-assured and independent.

24

Cafcass again

Since we were stuck with a new guardian, whether the kids wanted one or not, I complied and allowed interviews to take place between the Cafcass guardian and the children. I was torn over whether or not to agree to be interviewed myself. I'd had my fill of guardians, but in the end I reluctantly decided that if I didn't go and give my side of the story, she would be getting a very distorted picture of me from Jack.

I went on the bus to the Cafcass office, feeling apprehensive. My fears were realised. It was every bit as bad as I had expected. Mrs Hall, the new guardian we had been assigned, turned out to be the same Cafcass officer who had proved unsympathetic over my parking meter dilemma at court. It wasn't auspicious, but I decided to keep an open mind and not judge from one unfortunate incident at the beginning. I'd give her the benefit of the doubt and see what she could do for my children.

While I was waiting to be interviewed, I heard the screaming of a young infant. A tiny girl was brought, crying piteously, to her mother's arms by a Cafcass officer. It was an enforced contact session, between the little girl and her father, observed by a Cafcass officer. The mother was biting her lip, anxiously enquiring of the officer what would happen next.

In the hallway, with no thought for their privacy, a complacent-looking Cafcass officer outlined a plan for several sessions of supervised contact, leading on to unsupervised contact. The mother, fearful and hesitant, tried to object – tentatively trying to suggest parenting classes for the father and saying she was unhappy with the suggested contact. She was treated in a patronising manner and talked down.

It was an unpromising beginning. I was appalled by the scene. I hadn't liked the Cafcass office in London, but I'd seen nothing unprofessional like this scenario before. I sat glumly, waiting for my turn; wondering how many other mothers were going through this miserable ordeal.

It was clear to me when I got into the interview room that the new Cafcass guardian in our case hadn't read the court papers. She asked whether Jack's behaviour had been mainly verbal abuse. I stared at her, mystified and confused. I was embarrassed about tackling her over her ignorance. I waded in, floundering, trying to explain some of the abuse. Her response was: why did I go on to have four children with Jack if his abuse was so bad?

The response finished me off. I couldn't get angry. I was crushed. I began to feel guilty, as though I must be to blame for the abuse. Why didn't I leave Jack earlier?

I had often encountered the ignorance of lay people before who thought I could 'just leave', but I hadn't expected to find this attitude in the repertoire of a supposedly trained professional. However, it was only later when I repeated the conversation to my mother and to Eva and Orla on the phone that I began to get angry, in response to their outrage.

It's a misconception that you can just leave. We are not talking about a woman who is in a normal mindset. I began to adapt to abuse, my perceptions altered. In fact you're looking at the situation from an internalised negative view of yourself. It was only later, when I looked back at the situation I was in during the time of that relationship, that I understood how far my perceptions had been manipulated.

Another pernicious attitude which results from being abused is that you also begin to perceive the world as an unsafe place. Life is an enormous struggle and your trust in people gets undermined. You can begin to fear what is 'out there' as much as you fear your abuser. Better the devil you know. Also, by taking away your autonomy and making you dependent on him, the abuser makes you believe that you need him. An unhealthy dependence is created which keeps you in this destructive relationship.

These psychological issues are very real. You are not in a healthy place mentally, so you can't just up and leave the way a normally functioning person with proper self-esteem would. I am so far from that place now that it seems almost inconceivable I was ever in it. I was literally a different person. I was damaged and it took as many years being out of that situation to heal from it, as I spent in the abusive relationship.

I feel outraged now at the stupidity, the sheer ignorance, of the questions I was asked by someone who is involved in child protection. Rather than ask a man why he is abusive, she prefers to ask a woman why she puts up with it. 'It couldn't have been very bad if you were prepared to put up with it' was as far as her understanding stretched. When I think it over now, I feel shocked and appalled that such a person has any role at all in child protection, and if her attitudes are representative, it is not surprising that social services and child protection are in such poor condition in Britain.

Aside from the issues of ignorance and training of Cafcass officers, I often picked up a more personal attitude from some of the women who interviewed me. It was a kind of unconscious superiority. There were occasions when individuals detached themselves from you; when I got the feeling I was being blamed for the abuse. Their attitude was that such a thing could never happen to them.

It was as though I was blemished or tarnished by having been battered. I must be lacking in judgement in some way. I either provoked or invited mistreatment by my behaviour; or I should have seen it coming and avoided it.

It was the wrong question to ask. The question should not be: why is an abused woman bad at picking men? Such an idea rests on all kinds of dubious assumptions. The question really should be: why is abuse so widespread that women can't avoid it?

The children were equally unhappy with their new Cafcass guardian. They reported the set-up to her very clearly. They told her that their father had called a newspaper beforehand to witness the scene that was to take place, and that he had told them to kick the police when they came and refuse to go home with me; so it must have been evident to her that Jack had planned to attack me and set the children up. I knew firsthand that the children had told the Cafcass guardian what had happened because when I took the children for their interviews, my mother and I were asked to sit in the corridor outside the interview room. From our seat it was possible to hear Jools, who had a carrying voice, describe things exactly.

These events did not, however, get into her official reports to the court. Instead, she preferred to blame me for not supporting unsupervised contact.

25

'Mothers make it up'

I don't think any of the officials in the Welsh court liked dealing with a litigant in person. I didn't come across litigants in person at these small courts the way I had at the RCJ. In London I seemed to find fathers representing themselves on every corner. A lot of them helped each other. Sometimes I heard cruel jokes made about them by barristers, saying that they were ambulance chasers – always on the alert for other fathers whom they could persuade into the club for litigants in person.

I never came across any female litigants in person, so it was rather lonely from that standpoint while I was representing myself. I guess the system didn't favour women litigants. The more open to compromise and reason you were, the more disadvantaged you were by the system. As I saw it, family law was a crude mechanism for solving disputes. The stronger party was generally favoured; the louder and more assertive you were, the more likely you were to obtain a positive outcome. It was a vain hope that vulnerability would be protected; you really had to fight your own corner – something that battered women weren't well placed to do.

It's a well-known adage that one who represents himself has a fool for a client. Personally I don't think it's good for the legal profession to be so incestuous. Any profession that can't stand challenge from outsiders will be the poorer for it. Sometimes a litigant in person is good for making people think about why they do certain things. Never being questioned is the quickest route I know of to poor practice.

But there was no doubt they found me an annoyance. Judge F kept trying to pressure me into getting legal representation. I also got up the nose of the children's solicitor. She and the guardian invited me to drink coffee with them and discuss matters during a recess. I brought up the case of Re L and asked how it was that Mr Charming had been able to get away with never making any reparation for his behaviour, which was a key requirement mentioned in the CASC guidelines. The children's solicitor cut me off. 'We know Re L, thank you.' She had taken it upon herself to speak for both of them.

Her obstinacy in not consulting the children she had been appointed to represent was a burden, and it took a lot of pressure off when she suddenly quit her post with her firm. She had a heavy-handed approach and it was a relief to have her gone. Before her resignation she seemed regularly to have the ear of the judge, often going in to discuss cases alone with him. On one occasion she hastened to reassure me that it wasn't my case but someone else's they were discussing in private. It did nothing to ease my mind. Someone else's case this time, mine next time, I thought. When I heard later that she had gone on to become a judge in another area, I felt sorry for the children whose cases would come before her. I knew her attitude would have repelled my own children; she was working from theories about children – she hadn't even bothered to meet my children to see if her theories matched their reality.

The solicitor appointed in her place came from the same office, although her mild manner was completely the opposite of her colleague's. Unfortunately, a train of events had already been set in motion in which the new solicitor and the guardian showed themselves to be weak and ineffectual at protecting the children's interests.

The hearing dawned at which all parties were to give evidence. I brought up the question of Re L and the CASC guidelines. The judge asked the guardian, on the witness stand, whether she knew the Re L case. The Cafcass officer was forced to admit that she didn't know it. I was astounded. Here she was, employed to protect and safeguard my children, in a guardian's role, and she didn't know the seminal case. Shouldn't such ignorance have consequences?

Wouldn't the judge show concern, pursue the fact that she lacked the basic skills and informed perspective that she needed to be involved in child welfare? No, he had the case photocopied for her so she could look at it over lunch. But he was not willing to challenge her about her lack of research and minimal grasp of the issues. In fact, the judge was not only willing to let her ignorance go unchallenged, but he was cosily chummy with her, remarking to her on the witness stand, 'You and I know that mothers make it up.'

When he uttered this I was knocked for six. One sexist comment (like the one he'd made at an earlier hearing) could, just possibly, be a throwaway comment; a second blatantly sexist comment was part of a trend. There was no doubt that this judge was prejudiced against women. In this court, however, the judge held a position similar to a feudal lord.

I looked around. Why was no one else objecting to this outrageous piece of sexism? I looked at my husband's barrister, an articulate, able and confident woman. Surely she would object to this deliberate demeaning of her own sex? Not a flicker there. The Cafcass officer to whom it was addressed wasn't objecting either. True, she didn't look happy, but she didn't have the courage to respond. There was a court clerk present. I looked at him. Was he too used to these kinds of comments to turn a hair? Was the court culture so sexist and so deeply ingrained in its attitudes towards women that no one was going to stand up and remonstrate with the judge?

I too was a coward. I bottled it. I wanted to stand up. I wanted to leave the room. The judge was so biased against women that I stood no chance of a fair hearing or of getting a good outcome for the children. But I was afraid of arousing the judge's wrath. I had already been turned down by the appeal court, so there was no escape route. If I complained about him, I would still be stuck with him. So I sat there and said nothing. I was as complicit as all the other guilty people in that room.

Judge F's sexism was illuminating in another respect. It suggested a possible reason why the Cafcass guardian had produced such a bland, wishy-washy report. Maybe she didn't dare to write a report that held a man accountable for domestic violence, or that supported the children's wishes not to have any unsupervised contact, because she knew she would get short shrift from Judge F. It was understandable, but it didn't excuse her complicity.

On occasion I overheard the private opinions of one or two legal representatives who had to deal with Judge F that he was rude and cantankerous in court. So it wasn't merely the litigants who had to put up with his waywardness. Unfortunately, the judge's blustering was ineffectual. It cowed people, including the legal professionals who had to endure his hectoring manner, but it achieved nothing in terms of practical results. He continued to give directions and instructions which were never followed through.

One example was that Mr Charming had been ordered to seek permission before filing any more statements. My ex-husband's filings at court had become ridiculous. He filed statement after statement. If one set of arguments didn't convince, he would shift his ground to another. One statement he made on the subject of parental alienation amounted to 150 pages, and he turned up with it on the day of a hearing instead of filing it beforehand. The judge railed against this and made an order about it, but nevertheless continued to let this kind of behaviour pass.

When he gave evidence, Jack admitted that he retained his divorce settlement. It was a sizeable sum of money which should have disqualified him from receiving legal aid. Jack's admission went uncommented by the judge and legal representatives. I was sure my previous London solicitor would not have allowed such an admission to go unremarked if she had heard it. She was scrupulous where legal aid was concerned. I was perturbed by the laxity of these officials.

I realised that I'd probably done myself down through representing myself in front of Judge F. Yes, it enabled me to ask hard questions of the judge and the officials involved, but my lack of official status also made it impossible for me to hold them to account or to question them and have those questions taken seriously. Additionally, I didn't have the confidence to cross-examine the guardian or Jack on the witness stand. This was an unsympathetic judge I was standing in front of, and cross-examination carried its own dangers if not done properly. I gave in and employed a solicitor.

I asked for a transcript of this evidential hearing. I made the request through the new barrister who was employed to represent me. But I had made myself unpopular by representing myself and bringing inconvenient truths to his attention. Judge F's refusal of a transcript was curt. 'No, on her head be it. She would insist on representing herself.'

26

The children's voices and making complaints

⚖️

Seventeen months of hearings passed. Judge F had moved courts and our case went with him to the court where he was now sitting. He clearly found our case as stressful and unpleasant as the parties involved. At a hearing in Rhyl, he ruefully commented to one of the barristers that the name of Charming would end up carved on his coffin.

The number of hearings in front of Judge F was approaching double figures and finally, on the recommendations of the Cafcass guardian, he ordered unsupervised contact to take place. This time it was the kids who revolted. They were absolutely distraught: fed up with their father dragging them through court yet again, sick of guardians who didn't listen to them and angry at not having their voices heard, they refused point-blank to go.

Ben was particularly furious. He had been the one heavily leaned upon in the set-up at Christmas and he had suffered the most emotionally. He had consistently maintained that he didn't want unsupervised contact. He had been willing to see his dad in the contact centre, but he didn't want to be put in any situation again where his dad was able to exercise control over him. He couldn't understand why his guardian had failed to grasp this point and why she had failed to mention the set-up in her official report. He was keen to see his guardian as soon as possible, to ask what had gone wrong and to make sure he got his views across unmistakably.

Astonishingly, the judge was forced to rescind his order for unsupervised contact. It was the first time I'd seen a judge back down in this way. At first it appeared hopeful. The judge appeared to be cross with the guardian. Clearly something had gone wrong here. The guardian hadn't got it right because the type of contact she had suggested was anathema to the children. Initially it looked as though he was going to attribute blame to the correct cause. He had some rude things to say about guardians, blustering irritably, 'what use are they?' For once I wasn't bearing the brunt of a judge's anger; I was thankful for that, at least!

The guardian wasn't present for the hearing at which Judge F rescinded his order. She was on holiday. He ordered that she re-interview the children upon her return.

As a safeguard against his guardian not passing on his views again, Ben wrote his feelings down, explaining all about the Christmas set-up. He put such effort into it that it was touching. He wrote his notes with his best handwriting pen, lying on his bed and occasionally calling me in to consult me about spelling. At his interview with the Cafcass guardian, he gave her his carefully written notes.

When he came out of the guardian's office, he asked her to be sure to give his notes directly to the judge. For some reason she was reluctant to promise this. It appeared she was trying to dissuade him. She told him that if she gave his notes to the judge, Ben's father would see them. We didn't understand the purport of her objection.

Ben seemed flat and disappointed, which wasn't like him. Normally he was a confident, self-assured and resilient child. He felt the interview had gone badly and that he hadn't been listened to. 'The guardian gave me a hard time,' he said. 'When I told her things, she kept saying "why is that?" as though she didn't believe me. And she didn't ask me any questions about my notes and the set-up: I wanted to talk about that.' He seemed crushed and I felt furious and upset on his behalf.

'Shall I ring her up and tell her how you feel?' I asked him. He was too despondent that evening and thought it would be pointless. Next day he appeared cross and determined. He had recovered his resolve. 'I want to ring up the guardian and ask for another interview,' he insisted. He was so angry at the way he had been treated that he wanted to do it himself.

I didn't want to put my son in the position of suffering another rejection. I explained to Ben that the guardian might not be happy if he rang her direct and I suggested preparing the ground for him so that he could have another interview. I telephoned her myself and told her that Ben had been upset after his interview; that he'd wanted to talk about his notes, and that she'd apparently kept repeating 'why is that?' which had made him feel disbelieved.

I was annoyed on Ben's behalf when the guardian indicated that she wasn't willing for the children to phone her directly. She felt they were not old enough and I should be the one to ring. I felt if a child was showing enough maturity to ask for more responsibility he should be given it. He was chafing at the bit, angry at having other people always speaking for him. Even though he trusted me to say what he wanted me to say, he still wanted to do it himself. He wanted to feel his voice was being heard. I supported him on this.

The guardian had completely the wrong way of handling Ben. The trouble was she didn't want to take any advice from me, the person who knew him best of all, on the most effective way to handle him. It seemed to me she was so determined to do and handle things her own way that she was like a bull in a china shop.

We had suffered two inept guardians by now. I felt a kind of weary disgust at their performance. In addition, the two guardians we had been assigned seemed to be of low intellectual calibre compared with other professionals around. They were deferred to by judges simply because of their position. You couldn't challenge a guardian or Cafcass officer; the judges just wouldn't have it. Even if the guardians' reports were badly written, the conclusions illogical, their research and knowledge minimal and even if they contradicted an expert, they would have the last word. I could see the problem for judges. If you start admitting that social workers, Cafcass officials and guardians aren't up to the job, the whole system falls apart because there is no one else to do the task of child protection.

Nevertheless it was disappointing. Is it too much to hope for people who have intelligence as well as a sympathetic manner with children to be appointed for roles in child welfare? Our Cafcass guardian, unlike the NYAS one, had a very good way with children. Her manner appealed to them. But she didn't seem to have the wherewithal to stand up to other professionals and argue the children's case. She was the sort of person I could envisage working in a nursery; someone you'd think was kind and whom you'd be glad to leave your children in the care of. But having a nice manner isn't enough in child protection. You need to be more than usually intelligent and on the ball. And you need some awareness of how perpetrators work.

The next court hearing was a shambles. The court schedule was

over-stretched. We were the last case on the list. The penultimate
case was dragging on and on. I hated being last because the court at
Rhyl had a very small waiting area and sometimes I was left alone in
the room with Jack after all the other cases had finished. It was
stressful. I didn't like being alone with him. One time I was terribly
thirsty but I couldn't leave the court to buy a drink in case we were
called in before the judge. Jack was sitting right next to the only water
dispenser reading a book, holding it up provocatively so I could see
the title: the subject was parental alienation syndrome.

The guardian left before our case was called, saying she was
required elsewhere. On her way out she told me that she had brought
Ben's notes to court but that the legal representatives had told her
they would need special permission to file, so it hadn't been done.
Basically the judge was not going to see Ben's written notes, after all
that had happened.

I went home and thought things over when I was in a cooler state
of mind. This situation was self-evidently absurd. The guardian
needed special permission to show the judge my son's notes? Judge F
had specifically requested the guardian to re-interview my son; he
was waiting to hear the outcome of that interview. It defied logic that
they were hanging on to Ben's notes because they would need
'special permission' to show them to the judge. These people looking
after my son seemed to lack all common sense.

I was perturbed for another reason. The guardian was there to
give instructions to the solicitor and barrister. They weren't meant to
be giving instructions to her. She was supposed to be in charge. Why
didn't she just tell them to seek special permission if they needed it,
instead of meekly doing as they told her?

Over the next few months I chased up my son's notes and the
issue of the judge seeing them, but to no avail. I made phone calls
and I wrote letters. The children's solicitor simply didn't bother to
answer any calls or letters. My son kept asking me at intervals
whether the judge had seen his notes and what he thought of them.
Finally, I had to tell the children that I couldn't get the notes filed. At
my wits end, I made an official complaint about the children's
guardian. I complained to her superior at Cafcass about the situation.
Her superior told me that I should bring up the issue with the judge. I
then wrote to the judge with a chronology and an explanation of
what had happened, telling him that the children, especially Ben,
were very upset by the behaviour of their representatives and that
they were stonewalling us. He ordered his clerk to write to the

children's guardian asking her to respond to my letter. What followed was a blank silence.

The guardian simply didn't bother to respond to the judge's instructions and neither did he bother to make her. After some time I wrote back to the judge's clerk to point out that the guardian had ignored the judge's directions and that I had received no response at all. This time it was the judge who didn't bother to respond. Clearly he didn't care whether or not the children's guardian had failed to report the children's views and I had my doubts about whether he had even expected the guardian to respond to the clerk's request. This was evidently an exercise in nothingness to them. The fact that the kids were anxiously awaiting an outcome was of no account.

By this time, my two older children had become incensed by the pretence that they were being listened to at court. The officials came with their clipboards and notepads and tick boxes, but they didn't actually allow the children's views to penetrate and change the course of events. It was purely token listening, that's all. The children had no real say in matters. The professionals were paying lip service to the idea that everything was in the children's best interests; but their best interests in practice didn't include treating them as young human beings and taking their views into account.

I supported Madeleine and Ben in their opinion and in their desire to have a proper voice in the process. I decided to find out all I could about their legal rights. Part of me was simply puzzled by what I found. When you look into it, on paper children have a large number of rights to be involved in decision making. There were odd rare cases I found on the internet where children had sacked their guardians and taken the reins, making their own decisions. Why shouldn't my children form one of those rare cases? They wanted to be in control of their own lives and have more say in what affected them so deeply; it was my role to facilitate that by finding out what their rights were and enabling them to demand those.

Of course, this drew them closely into the judicial process, politicising them in the wider sense, early in life. I was not one hundred per cent comfortable with this. But on the other hand, by denying them that knowledge and information, I was leaving them at the mercy of a chaotic court process which had left them feeling powerless and angry. What was worse, being made to live a life they were unhappy with and enduring contact which was physically and emotionally unsafe, or giving them the knowledge they needed to fight for their own rights in a system which wasn't listening to them?

Since the Family Proceedings Rules 1991 no. 1247 allowed for children in private law proceedings to ask the court for the removal of their guardian ad litem and to conduct the proceedings without one, it seemed to me that in theory the children had a means of redress. Giving them this information and knowledge of their legal rights was empowering them to express their wishes and feelings.

Ben and Madeleine wanted the right to sack their guardian and be allowed to instruct a solicitor so that they could have a proper say on the issues relating to them. But although in theory they were entitled to all these legal rights and safeguards, enforcing them was another matter completely. My solicitor suggested that I contact the children's commissioner's office, saying they had been helpful to her in the past when children had required separate representation.

The office for the children's commissioner was not, however, very helpful. The person I contacted was offhand and said that the children's commissioner had no powers in the legal arena. The most they could do was to raise awareness in political circles and with the relevant authorities that children were not being given an adequate voice in the family courts. She suggested that I try complaining to the Legal Complaints Service about the children's solicitor.

My children had tried to enlist the help of their solicitor with regard to their ineffectual guardian, saying that she had not reported them properly. The solicitor had granted my elder son a token interview to ensure that 'his voice was heard'. But it turned out to be a meaningless interview. His voice wasn't heard because it made no difference to events.

In fact, the children's solicitor was chummy with the Cafcass guardian; they regularly had coffee together in the rooms reserved for professionals at court, and they were always meeting around the courts and involved in the same cases. No way was she going to take my children's side against a fellow professional, even though she was employed to act for the children.

It was a difficulty that hadn't arisen in London. The sheer number of solicitors' offices, barristers' chambers, judges and child professionals meant it was easier in the city to preserve a proper formal distance between professionals. Chumminess could be avoided in London, but in rural areas and small towns there is a 'club' mentality in which the professionals cohere.

In an ideal world, professionals would be able to strike a balance. There need to be good professional relationships between organisations, so that individuals in one agency can pick up the phone and discuss child safety issues with someone in another agency; but that shouldn't degenerate into a situation where there is a lack of proper distance and a corresponding willingness to overlook a fellow professional's failings.

Another example of how closed and circular the system was came in the form of the answer I had from the body to which one makes complaints about solicitors. The Legal Complaints Service said that they couldn't accept a complaint from my son or from me on his behalf. If a child had a guardian, only that guardian could make a complaint about the children's solicitor. As I pointed out, the children's guardian was the problem to begin with; we were only complaining about the solicitor because she wouldn't act for the children in complaining about the guardian.

We were completely manacled in trying to make a complaint. The system had the illogic of requiring a guardian to make a complaint about herself! The sheer stupidity of the system and how it was riddled with holes and tripwires for children made me gasp. Where children were concerned, you couldn't say there was a complaints procedure. The whole thing was chaotic.

The complaint I had made to Cafcass had a number of elements. The main part was my children's complaint about the way they had been denied a voice in proceedings because of their guardian's failure to report the set-up and other allegations; but I complained to Cafcass on my own behalf too. I felt the line of questioning that had been adopted by the guardian about why I had gone on to have four children if the abuse was so bad, her squeamish reluctance to hear the gory details of abuse and her lack of concern about the psychologist's domestic violence report were so far from the CASC guidelines and what had been intended by Re L that it needed making a fuss about.

My initial complaint was rejected by the Cafcass guardian's immediate superior. Since part of the complaint was the children's complaint, however, I decided that I couldn't let this go as I had so often in the past. The children were depending on me to fight this battle for them and to win.

Seeing no other option, I enlisted the help of my local MP. I was suitably impressed by his efficiency and willingness to help. I am convinced that his interest in the case and his willingness to ask questions and raise issues on our behalf was the only reason that Cafcass agreed to consider my complaint at a higher level, drafting in a director from another area, who was independent of the original Cafcass office, to consider the matter.

Although I had lost my early appeal against Judge F, the fight had not entirely gone out of me and I decided I still had to make the effort to address some of the issues that the case involved. Judge F had made two overtly sexist comments during the two years we had been in front of him and I felt it was time he should be held accountable for them.

Once the case was over, I complained to the Office for Judicial Complaints (OJC) about the sexist comments. The OJC cannot accept complaints against judges until after a final order is made. They do not investigate before a case is closed because it is deemed interference in the judicial process. In one way, I can see the point of this. If malicious complaints were made or litigants made complaints simply because they were unhappy with the outcome of their case, the justice system could not operate. Cases might grind to a halt if they investigated anything and everything, and the complaint might be wrong; meanwhile justice would have been unjustifiably delayed.

The fact remains, however, that if you have a genuine complaint, you have to watch your case going wrong and there is nothing you can do to stop it; no complaint you can make that will be heard. In some cases the judicial process needs interfering with because justice delayed may mean no justice at all. At present you can only allow a case to go wrong and then tinker around trying to put it right.

And so it was. By the time I was able to lodge a complaint with the OJC about the sexist comments, my case had taken two years to come to a final conclusion, and then it took the OJC another year to investigate it. By that time the earlier tapes had gone missing from the court and the tape with the later sexist comment, I was told, never existed because the tape machine was broken at the time.

The OJC seemed not to care that the tapes which would have shown a judge behaving in a sexist manner were missing. The attitude of their investigating officer was: tough luck, the tapes are missing, your complaint is dismissed. She seemed totally uninterested in why the tapes were missing and who was responsible for that negligence. It simply wasn't of interest to her.

Even worse, the investigation was full of inconsistencies. Very early on, the case worker had told me that she was listening to the tapes. Since it did not make sense for my complaint to be dismissed if they had listened to the tapes, I complained to the Judicial Appointments and Conduct Ombudsman, asking him to look at the botched investigation conducted by the OJC. My complaint to the ombudsman was upheld and the OJC agreed to reopen the investigation. By now I was experiencing sheer incredulity at the massive inefficiency and complete rottenness of the whole system. Wasn't there a single competent, intelligent or caring person in the whole court system?

27

In the Court of Appeal a third time

⚖

Judge F, of course, had rescinded his order for unsupervised contact because of the children's refusal to go. He had blustered for a time about the guardian's failings, when she wasn't there; but in the end he wasn't willing to hold her to account. It was impossible to get him to hold a hearing at which we could air the children's complaint. Both my own direct requests and my solicitor's went unanswered. He simply didn't bother to reply. Instead he decided to hand his final judgment down in writing.

There was no going to court to listen to the judgment, so no chance to raise any issues there. The professionals had so boxed us in that there was nothing we could do about it. Since he couldn't make the children go, the judge instead substituted an order for indirect contact. On paper the kids had won. But I could see it was not a real victory. For one thing, there were too many loose ends.

Whenever you go to court it is the last report that counts and which is influential. The last report in our case was the guardian's, from which the children's allegations and the set-up were missing. I knew we could not leave this to stand. I had allowed things to go unchallenged in the past. The NYAS guardian had gone unquestioned and it had led to near disaster for our family. Leaving the Cafcass guardian's report unchallenged was dangerous. I knew how it would look to a future judge. It would appear that we, the parents, had quarrelled one Christmas and that we should be able to move on from that. Since the real underlying psychological issues were absent from her conclusions, we were at risk from future contact applications from Jack.

Jack was litigious. Gaining ground in court only encouraged him to continue because he then felt he was getting somewhere. Unless a proper expert made the court accept that he was using these court proceedings abusively, we would be at continuous risk from litigation.

We had to get the children's allegations, the previous psychologist's report and the guardian's failings accepted, otherwise the children faced a life of court until they were grown up. That was why I wouldn't let my complaints drop even though on paper we had a final order. The legal representatives in Wales seemed to think it was all over. When I told them that Jack would come back, they dismissed it. He had no grounds for appeal, I was told. Even his own barrister thought he had no grounds of appeal and he wouldn't get funding for it. I didn't buy it. I knew he had the luck of the devil. Or rather that the system favours the rights of violent fathers over the rights of children. He seemed to have the right to go to court endlessly. But where were the children's rights to a decent, normal upbringing, away from conflict and perpetual litigation?

At the last brief session which had taken place in Rhyl, the children's solicitor and the Cafcass guardian knocked on the door of the tiny private room where I was talking with my barrister. They asked if they could say goodbye to the children, since the case was over. I stared at them uncomprehendingly. They thought it was all over? Had they learned nothing about Jack in the two years they'd been dealing with the case? Did they really think he wouldn't be back? He had already asked Judge F for leave to appeal his order – although, of course, the judge had turned him down, just as he had refused me permission to appeal earlier on in the case.

I was also sickened by the audacity of the children's representatives. The children were feeling let down, angry, hurt, betrayed by them. And they had the brazen cheek to come and ask to say goodbye. Could they really not understand what they had done? My eldest son was ready to bite their hands off, he was so angry. My barrister stepped into this embarrassing impasse and suggested that they wait to see if Jack succeeded in getting an appeal or not. Saying goodbye might be premature.

My predictions came true. Jack got his appeal. He had to represent himself at the Court of Appeal, but he managed to persuade three senior judges that Judge F's case management was poor enough to send the case back for a rehearing in front of another judge.

It gave me no pleasure to be able to say, I told you so. In fact, I was cross. I had complained about the judge's case management two years before, and things could have been put right at that point if Lord Justice Scott-Baker had so chosen. Instead the case had run on for two years, only for us to be told that Judge F had made mistakes.

I was unable to get to the Court of Appeal for the hearing in London. My solicitor and barrister represented me in court. They felt we should go in 'under the radar'. I was in two minds but felt, on balance, that this approach was probably right. The trouble was that we were in an impossible position. Judge F had handled the case very badly and we had genuine complaints about him; but on the other hand, we wanted his very last order, for indirect contact, to stand. This was the order he had been forced to substitute for the earlier order of unsupervised contact.

It had been the order we wanted, but it had not been granted for the right reasons. He hadn't wanted to grant it, but he had been forced to when the children rebelled. He had been unwilling overtly to acknowledge that Jack was a risk to the children because that would contradict the Cafcass guardian's erroneous assessment of him. The judge's line of reasoning was missing from his judgments, of course, because he had been all over the place with his decisions. It left his order vulnerable to appeal by the opposing party – to Jack.

We were in the invidious position of not approving Judge F's handling of the case but being forced to look as though we did because we didn't want his order to be dismantled. I wanted the Court of Appeal to know the children were unhappy, but if we let the judges know that, they might re-open the case; and then the children would suffer from protracted proceedings again. It was like having a cleaver through my mental processes.

Judge F had not examined the Cafcass officer's evidence at a hearing. That was one of the grounds on which Jack's appeal succeeded. I thought I could suggest a reason why Judge F had not held a hearing to examine her later evidence. If he had, it would have opened a can of worms. He would have been forced to go into my children's complaint against her and her failure to record their allegations.

The appeal court judges noted that my son's handwritten notes were not in the bundle. They were absent even though I had specifically written to the children's solicitor, on Ben's request, to say that he wanted his notes to go to the appeal judges. The children's solicitor and the guardian made sure that none of the complaints raised about them found their way to the appeal court.

I wasn't at the appeal, of course, but I read the judgment afterwards. I felt my children were let down badly by it. I wondered if, had the judges known of the fight my son had had with his guardian to get his allegations before a judge, they would have been so ready to praise her, as they did in their judgment. It was stomach turning given the reality of the children's predicament. I could see the reason for their talking her up. Jack was claiming that the courts were biased in favour of women and he was claiming that Judge F and the Cafcass guardian exemplified that bias. In order to counter Jack's accusations of bias against men, the appeal court judges were put in the position of defending her impartiality and lack of bias towards him. Naturally, their praise of her, protecting her position from Jack, left our flank exposed.

My barrister, an intelligent woman with a more perceptive attitude than many of the barristers I'd previously come across, explained the appeal judges' concerns about Judge F on her return from London. She mentioned a throw-away comment by one of the senior judges when she'd tentatively tried to introduce the idea that I had made a complaint about the judge. Apparently the children's barrister had chipped in with a contribution that I'd also made a complaint about the guardian.

I understood that one of the appeal judges said in an aside, 'What's wrong with these people?' Of course, he didn't know what had gone on behind the scenes; the judges only saw the evidence presented to them. He didn't know anything of the horrors the children had had to cope with. Nevertheless it was wounding to hear these uncomprehending comments.

A decade on from Re L, judges are still unaware that abusive men are regularly very manipulative and play the court system, that they put on convincing performances to fool the courts into thinking they are good parents, and that women need real protection in these circumstances.

Once again I had to put up with the suggestion in the judgment (how many times had I heard this over the years?) that the case involved a low level of violence. When were judges ever going to get the point that I continually made? It wasn't about the violence; it was about wider forms of abuse, and it involved Mr Charming's ongoing controlling behaviour towards me and the children, and his attempts to undermine my relationship with them. Neither did I like his behaviour referred to as 'low level'. By now I rejected that perception by judges. There is nothing low level about a man trying to run you down in a car or smashing a light over a baby's head. It was simply insulting.

After this, our third outing at the appeal court in the span of seven years, we started again with hearings in Wales in front of a new judge, Judge H. In the end, the children's refusal to be represented by the Cafcass guardian and the solicitor who had let them down so badly gained them their wish: the pair were forced to resign, not because we could make them responsible for their actions and hold them accountable, but simply because the children would not be represented by them any longer.

A new guardian was appointed from the Wrexham area. I was bemused in my interviews with her. She was based nowhere near the Llandudno office and yet she was using identical language to the guardian who had just resigned her position. The fact that different Cafcass officers used the same language suggests that they are trained to think in the same way. I found this unsettling. It told me they are trained to see parents as equally culpable, as quarrelling. Again there were no perpetrators in the equation.

I realised then that there was something fundamentally flawed with the way Cafcass and the family court operate. They are a crude mechanism for settling what they term 'disputes', in the same way you might settle a land dispute or a financial claim. The stronger party gets more out of the deal and the weaker party has to give more. This way of doing law was so ingrained that it was virtually impossible for them to handle domestic violence cases, where the weaker party is supposed to be protected.

The guardians I had come across had another unfortunate trait in common. They tended to anticipate what a judge was likely to think and to write their reports to fit this perception. The whole system was self-reinforcing. Since they anticipated that domestic abuse would be downplayed, that emotional forms of abuse wouldn't count, that children would be sent for contact anyway, they produced reports reflecting the likelihood of that outcome. They never had the intelligence or the independence of mind to challenge it. One would almost think they were likely to suffer a penalty from standing out or coming to a different conclusion.

If cloned reports reach judges, they in turn will produce identikit orders. It's no wonder really that some judges think women make it up and exaggerate the effects of domestic abuse, if the reality of the situation is not conveyed by Cafcass reports.

I also see a fundamental conflict of interest which Cafcass officers face. Part of their remit is to encourage contact. Yet if one is appointed as a children's guardian, one is supposed to report their wishes and feelings. When the child expresses a desire not to engage in contact, a guardian should protect that child, report their wishes and not force them into a potentially abusive relationship. The two things do not sit happily together; the roles are contradictory and mutually exclusive.

I found the new Cafcass guardian unhelpful. After one interview with her, the older two children were equally dismayed. Madeleine told me afterwards that she had said to them that a judge might think it was reasonable for them to have contact with their father. Apparently she likened her role to that of a parent: one who sometimes has to take decisions which are in a child's best interests but which a child may not want; as, for instance, a parent might make a child wear school uniform. As Madeleine pointed out to me later with ruthless logic, the new guardian wasn't their parent and wasn't comparing like with like. Madeleine could argue good reasons for wearing school uniform, but she couldn't see why it was in her best interests to force her into a relationship with a man who continually put her under pressure with his obsession about residence, and who wanted to control even her basic bodily functions such as eating and going to the toilet. She said in that wry comic way she has when seeing through the absurdity of certain adults, that it was quite obvious after one interview which way the new Cafcass guardian would be leaning. There was no doubt she would be pro-contact; she'd given that away.

I felt my daughter had hit on an important logical absurdity which both Cafcass officers in Wales had fallen into. They expected me to encourage contact and yet they took no precautions to ensure the children were safe. I received criticism for not supporting contact more, but the role of Cafcass should have been to ensure the emotional, physical and psychological safety of the children. If contact was not safe for them, Cafcass should not have expected me to support direct contact.

I challenged both Cafcass guardians on this logical contradiction in the position they held. Neither was willing to say overtly that direct contact was safe for the children. I suppose they didn't dare, since that would have contradicted the DVIP's conclusion that Jack was a high risk to the children. On the other hand, neither of them would explicitly respond to my challenge that contact was risky. I was left to infer their position by the fact that I was criticised for not doing more to encourage the children to see their dad. They made it obvious by the stance they took, but neither of them would court controversy by explicitly stating their views. This lack of transparency and honesty in their reporting was frustrating. I felt they should get off the fence and take a view, but instead they chose to remain neutral. I didn't think this was a defensible position for them to take when children were involved.

Madeleine and Ben could see the impossibility of having the new guardian as their representative. They each felt strongly that she wouldn't help them and expressed the desire to instruct a solicitor. Judge H did not put up any opposition to the children instructing a solicitor. I could see the new guardian wasn't wildly enthusiastic about the idea, but Madeleine and Ben were so strongly in favour of having their own solicitor that she did not actively oppose it. A solicitor was found for the older two children and the guardian continued to represent Jools and Mia, who were too young to instruct a solicitor.

An early order in the new case in front of Judge H, before the new guardian was on board, ordered the guardian to consider two things. One was whether the older two children should have separate representation and the other was whether Mr Charming should be assessed by a psychologist. I was extremely frustrated by the attitude of the newly appointed guardian. She hadn't been present at the initial hearing and didn't have a full grasp of the issues. I gathered in my first interview with her in Wrexham that, rather than taking up the judge's suggestion that Mr Charming should be sent for a psychological assessment, she was going to make the recommendation that all of us should be referred to a psychologist.

At the hearing which was convened to consider these two matters, my usual barrister, whom I had come to rely on for her grasp of the case, was away. The stand-in barrister advised me that I should go along with the recommendation, since a judge might consider me unreasonable for refusing to be sent to a psychologist. Without my own solicitor and usual barrister to rely on for support, I felt unhappy and backed into a corner. The Cafcass officer's approach was a clear departure from common sense, but I didn't know where to start in explaining the convoluted history behind the case, in order to justify myself.

Once I got home in the evening and recovered my poise, I decided I wasn't having any of this nonsense. Mr Charming and I had both been seen by a psychologist previously who had made clear recommendations about Mr Charming's behaviour and what needed to alter. Unless he could develop some insight and make an effort to change, it was useless sending the whole family to a psychologist. Not only would it be unwelcome to the children; it would also be unnecessarily intrusive. With the limited contact which had been going on over the last few years, the children had come on in leaps and bounds; I wasn't minded to set that back.

In any other arena a professional would be expected to give sound reasons for her recommendations. In court, so far as I could see, Cafcass officers were virtually never challenged about their reasoning. What did the Cafcass guardian think would be achieved by sending all of us to a psychologist? The illogic of it was intensely annoying. Nothing that we said or did could achieve a change in Mr Charming; and without his first step it was pointless sending the rest of us for counselling.

I was confirmed in my views later on, after the Cafcass guardian's solicitor had sought out a number of psychologists with a view to doing an assessment of us. One psychologist turned down the case, saying that men who claimed parental alienation syndrome, as Jack was, were impossible to work with. Another psychologist took the same view, that such men could not usually be counselled since they found themselves unable to accept what the therapist was saying to them. This accorded with my own experience of Jack and also with what the DVIP psychologist had said back in 2003 – there was no possibility of Jack making any progress; he was too stuck.

Despite apparently having read the DVIP and in light of what several reputable psychologists were now saying, the guardian still seemed to think that counselling was an option. She might have been on autopilot; it just didn't seem to register with her that Jack was a genuinely impossible case.

She had also boxed the judge in by making her recommendation. Judges have to give reasons in their judgments for not going along with recommendations from Cafcass. Looking ahead and knowing Mr Charming's track record for appealing, I could see him using her suggestion as a loophole for going to appeal.

I had learned by hard experience in front of Judge F that no matter how incompetent a Cafcass officer was, it didn't help your case to oppose their reports. Having better arguments and common sense on your side, and even a psychologist, didn't win you the day. I wasn't going to agree to the children being subjected to more intrusion and I withdrew my request for Mr Charming to undergo a psychological assessment.

I had pinned my hopes on another psychological assessment for

Mr Charming. One reason is that I knew there was no way any psychologist worth their salt could fail to pick up Mr Charming's peculiar intransigence and the extreme degree to which he wanted to control me and the children. It would also be safer for the children if he was examined and his behaviour properly explained.

The DVIP report had been excellent, but it had assessed Mr Charming's behaviour for risk rather than explaining its possible causes. I personally felt it would be helpful for the children in the longer term, when they were older, to understand their father's behaviour. I had long got past the stage of anger towards Mr Charming for his behaviour towards me. I had almost come to feel sorry for him. There can't be much worse than being stuck in a particular unhealthy and unpleasant mindset. There was no doubt he was suffering, locked in by his anger towards me, the thwarting of his desire to control and his sense of loss. He had lost a great deal: his home and his family. And he had no way mentally of moving on from those feelings.

At present, the children were angry towards him. I felt compassion would come if they had a proper explanation for his behaviour. You can't really blame someone for lack of insight. If you don't have it at all, how do you develop it? I felt the Cafcass guardian's lack of perception in picking up on Judge H's order and going along with it, instead suggesting that the children should be subjected to yet more proceedings and intrusion, had deprived the children of a real opportunity to understand why things were as they were. In addition, I believed that deep down the children might be taking on some burden of guilt for the failure of the relationship with their father. A proper explanation of the causes of it would, I thought, help to relieve them of this and perhaps increase their self-esteem as they came to accept that it was not their responsibility.

Cafcass said they tried hard to fix things; but they only worked at putting pressure on us to do things their way. They didn't try hard at all to understand our position. Our position was in line with all relevant guidelines and legislation on domestic abuse. It was Cafcass Cymru's position which was out of step with up-to-date thinking on domestic violence.

However, it was brought to my attention very starkly in Wales that the legal professionals did not see it as their business to challenge Cafcass on their practices. It never occurred to a judge, for instance, to ask whether Cafcass was following its own guidelines on performing or seeking independent risk assessments in cases involving domestic abuse. I felt this was a mistake on the part of professionals.

When tragedies have occurred in child protection, it is often the case that someone in one organisation or another has spotted failings in the system. But each organisation only seems to be responsible for its own practices; they don't see it as their responsibility to police another body, even if that other body is failing children. Since the system of child protection only works if the judiciary are aware of how Cafcass should proceed and vice versa, this mutual hands-off approach is not good practice.

I was still pursuing my complaint against the previous Cafcass guardian. I had asked for an explanation of how Cafcass Cymru had assessed the risks in our case. The area director of Powys had sent me a copy of a document called *The Domestic Abuse Assessment Toolkit*. This apparently was the document which should inform the practice of Cafcass Cymru in cases involving domestic abuse.

I read the toolkit. It was sound, rooted in the work done by Sturge and Glaser and the CASC guidelines. It was very much along the lines by which the DVIP had carried out its risk assessment. There was nothing in it that I didn't recognise. Risk assessments were to be carried out; there were specific indications of risk, such as a perpetrator minimising or denying their abuse. Nothing controversial there – except that current Cafcass practice was nowhere near modelled on this document. Where was our assessment of risk and the challenge to Mr Charming to change his behaviour?

The first Cafcass officer's immediate superior had rejected my complaint, telling me that they had a specialist evidence-based Domestic Abuse Assessment Tool to assist in the management of cases where domestic abuse had been identified, and that all relevant toolkits and best practice guidelines had been adhered to.

I was annoyed by the summary dismissal of my complaint and wrote back to the superior to point out that her junior officer's method of procedure didn't meet any of the published standards and guidelines. The CASC guidelines and the work done by Sturge and Glaser, all good practice since the year 2000, required that a man should acknowledge his behaviour and show willingness to address it. I asked for my complaint to progress to a more senior level. Without the help of my local MP I very much doubt that the complaint would have gone any further, but following questions he raised with them about their own procedures relating to risk assessment, it progressed to a Stage II complaint.

The complaint would normally have been investigated after a final hearing in the case. Unfortunately, the investigation never got off the ground because Mr Charming appealed and the investigation was suspended until after the appeal. Mr Charming's appeal was granted and the case came before a new judge. Cafcass refused to investigate my complaint in these circumstances, saying the case must come to a close first.

As I pointed out, this was subjecting the children to a huge delay for no proper reason. Surely a decent complaints process should have been able to investigate a complaint concerning children much more quickly than they were doing? We had already been two years in front of Judge F and it had been nearly another year before the case got to appeal; and how long would it take the case to be heard after that? Resources and the court schedule seemed to be seriously overstretched; the likelihood of a judge being able to conclude a case quickly was minimal.

Cafcass argued that investigating my complaint could be seen as interference in the judicial process; as attempting to influence the new guardian or the new judge. Their reasoning was faulty: if our complaint was found to be genuine and the children's allegations were found not to have been reported properly to Judge F by the old guardian, then these facts needed bringing to any new judge's attention. This would not be exercising improper influence but simply bringing facts to a judge's notice which should properly have been presented before. Obviously it would carry a great deal more weight if the superiors at Cafcass came to the conclusion that the guardian had not carried out her duties adequately than if I simply pointed it out at court.

I had also heard of a case in another area which was investigated while proceedings were ongoing and the Cafcass officer was found to be at fault. No one had said in that case that the judge shouldn't have known about it before the case concluded. It was an absurd piece of logic for Cafcass Cymru to take the position that a judge shouldn't be influenced by the correct facts rather than by errors. It also seemed a ridiculously scrupulous stand to take, since we now had a new guardian and a new judge. What harm could be done by investigating those individuals who were off the case now that they could no longer be improperly influenced?

Cafcass however wouldn't progress the investigation, even if it meant leaving us on the back burner for years. I decided to see if I could unravel some of the obscurities in their proceedings for myself. I asked if I could be allowed to see the original Cafcass guardian's case notes so that I could judge her methods for myself. There were clear discrepancies between her conclusions and what the domestic abuse toolkit said should happen and I wanted to see the documents relating to those issues. What followed was a series of letters that rendered the process as opaque as a mud bath.

One Cafcass individual wrote to me to say that the domestic abuse toolkit was not in use during 2006, so there were no documents to see and she couldn't help me any further. When I wrote back to point out that I had a letter from the superior at that office a year before saying that all toolkits had been adhered to, I was told there was a mistake and that an early version of the toolkit had been in use but not the later one. I hadn't distinguished between toolkits, early or late versions, at that point, so why this had been introduced I couldn't say. I was only interested in getting hold of any objective guidelines, toolkits or lists of procedures which were in use at the time, so that I could compare the guardian's methods of proceeding against those criteria to see if she had carried out her statutory obligations with regard to child protection.

The area director in another area had supplied me with toolkit version 2, presumably under the impression that this was the version in use during 2006. The guardian's assessment of matters certainly didn't correspond with that version of the toolkit. I asked for the earlier version of the toolkit so that I could see how it differed from version two. I was sceptical that it would differ very much in terms of requiring risk assessments. However, the earlier version of the toolkit was not forthcoming and I was told that my request might be passed on to the superior of that office, who was returning from leave some time in the future. This turned out to be the same superior who had initially rejected my complaint and told me that all standards had been adhered to. Clearly this was going nowhere. You couldn't call this a complaints procedure; it didn't even have the basic elements of a complaints process. If they had deliberately set out to be as difficult, uncommunicative and secretive as possible, they couldn't have done a better job of being obstructive.

This only increased my resolution to get to the bottom of things. My attitude towards Cafcass was: you have promised me a certain level of service and you have legal responsibilities to safeguard children; no way are you going to deliver to my children a lesser service than you promise in your published guidelines.

Yet another person at Cafcass – and I seemed to be passed around from office to office and person to person – told me that there was a process to go through if I wanted to look at the case notes. The notes were covered by the Data Protection Act and I would only be allowed personal information which related to me; and even if a document related to me, it didn't mean I could have the whole document. This was clearly one of those standard letters which no one knows the meaning of, churned out from a machine.

Even with two degrees in English, I couldn't decipher what the letter meant. It sounded very much as though I couldn't have any information which related to anyone else. However, this would clearly be nonsense, since there couldn't be anything in the guardian's case notes except what had been covered at court, which I would already be party to. By this time Cafcass had proved to be so obstructive that the thought crossed my mind that they were using the Data Protection Act simply as an excuse to withhold the case notes. They appeared to be suggesting that I would be receiving a heavily bowdlerised version of the case notes from which I wouldn't be able to glean anything.

I didn't want to pay £10 and provide my ID, as requested in the standard letter, if I wasn't going to be able to see the Cafcass guardian's notes more or less in their entirety, so I wrote back asking for clarification about what I would be allowed to view and asking how and why the Data Protection Act applied in this case. An answer to my request was not immediately forthcoming.

In high frustration I asked my MP if he could take the matter up again. I was after something very simple: a transparent complaints procedure and simply to know how the risks to my children had been assessed by the person responsible for protecting them. Cafcass's inability to handle simple requests lost them any of my confidence. Not only did they not have a clear and direct line of responsibility, but they couldn't answer basic questions with straightforward information. Their attitude was wrong and they simply were not accountable.

Unless my complaint was upheld by Cafcass, I could see I wasn't going to get anywhere in court with the children's allegations. The new judge, Judge H, was courteous and appeared to be listening intently to the evidence presented to him. He gave my ex-husband, as a litigant in person, every chance to present his case well without making me feel disadvantaged. He had an authoritative but respectful way of conducting the proceedings. There were none of the personal comments and subjective opinions I'd had to listen to from the judge who came before him. By contrast this judge was impassive, revealing very little of what he was thinking. However, you get an instinct for judges when you've seen so many of them. My instinct about this one was that he would be fair minded and that he would come to the right conclusions if we presented him with enough evidence.

The problem in family proceedings was always bits of paper. I had seen before how things always fell apart unless you had the bit of paper proving your point. This is extremely difficult in a case involving the kind of abuse I was alleging. Control manifests itself in an attitude and some of the things my ex-husband demanded from me could equally have been the result of concern for the children. Often it wasn't, but attitudes are difficult to expose unless those judging have seen a man over a long enough period of time. It helped that Jack was representing himself during the year that we appeared in front of Judge H. He could conduct himself well for a short time, but being subjected to pressure and intense questioning for sustained periods revealed his character. After a time he couldn't help justifying the slaps he'd dished out to me and the attitudes he otherwise tried to keep hidden.

I couldn't prove that Jack had been running me down and directly undermining me with the children. This all took place with the children behind closed doors, and the first Cafcass guardian had let them down by failing to report it. I didn't see a way to get that before a judge as hard evidence. Going into the Cafcass saga before the judge didn't seem the right route. It would have opened up wider issues, probably lengthened proceedings and with no guaranteed outcome. My legal advisers thought I had enough current evidence to win the case. I could see for myself that their judgement was correct. From a legal point of view, it made sense to keep the issues as narrow as possible. So long as the outcome was the order we had asked for, it didn't make sense to bring up wider issues. It also made sense in terms of bringing court to an end as quickly as possible. Psychologically, however, I felt cheated.

When you have suffered abuse and an injustice following it, there is a psychological need to have that recognised and put right. I could see that where the court was concerned we were going to have to let go of the children's allegations and views expressed to their first Cafcass guardian. But it left me with a sense of injustice that the children had not been treated fairly and that we had been forced to suffer more years of court simply because the case had not been handled properly the last time around.

The bits of paper necessary to win the case were more current than my son's previous allegations. There was a recent letter written to a school by Jack. Since he had been prevented from knowing where we were living and where the children went to school, he had tried a little detective work of his own, randomly writing to a school in the area to ask if the children were registered there. The letter was derogatory of me, implying that I was mentally ill. It was couched in very emotive language and omitted to mention that there was a court order in place keeping the identity of the children's schools from him.

The other pieces of paper were copies of websites on which he had posted, under his own name, things in a similar vein; plus a teen health website on which he had said that girls who were not virgins were 'fair game' to 'practise sex' on. The websites were revealing of his attitudes towards women, without any input from me. There was also an email from Jack to Madeleine, whom he had located on Facebook, in which he recommended a book on parental alienation syndrome to her.

In my written statements, I had relied mainly on what Jack wrote and posted. What he said about himself was far more revealing than anything I could allege. I was also relying on his behaviour in court. I knew from old that he could not sustain the concerned parent act for very long without bursting into some kind of angry tirade against me. I couldn't prove that Jack was running me down to the children in private, but I could show that it was likely he was doing that, given what he was writing about me to schools, to complete strangers on the internet, and also in his email to my daughter.

Evidence was given on the witness stand over a period of three days in late 2009. On the first day of evidence giving, Jack came with a McKenzie friend. It was a friend we had in common. I'd known this friend of Jack's independently. We'd been introduced in my university days. It's always hurtful and difficult to see a former friend ranged alongside the opposing party. I tried to shut my mind to that. Jack was in the box first. My barrister took him through the findings of previous judges and asked him if he accepted them. There wasn't a single finding that he would admit to.

On the second date for evidence giving, I was in the box. It was harder than I'd expected. Jack had made a mess of cross-examining me once before in 2002; he seemed to have learned something from then. His case was that he'd previously had a reasonable relationship with the kids, and that as he'd had very little contact with them over the last couple of years I must have alienated them. He had a couple of DVDs which he'd filmed showing footage of the kids on bicycles, having a good time with him in the park in London, to show how his relationship was with them in the old days.

I hated this sort of evidence. Visual images tended to influence people. But they only showed certain limited aspects of his relationship with them. I knew he was good with children generally – he was a good teacher – but, to my thinking, his influence on our children's attitudes was much more crucial than whether he could give them a good time in the park. I didn't believe it was in their best long-term emotional interests to be exposed to their father's attitude towards me and towards women in general. The attitudes he expressed on the web, that women were 'fair game', were abhorrent. I didn't want my sons growing up regarding women in a predatory way, and being disabled from genuine relationships with women. Neither did I think that in the long term he would treat my daughters in a way that would enable them to hold their own in relationships. Nothing in his expressed attitudes towards them and what he wrote on the web showed that, left unsupervised, he could be a good parent.

Along with questioning me, Jack had a tendency to give long speeches while he was cross-examining. The judge several times had to remind him that he was meant to be questioning me and not presenting evidence. I found it difficult to answer a number of Jack's questions. He was very repetitive, trying to trip me, looking for an admission, looking for any way to catch me out on something. It was hard thinking up fresh ways to phrase answers that I'd given many times before.

Jack was aggrieved at being treated as a child, as he saw it. He argued that giving children too much say in whether they saw a parent or not gave them power that they shouldn't have in reality. I felt this was a point that needed debating generally. Not there in that courtroom at that particular moment, but by legislators, legal professionals and everyone involved in children's welfare.

As I pointed out to Jack, this wasn't the time to debate the legalities, the scope of the Children Act and how much decision-making ability it gave children over their own affairs; nevertheless the law did allow them a say in contact matters. The judge later told Jack that the children's wishes were not and could not be the predominant factor in law; he had other considerations to take into account.

There was a spectrum of opinion here in the courtroom about how much weight should be accorded to children's wishes. Jack thought the children's wishes should be given no weight at all. Too bad if a child didn't want to see a parent; the child was a minor and should do as it was told. It couldn't psychologically harm a child to see a parent; they needed a reality check to see that he was not harmful to them, and the law should not be allowing them a say on this.

As the judge explained, he was bound to give their wishes and feelings consideration; the law compelled him to do so. How much weight was attached to their feelings depended on the particular circumstances of a case. He said the law did not allow him to make their wishes and feelings the sole factor in his decisions.

I have no idea what the judge's personal views on the matter were. He was expressing himself in terms of what the law allowed him to do. I knew that in cases involving domestic violence the views of a child were supposed to carry more weight than they would in circumstances where there was no abuse – although in practice, to date, the children's wishes had not always been given the weight that should have been accorded to them.

My personal views go further than the law currently allows. I would argue that children's views should carry a great deal more weight than they presently do, even in cases not involving domestic abuse. I think there is still a relic of the Victorian era present in our legislation, and particularly in the application of family law, which regularly doesn't match even the more civilised written guidelines we have; an attitude that children shouldn't be involved in decision making; a paternalistic attitude which sees children as inferior to adults, needing to have matters kept from them.

Even if we, as adults, believe that seeing a parent is in a child's best interests, you can't legislate for relationships. If a child develops a dislike of someone or an objection to the way they are treated, if a relationship stops working, you can't make a relationship work simply by ordering it to work. Relationships are two-way and involve listening and receiving as well as transmitting. If one party is not good at receiving, it doesn't make sense for the other party to be forced into a futile one-sided attempt at relating. In an ideal world it may be better to have two parents, but courts can't bring about an ideal world by order. Legislating in the delicate area of relationships is fraught with danger. It has long been a principle in English law that the state should meddle as little as possible. I think that principle is being abandoned where a court tries to force children into unwanted relationships. It's not a healthy thing to do.

I felt my children had shown a great deal of insight into their father's behaviour, into the legal system and into some of the individuals they came into contact with. They could see when their representatives weren't up to scratch and it insulted their intelligence to gloss over that fact and to ignore their ability to make decisions for themselves.

I accorded my children a lot of independence in our home. Having been so minutely controlled during my marriage, I was acutely aware of issues of control and determined to keep control of my children to an absolute minimum. I had home-educated them at various periods and they were used to a high degree of autonomy, including a large say in how they were educated – while they were taught at home, their education was led very much by their interests rather than being highly structured. Used, as they were, to thinking independently, the control and intrusion of the court was all the more irksome and incomprehensible to them.

I had asked for a section 91(14) order to prevent Jack from re-litigating matters in future. This order would prohibit the matter returning to court for a period of time. I was annoyed and upset to see that the new guardian had picked up on this suggestion and asked for the order to be applied to both of us. I felt that was unjust. It had been necessary to ask for certain orders against Jack in the past; but I felt I couldn't be held equally litigious, since it was justified asking for an occupation order when we were homeless and for a non-molestation order. I commented on the witness stand that I felt it was sending Jack the wrong message to apply the order to both of us. He would regard it as saying that our conduct was the same.

My mental health was raised. Jack quoted at length from my GP's letter. It was embarrassing and hurtful but no more than I had expected. I knew I would be hounded about my mental health; all I could do was to stay calm and treat the issue with the contempt it deserved. I pointed out the difference in our behaviour: how I had scrupulously avoided running him down to the children but that he did not reciprocate; he thought it acceptable to write to a child's school that I was unstable and that his children had been hidden from him. I'd also lent him my house for contact whereas he'd had to be carried out of the marital home in handcuffs after the occupation order. Our conduct wasn't comparable.

I also pointed out that he spoke a lot about his rights but never about his responsibilities; that he hadn't contributed so much as 50p towards their upkeep in the last eight years. This hit a raw nerve and he began to bluster, in a temper, about how I had ruined his life by leaving him; that I should have kept my marital promises; that I had taken a large part of his assets and why should I expect any money when he wasn't seeing the children? This was the Jack I recognised: one who could never keep his cool when challenged. He couldn't discuss an issue he found emotive without losing his temper.

When I went on to say that it was unacceptable that he found it legitimate to slap me on occasions when I disagreed with him, he told a story about a friend of his who had recently been admitted to hospital and who, after becoming 'hysterical', had had her face slapped by a nurse. 'It isn't Victorian and a slap on the face is still used nowadays,' he summed up, as though we were unenlightened souls who needed setting straight about the old-fashioned merits of hitting someone.

The Cafcass guardian was the last to give evidence. I had asked my barrister beforehand to challenge her on three specific points: one was why she'd suggested that the 91(14) order should apply to both me and Mr Charming; the second was whether she'd conducted a risk assessment; and the third was whether she'd challenged Mr Charming about his violence towards me.

I did not like her answer to the first question. When challenged with the facts, she had to concede that most of the legal applications had sprung from Mr Charming and not from me, but instead of conceding that the order shouldn't therefore apply to both of us since we were not equally litigious, she shifted her ground and added a point that she had not made before in either of her reports. She said that applying the order to both of us would send a clear message to the children that they were safe and secure from further litigation. It was for the children's sake, she stressed.

I felt this was dishonest. She had only come up with this reason when my barrister challenged her view of whether I was as litigious as Mr Charming. If she had really been concerned to protect the children from further litigation, she would have suggested a section 91(14) order herself. Such an order was nowhere mentioned in any of her reports, however. I had come up with the idea myself after finding cases on the internet where long-running litigation had been brought to an end with such an order.

The guardian's position was illogical. I would hardly ask for an order barring future litigation if I had any intention of returning to court. The children had absolutely no need of any reassurance that I wouldn't be returning to court voluntarily. They were in no doubt of my sentiments on that score, and in fact they shared my feelings. We were united on that.

I felt cross that the guardian was speaking for the children here when the older two children had rejected Cafcass as their representative on the grounds that the guardians from there had not adequately represented their views to date. It was a cheek of her to offer that view on behalf of the children when I knew it would be rejected by them if they had been asked.

However, the children were not there to ask and I was pretty sure that in their absence the guardian's view would carry the day. It would be hard to argue against the ground she had taken, even if it was an opportunistic change of tack when she had been caught off guard on the witness stand. If we continued to argue against her view, it might appear that we were arguing against sending the children a message that they were secure from any more litigation.

My barrister did make the point that the no order principle should apply here, since there was clearly no need for the order to apply to me, but once she had made the point, we had to leave it. The important thing was to get a 91(14), whether it applied to us both or not. Such an order would prevent the children's childhood from being wasted by any more intrusive proceedings.

I felt that the qualities which made the judge a decent one in this case would also work against us on this point. He clearly wasn't going to see someone humiliated in court, least of all a professional. His professional courtesy – unlike his predecessor he treated all the professionals, and Jack, with courtesy – wouldn't allow him to countenance the Cafcass officer losing face.

My barrister went on to ask her whether she'd conducted a risk assessment. Her reply was that she hadn't. My barrister responded with 'Why not?' I waited for her reply with interest. From the Cafcass domestic abuse toolkit, I knew that risk assessments were supposed to be carried out in any case like ours. I wanted to know how she'd justify not doing one.

It was the first time I'd seen the Cafcass guardian flustered. She was evidently on the spot. She floundered slightly, obviously searching around for an acceptable answer. She came up with the defence that she'd merely been following on in the case; that a risk assessment had already been carried out by the DVIP and she accepted that. I could hardly believe my ears. At last a Cafcass guardian having to concede that the DVIP report counted and they accepted it? The barrister reiterated her point, driving it home: 'You accept the DVIP?'

Of course, the DVIP assessment was the guardian's excuse not to conduct a risk assessment herself and it got her off the hook on the witness stand, but it was disingenuous. If she accepted the DVIP assessment, she presumably accepted its conclusions that Mr Charming had no insight into his behaviour and that he was a high risk to the children who shouldn't have unsupervised contact. It also recommended a perpetrator programme for Mr Charming. Despite her assertion that she accepted the DVIP assessment, it wasn't backed up by what she had written in her reports. There was no challenge anywhere in her reports to Mr Charming's behaviour, no indication that she regarded it as harmful and no suggestion that he should undertake a perpetrator programme. Rather there was the implicit assumption that it was 'six of one and half a dozen of the other', since both the suggested orders, sending Mr Charming for a psychological assessment and the 91(14), were transposed into her own suggestion of making everything apply to both of us. Her logic was all over the place and it did her no credit.

My barrister asked her if she had offered any challenge at all to Mr Charming on his behaviour and required him to acknowledge past findings. Apparently she hadn't done this either. I reflected that Cafcass Cymru might as well tear up their toolkits and statutory obligations for all the influence they had on their officers' methods of dealing with domestic violence.

Neither the previous NYAS guardian nor the first Cafcass guardian had paid any attention at all to the conclusions of the DVIP. Each of them had decided the children should have unsupervised contact, and had pushed, manoeuvred us and pressured us to fit their own conclusions. However, the history with the guardians wasn't before the judge and neither were they on trial here. It was Mr Charming and I who were on trial and all we could hope was that the judge had read the DVIP for himself and saw that the methods and conclusions of the current Cafcass guardian were out of step with it.

I nearly laughed out loud when the latter, under cross-examination, mentioned her concern about the letter sent to the school by Mr Charming. It was clear to me that she was just bending with the wind. Seeing my barrister taking a very strong line over the letter, she took a stronger line herself. When she said that she had expressed concern about the letter in her report, I recalled my own feelings when I had read that same report. She had nowhere said the letter was derogatory. She had merely said that I 'perceived' it as derogatory. I remembered commenting to my legal advisers that she was sitting tight on the fence, determined not to take a personal view.

Pushed by my barrister, she had to agree that Mr Charming had zero insight into his behaviour. I felt aggrieved that it took cross-examination to force these acknowledgments out of her. She should have been more proactive on the children's behalf, taking a strong line in her reports regarding his behaviour. Her reports were mild, wishy-washy nothings, not helpful to me and the children at all; and on a couple of matters she had been positively damaging, such as not taking up the suggestion of sending Mr Charming for an assessment on his own but making it apply to both of us.

Even a 91(14) order would keep the children safe and free from litigation for only a limited period of time, not until they were grown up. If such an order were applied, it would still leave the children feeling that it was just a matter of time until we came back to court. A proper report by a psychologist on Mr Charming might have given the children greater protection in the future. The Cafcass guardian could have been more helpful in stressing the risks to the children from Mr Charming's behaviour, rather than taking the line of least resistance. She pinned responsibility for her support of indirect contact and the 91(14) on the fact that the children were tired of court, with no suggestion of risk to the children at all. Our experience of Cafcass in Wales left me feeling incredibly let down, and the children feeling they wanted as little to do with that organisation as possible.

The judge delivered a long and thorough judgment on the third afternoon of the case. As with Judge K some years back, he summed up the evidence first before arriving at his conclusions. This was always the difficult bit, hearing the evidence being gone over and not yet knowing what bearing it would have.

His thoroughness on the matters relating to the children and his strong line on the letter sent to the school made up for the guardian's weakness on these points. On the matter of the section 91(14) he did follow the guardian's line and made the order apply to both of us, but he took the sting out of it by stressing that he wasn't comparing my conduct with that of Mr Charming, but rather sending a clear message to the children, who had already been robbed of a great deal of their childhood through excessive litigation, that it wasn't going to continue. I could live with that. No judgment is going to be perfect because no judge is omniscient, but the judgment was as good as it was possible to be under the circumstances. I did feel that, more than any judge we'd had in a long line of judges, this one was absolutely focused on what the issues would mean to the children. I came in for some mild criticism but I'd have to take that on the chin; it was nothing compared to what Mr Charming had to sit and listen to.

His behaviour and websites were gone over in detail and the impact on the children painted in stark terms. I don't know about Mr Charming – I couldn't tell what he was inwardly feeling – but if it had been me, I would have been squirming by the end of that judgment. It was accomplished without any personal remarks or bluster, just a thorough, reasoned and logical laying bare of his motivation and behaviour. The judge did not leave any loopholes; he read Mr Charming's letter into the record so there would be a transcript of it; he went over every piece of evidence, leaving nothing out.

I had been scared after the judgment by the previous Judge F, knowing it left us vulnerable to appeal because it was weak on reasons and analysis of Mr Charming's behaviour. It hadn't even mentioned that he disavowed all the past findings of violence against him. I had no such doubts about Judge H's judgment. He had left nothing to chance and nothing that could be disputed, giving reasons for each of his conclusions. I felt close to tears at one point when the judge commented that Mr Charming had bullied me on the witness stand. He remarked that my barrister had had to step in at several points to restrain him and that he himself could have stepped in more often, but that he had allowed Mr Charming to continue on a couple of occasions because it had been revealing of his mentality. I had not really given a thought before to how I had been cross-examined; I had expected it to be unpleasant. He had always been contemptuous towards me in our home; I didn't expect anything different from him when I was on the witness stand. It was unexpected to find any sympathy coming my way on this. I felt grateful for it.

Judge H pointed out the contradiction in Mr Charming's statements when he claimed that I was alienating the children; in fact, the evidence revealed that it was the other way around. Everything he had written and said both to the children and to schools, and to strangers on the internet, and what he had said on the stand pointed in the other direction. The judge also commented on the 'astonishing' story of a nurse slapping a patient that Mr Charming had used to justify his violence towards me, remarking that a slap in the face was an assault that could lead to criminal charges and that such violence had no place in a relationship.

I remember once being stunned at the end of a judgment in front of a very different judge. Mr Charming seemed like this now; dazed rather than his normal ebullient self. He had asked at the beginning of the judgment whether he could make his own tape recording of it and had been refused permission. The judge told him that he could have an official transcript and arranged for that to take place. Mr Charming had said in no uncertain terms in his summing up before the judgment that he intended to go back to the Court of Appeal and to the European Court of Human Rights if he didn't get an order for direct contact. After the judgment his bullishness diminished somewhat.

So in late 2009 we finally had an order along the lines of what the psychologist recommended back in 2003. It had taken all those years, going round the houses, to come back to exactly the same spot. We also had an order preventing further litigation for two and a half years.

28

Finding a voice

In many areas of society we are opening up institutions, organisations and the professions for scrutiny. The Freedom of Information Act has given access to those wanting greater openness and accountability in government. But who is going to scrutinise the judges, Cafcass and those officials who work in the secrecy of the family courts? At present no one adequately scrutinises the family court system or the judiciary. Groups regulating themselves have generally been found to need independent regulators. It is a principle recognised practically everywhere else that there need to be independent regulatory authorities.

My feeling is that the judiciary as presently constituted and the family court as it operates now isn't the right set-up to consider complex family cases. The judges have no contact with the mothers and children whose situation they have to consider; they are cutting corners and failing to investigate issues properly due to lack of time in the court schedule and lack of resources; often they are judging difficult psychological issues with no proper expertise to hand. Since children are not followed up in the longer term, they cannot even be confident that good outcomes are being achieved.

Our crushing experiences at court were instrumental in inspiring me to form the campaign group Children's Voices in Family Law (CVFL) along with other mothers who had also suffered in the courts. Our research confirms that the problem of judges failing to understand the effects on children of witnessing domestic abuse is widespread.

We also discovered that judges receive barely any training in domestic abuse. Aside from a very brief induction, training is optional and it is perfectly possible for judges to sit for years in family cases without updating their knowledge or skills, even though research in the field of domestic violence has increased immeasurably. They rely on in-house training: passing on their own experiences to new judges, which in practice means passing on old myths and stereotypes.

My belief is that victims of domestic abuse and children need greater protection and legal rights. I disagree with the senior judges who heard the cases involving domestic violence in the year 2000 which considered fathers' contact with their children. They felt that domestic violence should not necessarily be the main factor in such decisions.

I believe they were wrong; that domestic violence should constitute an automatic bar to contact with children. I think the onus should be on the abusive parent to prove they are fit and that they can make a contribution to their children's lives and not undermine the residential parent; that they should be required to undergo therapy. If they refuse, it should prevent unsupervised contact resuming. Unless judges send a very strong message to abusers, making it clear that abuse in all its forms is totally unacceptable, nothing will change. The current emphasis is always on contact, regardless of other factors and despite the fact that there is a growing body of research which suggests that children who have witnessed domestic abuse may do better with little or no contact with the abusive parent.

In his letter to me Sir Mark Potter, the head of the family division, referred to the fact that judges are exposed to issues of domestic violence; they see it enacted by actors, for example. I found this response oddly comical as well as alarming. However skilled actors are, it is not the same as coming face to face with women who have suffered at the hands of a violent man and also at the hands of the courts. Acting out battering misses the point – its long-term psychological effects cannot be conveyed in a show put on for the purpose of training judges in a spare afternoon or two. The judges need to listen to real victims of the system, not be at one step removed from them.

It might also be of help in cases involving domestic abuse if they gave out a questionnaire to each woman after a hearing, asking about any problems she might have with the court service. If the surveys were anonymous, they might get an honest picture of what is happening on the ground.

It seems self-evident that the decision-makers should speak directly with those whose lives their decisions affect. As in some other jurisdictions, I also believe that judges should speak with the children and not merely rely on a system of Chinese whispers. I once heard a Cafcass official say that some judges don't feel they are the best people to talk to children and don't always feel capable of doing it. The absurdity of this is surely obvious? If a judge is incapable of relating normally with a young human being for whom he is making vital decisions, then he shouldn't be in a position to make those decisions.

Aside from engaging with women and children in domestic abuse cases, I believe judges should also request the help of domestic violence specialists on how to handle these cases, to help bring about a shift in focus. Presently, cases are viewed very much through the eyes of the legal professionals – people with limited training in this area. Often the professionals receive a degree of training and feel it qualifies them to assess DV cases. They frequently end up doing more harm than good. The people best placed to help are DV agencies. If courts were required to involve DV agencies in the training of judges, lawyers and Cafcass officers this would be a huge step forward in tackling the scourge of violence against women. It would be helpful in bringing about a victim-focused approach. Unless such practical measures are implemented, it is fair to regard with scepticism judicial and establishment claims that they take domestic violence seriously.

There are numerous ways in which the family court system appears to operate for the benefit of the legal professionals running it rather than for the benefit of the victims. Not only are cases allowed to run on for too long, but there is an inbuilt scepticism about domestic violence. It is easy enough for anyone to understand how physical beatings would cause a woman to object to unsupervised contact with children. However, there is a real lack of understanding that other forms of less obvious abuse – harassing, undermining and using the court system as a form of intimidation – can have a profound effect on a victim and on the children's family life.

During the years of court, you could never say our lives were normal. The courts and Mr Charming's manipulation of the system affected our lives deeply. For a long period I used to make a huge effort to try to shut it out. It led to feeling continually strained.

It is a pretty abnormal way of living and the kids deserved better. I made a huge effort of will not to let my stress affect the children –

not to take my anxiety out on them – but sensitive children will be affected. It was not the life they were entitled to. My children certainly have strong views on the way the courts have allowed their lives to be so badly affected by continuous litigation and the intrusive line of strangers who came knocking at our door.

It has been too easy for judges and other professionals in the system to lay the blame on 'warring and intransigent parents' without looking at the part they play in matters. If someone has genuine reason for fearing abuse by an ex-partner, some effort should be made to discriminate carefully in a case and not unthinkingly to label both parents.

When I look back over my experiences, I also find it significant that in the time I worked for an MP there was not a single letter from a woman regarding domestic abuse. Not one. It is clearly a hidden problem and unless women approach their MPs and bring it to their attention, they are not going to know just how big a problem it is. There is no substitute for a woman using her own voice and telling it like it is.

There are plenty of high-profile groups representing fathers' interests and because they are so vocal they are getting more than their fair share of the limelight as well as public and political sympathy; sometimes for the wrong reasons. Who knows whether judges on the bench aren't being subtly influenced by media depictions of hard-done-by fathers, cheated out of their parental rights by vengeful mothers? It may not consciously affect a judge's decision making in a particular case, but when he diminishes abuse and lets a perpetrator off lightly, you can't help wondering. After all, it would have to be a block of stone that isn't influenced by the prevailing wind, by images of the stunts performed by Fathers4Justice, and the utterances by prominent politicians in favour of increasing fathers' rights and punishing mothers who refuse contact.

I believe that there should also be an independent inspectorate for family court judges, comprising domestic abuse experts. For too long they have been both judge and jury in their closed courts. It is never a good thing to have members of their own profession performing the scrutiny. A lay panel observing hearings and making recommendations would be beneficial.

Merely allowing observers at family hearings, whether medical professionals or the press, wouldn't provide a complete solution to the problem of accountability; nor would the Court of Appeal's recent practice of publishing its judgments. In the judgments one only gets a perception of the facts through a judge's eyes. The same facts, as in my own case, may appear in a wholly different light to the litigants. The judicial facts in my case sometimes conflicted with the views of the psychologist, the police and social services. And even within the ranks of the judiciary there had been wildly differing interpretations of the same facts. Lay observers would need independent access to the statements and reports in a case; merely sitting in the courtroom and watching does not produce anything like a whole picture.

Allowing observer status to certain individuals would not affect the independence of the judiciary, since they would not have power to overturn judicial decisions; but it would bring a light into a closed and jealously guarded system, which can only be a good thing. If judges can't rise to the challenge of accountability and examining their own practices, then politicians should look at enforcing change.

I am not convinced by the idea of 'naming and shaming', which is one idea being kicked around in relation to the family courts. My feeling is that if we had better training for those involved in protecting children, there wouldn't be a need for shaming people. Neither should I like the only scrutiny of the family courts to be performed by the press. One can see how colourful characters and high-profile cases, which might make entertaining reading, might predominate over more serious issues.

The judiciary has become very jealous of its own privileges and resentful of what it deems interference by politicians. But no body of professionals should be above scrutiny, particularly not one which has peculiar power in society. After all, judges do not make the laws; politicians do, on behalf of people like you and me.

It is only right that the people on whose behalf the judges enforce the law should be able to see whether or not it is operating well. The law is not a possession belonging to a particular group of people; we all have an interest in it. There should be no place for the resentful and proprietorial attitude to the law which some judges display on being challenged or criticised. The law-makers and their constituents have as much stake and interest in the law as the lawyers and judges who operate it on their behalf. I believe there is also a case for electing judges the way they do in other jurisdictions so they are removable by popular vote. Members of society have a right to know what is being done on their behalf. And if the measure of how civilised and humane we are as a society is how we treat vulnerable people, I do not think we are performing well.

In addition to greater openness in the family courts, I believe there needs to be a one-stop shop to deal with complaints. The Court of Appeal is supposed to be the place where you can appeal judges' decisions, but in practice its remit is extremely narrow and inadequate. It can only deal with the most recent order in a case, and within a very limited time span. Moreover, the court can only deal with legal issues. If you have a complaint about a judge's conduct, it falls to the OJC to deal with; and it falls to Cafcass to deal with complaints made about a Cafcass officer. Solicitors and barristers have different bodies regulating them.

All the different individuals and organisations involved in court cases form what they call 'a system'. But as we have seen from the terrible failures in child protection in Haringey, for example, the more complex a system, the harder it is to get it to work properly. More organisations involved mean higher risks of failure in communication and increased risks to children. When officials exonerate themselves in these situations and talk about system failures, they are really referring to a whole collection of individuals not doing their jobs properly.

When a large number of people don't perform in their role to an adequate standard and let down those who are relying on them for protection, a usual response tends to be denial. There is collective denial about the family court system at present. Judges, Cafcass, NYAS, solicitors and barristers are in denial about the court system which is supposed to protect vulnerable children. I understand this because it's a human response and it is similar to the denial I experienced when I was suffering abuse at my husband's hands.

It is very difficult to admit sometimes that people can do bad things on a large scale, especially if the individuals involved are not badly intentioned or malicious. But the fact is that the way those involved in the family court system deal with domestic abuse causes real harm and damage to those families who are unfortunate enough to suffer their appalling interference.

One response to terrible failures in child protection which become public is to increase the complexity of the system by adding in extra layers of protection: extra checks, more tick boxes, more officials. It is an understandable response but it has been found that increasing the complexity of systems merely increases the risk of human error. Systems need to operate as simply as possible and they need to be transparent and accountable enough for any person of ordinary intelligence to grasp.

Rather than increase the complexity in domestic abuse cases I would suggest simplifying the procedures. Reversing the presumption of contact in these cases would help because it would automatically make the victim and the children safe without having to conduct endless investigations into whether contact is safe or not. I would also suggest that the resident parent should be the one to set the level of contact. In a family where abuse has occurred, it is the resident parent who is best placed to judge the effects of contact and the stresses and strains it places on the family.

I can hear the protests from fathers' groups already on that last suggestion. But I am talking about allowing the resident parent to decide specifically in cases where domestic abuse has occurred, not in cases generally. I think it is reasonable where there is one abusive parent and one non-abusive for the non-abusive parent to decide the level of contact. Clearly an abusive parent has a degree of impaired judgement and a diminished capacity for proper parenting, along with a propensity to abuse their power; it makes no sense for that person to have equal say.

I also believe this option would lead to less obstructionism in regard to contact, which is the issue many aggrieved fathers complain of. If a woman is guaranteed her physical and emotional safety and is assured that the new family dynamics with her children will not be upset or threatened, she is much more likely to be positive about contact. In the present situation, where women are forced to give more than they believe is safe, the temptation for the woman to obstruct contact is a lot greater.

It also reduces the potential for conflict with an ex-partner. There is nothing like going to court to fan the flames of conflict. Putting a controlling father in the position of 'losing' in the courtroom is calculated to make him mad with fury. It doesn't increase women's safety and security. It would be better to have a proper procedure and a blanket 'no unsupervised contact' rule – which could be reversed in individual cases if a perpetrator got professional help and made the required changes in behaviour – than to have the victim and perpetrator fighting contact issues out in the courtroom.

We should be honest about how much time the judiciary can devote to private law cases and how much of a burden the public purse is bearing. The legal aid costs of many of these cases are ridiculously out of proportion to the problems. It is quite possible that many domestic abuse cases are fuelled by individuals with psychological problems. Making simpler the principles on which such cases are conducted would provide a neater and less expensive solution than devoting endless judges, Cafcass officers, guardians, solicitors, barristers and court officials to produce reams of paper and to do a job they aren't even qualified for.

I think it is time that the judiciary moved on in their attitudes to women. Within the lifetime of many senior judges, it used to be the case that an adulterous mother automatically lost custody of her children and they went to the father. As recently as the 1960s Erin Pizzey was a hate figure amongst the establishment for setting up women's refuges. The generation that vilified her is now lauding her for her work with abused women. Attitudes towards women have moved on since then, but there is still a huge amount of progress to be made. No one should forget that these rights for women were hard won and have been around for very little time. Wholesale changes of attitude have yet to take place. If the judges who heard Re L expected a cascade to follow, they were wrong; similar outcomes for similar cases to Re L have slowed to a trickle.

There are many reasons why it might be difficult for mothers to speak for themselves. They are usually the ones looking after the children; a full-time job in itself. If she has suffered abuse, it is difficult for a woman to find her voice again. There must be a support structure in place to enable women to be heard, and they must be assured they will be listened to and treated as competent people, concerned first and foremost with the welfare of their children. It is better for a woman to have her own voice in this process than to give over speaking to someone else. That is what this book is about. It is written in the hope that women can find their own voices.